ŚRĪMAD BHĀGAVATAM

Sixth Canto

"Prescribed Duties for Mankind"

(Part Three—Chapters 14-19)

With the Original Sanskrit Text,
Its Roman Transliteration, Synonyms,
Translation and Elaborate Purports by

His Divine Grace
A.C. Bhaktivedanta Swami Prabhupāda
Founder-*Ācārya* of the International Society for Krishna Consciousness

THE BHAKTIVEDANTA BOOK TRUST
New York · Los Angeles · London · Bombay

Readers interested in the subject matter of this book
are invited by the International Society for Krishna Consciousness
to correspond with its Secretary.

International Society for Krishna Consciousness
3764 Watseka Avenue
Los Angeles, California 90034

Library of Congress Catalogue Card Number: 73-169353
International Standard Book Number: 0-912776-83-8

First printing, 1976: 20,000 copies

Printed in the United States of America

Table of Contents

CHAPTER SIXTEEN
King Citraketu Meets the Supreme Lord   79

CHAPTER SEVENTEEN
Mother Pārvatī Curses Citraketu   165

CHAPTER EIGHTEEN
Diti Vows to Kill King Indra   209

CHAPTER NINETEEN
Performing the Puṁsavana Ritualistic Ceremony   269

Appendixes

Preface

We must know the present need of human society. And what is that need? Human society is no longer bounded by geographical limits to particular countries or communities. Human society is broader than in the Middle Ages, and the world tendency is toward one state or one human society. The ideals of spiritual communism, according to *Śrīmad-Bhāgavatam,* are based more or less on the oneness of the entire human society, nay, on the entire energy of living beings. The need is felt by great thinkers to make this a successful ideology. *Śrīmad-Bhāgavatam* will fill this need in human society. It begins, therefore, with the aphorism of Vedānta philosophy (*janmādy asya yataḥ*) to establish the ideal of a common cause.

Human society, at the present moment, is not in the darkness of oblivion. It has made rapid progress in the field of material comforts, education and economic development throughout the entire world. But there is a pinprick somewhere in the social body at large, and therefore there are large-scale quarrels, even over less important issues. There is need of a clue as to how humanity can become one in peace, friendship and prosperity with a common cause. *Śrīmad-Bhāgavatam* will fill this need, for it is a cultural presentation for the re-spiritualization of the entire human society.

Śrīmad-Bhāgavatam should be introduced also in the schools and colleges, for it is recommended by the great student devotee Prahlāda Mahārāja in order to change the demonic face of society.

kaumāra ācaret prājño
dharmān bhāgavatān iha
durlabhaṁ mānuṣaṁ janma
tad apy adhruvam arthadam
(*Bhāg.* 7.6.1)

Disparity in human society is due to lack of principles in a godless civilization. There is God, or the Almighty One, from whom everything emanates, by whom everything is maintained and in whom everything is merged to rest. Material science has tried to find the ultimate source of creation very insufficiently, but it is a fact that there is one ultimate source of everything that be. This ultimate source is explained rationally and authoritatively in the beautiful *Bhāgavatam* or *Śrīmad-Bhāgavatam.*

Śrīmad-Bhāgavatam is the transcendental science not only for knowing the ultimate source of everything but also for knowing our relation with Him and our duty towards perfection of the human society on the basis of this perfect knowledge. It is powerful reading matter in the Sanskrit language, and it is now rendered into English elaborately so that simply by a careful reading one will know God perfectly well, so much so that the reader will be sufficiently educated to defend himself from the onslaught of atheists. Over and above this, the reader will be able to convert others to accept God as a concrete principle.

Śrīmad-Bhāgavatam begins with the definition of the ultimate source. It is a bona fide commentary on the *Vedānta-sūtra* by the same author, Śrīla Vyāsadeva, and gradually it develops into nine cantos up to the highest state of God realization. The only qualification one needs to study this great book of transcendental knowledge is to proceed step by step cautiously and not jump forward haphazardly as with an ordinary book. It should be gone through chapter by chapter, one after another. The reading matter is so arranged with its original Sanskrit text, its English transliteration, synonyms, translation and purports so that one is sure to become a God realized soul at the end of finishing the first nine cantos.

The Tenth Canto is distinct from the first nine cantos, because it deals directly with the transcendental activities of the Personality of Godhead Śrī Kṛṣṇa. One will be unable to capture the effects of the Tenth Canto without going through the first nine cantos. The book is complete in twelve cantos, each independent, but it is good for all to read them in small installments one after another.

I must admit my frailties in presenting *Śrīmad-Bhāgavatam,* but still I am hopeful of its good reception by the thinkers and leaders of society on the strength of the following statement of *Śrīmad-Bhāgavatam.*

tad-vāg-visargo janatāgha-viplavo
yasmin pratiślokam abaddhavaty api

nāmāny anantasya yaśo 'ṅkitāni yac
chṛṇvanti gāyanti gṛṇanti sādhavaḥ
(*Bhāg.* 1.5.11)

"On the other hand, that literature which is full with descriptions of the transcendental glories of the name, fame, form and pastimes of the unlimited Supreme Lord is a transcendental creation meant to bring about a revolution in the impious life of a misdirected civilization. Such transcendental literatures, even though irregularly composed, are heard, sung and accepted by purified men who are thoroughly honest."

Oṁ tat sat

A. C. Bhaktivedanta Swami

Introduction

"This *Bhāgavata Purāṇa* is as brilliant as the sun, and it has arisen just after the departure of Lord Kṛṣṇa to His own abode, accompanied by religion, knowledge, etc. Persons who have lost their vision due to the dense darkness of ignorance in the age of Kali shall get light from this *Purāṇa*." (*Śrīmad-Bhāgavatam* 1.3.43)

The timeless wisdom of India is expressed in the *Vedas*, ancient Sanskrit texts that touch upon all fields of human knowledge. Originally preserved through oral tradition, the *Vedas* were first put into writing five thousand years ago by Śrīla Vyāsadeva, the "literary incarnation of God." After compiling the *Vedas*, Vyāsadeva set forth their essence in the aphorisms known as *Vedānta-sūtras*. *Śrīmad-Bhāgavatam* is Vyāsadeva's commentary on his own *Vedānta-sūtras*. It was written in the maturity of his spiritual life under the direction of Nārada Muni, his spiritual master. Referred to as "the ripened fruit of the tree of Vedic literature," *Śrīmad-Bhāgavatam* is the most complete and authoritative exposition of Vedic knowledge.

After compiling the *Bhāgavatam*, Vyāsa impressed the synopsis of it upon his son, the sage Śukadeva Gosvāmī. Śukadeva Gosvāmī subsequently recited the entire *Bhāgavatam* to Mahārāja Parīkṣit in an assembly of learned saints on the bank of the Ganges at Hastināpura (now Delhi). Mahārāja Parīkṣit was the emperor of the world and was a great *rājarṣi* (saintly king). Having received a warning that he would die within a week, he renounced his entire kingdom and retired to the bank of the Ganges to fast until death and receive spiritual enlightenment. The *Bhāgavatam* begins with Emperor Parīkṣit's sober inquiry to Śukadeva Gosvāmī:

> "You are the spiritual master of great saints and devotees. I am therefore begging you to show the way of perfection for all persons, and especially for one who is about to die. Please let me know what a man should hear, chant, remember and worship, and also what he should not do. Please explain all this to me."

Śukadeva Gosvāmī's answer to this question, and numerous other questions posed by Mahārāja Parīkṣit, concerning everything from the nature of the self to the origin of the universe, held the assembled sages in rapt attention continuously for the seven days leading to the King's death. The sage Sūta Gosvāmī, who was present on the bank of the Ganges when Śukadeva Gosvāmī first recited *Śrīmad-Bhāgavatam*, later repeated the *Bhāgavatam* before a gathering of sages in the forest of Naimiṣāraṇya. Those sages, concerned about the spiritual welfare of the people in general, had gathered to perform a long, continuous chain of sacrifices to counteract the degrading influence of the incipient age of Kali. In response to the sages' request that he speak the essence of Vedic wisdom, Sūta Gosvāmī repeated from memory the entire eighteen thousand verses of *Śrīmad-Bhāgavatam*, as spoken by Śukadeva Gosvāmī to Mahārāja Parīkṣit.

The reader of *Śrīmad-Bhāgavatam* hears Sūta Gosvāmī relate the questions of Mahārāja Parīkṣit and the answers of Śukadeva Gosvāmī. Also, Sūta Gosvāmī sometimes responds directly to questions put by Śaunaka Ṛṣi, the spokesman for the sages gathered at Naimiṣāraṇya. One therefore simultaneously hears two dialogues: one between Mahārāja Parīkṣit and Śukadeva Gosvāmī on the bank of the Ganges, and another at Naimiṣāraṇya between Sūta Gosvāmī and the sages at Naimiṣāraṇya Forest, headed by Śaunaka Ṛṣi. Furthermore, while instructing King Parīkṣit, Śukadeva Gosvāmī often relates historical episodes and gives accounts of lengthy philosophical discussions between such great souls as the saint Maitreya and his disciple Vidura. With this understanding of the history of the *Bhāgavatam*, the reader will easily be able to follow its intermingling of dialogues and events from various sources. Since philosophical wisdom, not chronological order, is most important in the text, one need only be attentive to the subject matter of *Śrīmad-Bhāgavatam* to appreciate fully its profound message.

It should also be noted that the volumes of the *Bhāgavatam* need not be read consecutively, starting with the first and proceeding to the last. The translator of this edition compares the *Bhāgavatam* to sugar candy—wherever you taste it, you will find it equally sweet and relishable.

This edition of the *Bhāgavatam* is the first complete English translation of this important text with an elaborate commentary, and it is the first widely available to the English-speaking public. It is the product of the scholarly and devotional effort of His Divine Grace A. C. Bhaktivedanta Swami Prabhupāda, the world's most distinguished teacher of Indian religious and philosophical thought. His consummate Sanskrit scholarship and intimate familiarity with Vedic culture and thought as well as the modern way of life combine to reveal to the West a magnificent exposition of this important classic.

Readers will find this work of value for many reasons. For those interested in the classical roots of Indian civilization, it serves as a vast reservoir of detailed information on virtually every one of its aspects. For students of comparative philosophy and religion, the *Bhāgavatam* offers a penetrating view into the meaning of India's profound spiritual heritage. To sociologists and anthropologists, the *Bhāgavatam* reveals the practical workings of a peaceful and scientifically organized Vedic culture, whose institutions were integrated on the basis of a highly developed spiritual world view. Students of literature will discover the *Bhāgavatam* to be a masterpiece of majestic poetry. For students of psychology, the text provides important perspectives on the nature of consciousness, human behavior and the philosophical study of identity. Finally, to those seeking spiritual insight, the *Bhāgavatam* offers simple and practical guidance for attainment of the highest self-knowledge and realization of the Absolute Truth. The entire multivolume text, presented by the Bhaktivedanta Book Trust, promises to occupy a significant place in the intellectual, cultural and spiritual life of modern man for a long time to come.

—The Publishers

His Divine Grace
A. C. Bhaktivedanta Swami Prabhupāda
Founder-Ācārya of the International Society for Krishna Consciousness

PLATE ONE

In the province of Śūrasena there was a King named Citraketu, who ruled the entire earth. Although he had millions of wives, by chance he did not receive a child from any of them. One queen, however, having received a benediction from the great sage Aṅgirā, bore the King a son and thus became his most favored wife. This caused her co-wives to become extremely unhappy. These queens, burning with envy and unable to tolerate the King's neglect, poisoned the son. When the King heard of his son's death, he became almost blind and fell at his son's feet. Accompanied by his wife, who was lamenting for her dead child, King Citraketu began crying loudly in grief. While the King lay like a dead body beside his dead son, the two great sages Nārada and Aṅgirā appeared and enlightened him with instructions about spiritual consciousness. Then, by mystic power, the great sage Nārada brought the dead son back into the vision of all the lamenting relatives. The son then spoke to further enlighten the King. *(pp. 12–80)*

PLATE TWO

After receiving instructions from his spiritual master, Nārada Muni, regarding the falsity of the material world and material possessions, King Citraketu became greatly renounced. Fasting and drinking only water, for one week continuously he chanted with great care and attention the *mantra* given by Nārada Muni. Within a very few days, by the influence of the *mantra*, his mind became increasingly enlightened in spiritual progress, and he attained shelter at the lotus feet of Anantadeva, Lord Śeṣa, the Supreme Personality of Godhead. Citraketu saw that the Lord was as white as the white fibers of a lotus flower. He was dressed in bluish garments and adorned with a brilliantly glittering helmet, armlets, belt and bangles. His face was smiling, and His eyes were reddish. He was surrounded by such exalted liberated persons as Sanatkumāra. As soon as Mahārāja Citraketu saw the Supreme Lord, he was cleansed of all material contamination and situated in his original Kṛṣṇa consciousness, being completely purified. He became silent and grave, and because of love for the Lord, tears fell from his eyes, and his hairs stood on end. With great devotion and love, he offered his respectful obeisances unto the original Personality of Godhead. *(pp. 98–114)*

PLATE THREE

"O unconquerable Lord, although You cannot be conquered by anyone, You are certainly conquered by devotees who have control of the mind and senses. They can keep You under their control because You are causelessly merciful to devotees who desire no material profit from You. Indeed, You give Yourself to them, and because of this You also have full control over Your devotees."

The Lord and the devotees both conquer. The Lord is conquered by the devotees, and the devotees are conquered by the Lord. Because of being conquered by one another, they both derive transcendental bliss from their relationship. The highest perfection of this mutual conquering is exhibited by Kṛṣṇa and the *gopīs.* Whenever Kṛṣṇa played His flute, He conquered the minds of the *gopīs*, and without seeing the *gopīs*, Kṛṣṇa could not be happy. *(pp. 117–118)*

PLATE FOUR

The cosmic manifestation and its creation, maintenance and annihilation reflect the opulences of the Supreme Personality of Godhead, Kṛṣṇa, the absolute, infallible, beginningless person who is expanded into unlimited forms. He is the original person, the oldest, yet He always appears as a fresh youth. For material creation, Lord Kṛṣṇa's plenary expansion assumes three Viṣṇu forms. The origin of the material creation is Mahā-Viṣṇu, who lies in the Causal Ocean. While He sleeps in that ocean, millions of universes are generated as He exhales and annihilated when He inhales. The second expansion, Garbhodakaśāyī Viṣṇu, enters all the universes to create diversities in each of them. From the navel of Garbhodakaśāyī Viṣṇu has sprung the stem of a lotus flower, the birthplace of Brahmā, who is the father of all living beings and master of all the demigod engineers. Within the stem of the lotus are fourteen divisions of planetary systems, the earthly planets being situated in the middle. The third expansion of the Lord, Kṣīrodakaśāyī Viṣṇu, is diffused as the all-pervading Supersoul in all the universes and is known as Paramātmā. He is present within the hearts of all living entities and even within the atoms. Anyone who knows these three Viṣṇus can be liberated from material entanglements. *(pp. 120–125)*

PLATE FIVE

Once while King Citraketu was traveling in outer space on a brilliantly effulgent airplane given to him by Lord Viṣṇu, he saw Lord Śiva sitting in an assembly of great saintly persons and embracing Pārvatī on his lap. Citraketu laughed loudly to see Lord Śiva in that situation, and, within the hearing of Pārvatī, he spoke expressing his wonder. Not knowing the prowess of Lord Śiva and Pārvatī, Citraketu strongly criticized them. Lord Śiva, the most powerful personality, whose knowledge is fathomless, simply smiled and remained silent, and all the members of the assembly followed the lord by not saying anything. Citraketu's statements were not at all pleasing, however, and therefore the goddess Pārvatī, being very angry, cursed Citraketu, who had thought himself better than Lord Śiva in controlling the senses. *(pp. 169–180)*

PLATE SIX

Diti, the mother of Hiraṇyākṣa and Hiraṇyakaśipu, was overwhelmed with lamentation and anger because her sons were killed by Lord Viṣṇu for the benefit of King Indra. Desiring to have a son who would kill Indra, she began constantly acting to satisfy her husband, Kaśyapa, by her pleasing behavior. Desiring to purify his wife, Kaśyapa instructed her to accept a vow of devotional service. He assured her that if she adhered to the vow with faith for at least one year, she would give birth to a son destined to kill Indra, but if there were any discrepancy in the discharge of the vow, the son would be a friend to Indra. Indra could understand the purpose of Diti's vow, and so he outwardly became very friendly and served Diti in a faithful way in order to cheat her as soon as he could find some fault in her observances. Once Diti neglected to purify herself after eating and, having grown weak, went to sleep at an improper time. Finding this fault, Indra, who has all mystic powers, entered Diti's womb while she was unconscious, being fast asleep. With the help of his thunderbolt, he cut her embryo into seven pieces. In seven places, seven different living beings began crying. Indra told them, "Do not cry," and then he cut each of them into seven pieces again. Being very much aggrieved, they pleaded to Indra with folded hands, saying, "Dear Indra, we are the Maruts, your brothers. Why are you trying to kill us?" *(pp. 225–257)*

PLATE SEVEN

"My dear Lord Viṣṇu and mother Lakṣmī, goddess of fortune, You are the proprietors of the entire creation. Indeed, You are the cause of the creation. Mother Lakṣmī is extremely difficult to understand because she is so powerful that the jurisdiction of Her power is difficult to overcome. Mother Lakṣmī is represented in the material world as the external energy, but actually she is always the internal energy of the Lord. My Lord, You are the master of energy, and therefore You are the Supreme Person. You are sacrifice [*yajña*] personified. Lakṣmī, the embodiment of spiritual activities, is the original form of worship offered unto You, whereas You are the enjoyer of all sacrifices. Mother Lakṣmī is the reservoir of all spiritual qualities, whereas You are the support of all such names and forms and the cause for their manifestation. You are both the supreme rulers and benedictors of the three worlds. Therefore, my Lord, *uttama-śloka,* may my ambitions be fulfilled by Your grace." *(pp. 279–283)*

CHAPTER FOURTEEN

King Citraketu's Lamentation

In this Fourteenth Chapter, Parīkṣit Mahārāja asks his spiritual master, Śukadeva Gosvāmī, how such a demon as Vṛtrāsura could become an exalted devotee. In this connection the previous life of Vṛtrāsura is discussed. This involves the story of Citraketu and how he was victimized by lamentation because of the death of his son.

Among many millions of living entities, the number of human beings is extremely small, and among human beings who are actually religious, only some are eager to be liberated from material existence. Among many thousands of people who desire relief from material existence, one is freed from the association of unwanted persons or is relieved of material contamination. And among many millions of such liberated persons, one may become a devotee of Lord Nārāyaṇa. Therefore such devotees are extremely rare. Since *bhakti*, devotional service, is not ordinary, Parīkṣit Mahārāja was astonished that an *asura* could rise to the exalted position of a devotee. Being doubtful, Parīkṣit Mahārāja inquired from Śukadeva Gosvāmī, who then described Vṛtrāsura with reference to his previous birth as Citraketu, the King of Śūrasena.

Citraketu, who had no sons, got an opportunity to meet the great sage Aṅgirā. When Aṅgirā inquired from the King about his welfare, the King expressed his moroseness, and therefore by the grace of the great sage, the King's first wife, Kṛtadyuti, gave birth to a son, who was the cause of both happiness and lamentation. Upon the birth of this son, the King and all the residents of the palace were very happy. The co-wives of Kṛtadyuti, however, were envious, and later they administered poison to the child. Citraketu was overwhelmed by shock at his son's death. Then Nārada Muni and Aṅgirā went to see him.

TEXT 1

श्रीपरीक्षिदुवाच

रजस्तमःस्वभावस्य ब्रह्मन् वृत्रस्य पाप्मनः ।
नारायणे भगवति कथमासीद् दृढा मतिः ॥ १ ॥

śrī-parīkṣid uvāca
rajas-tamaḥ-svabhāvasya
brahman vṛtrasya pāpmanaḥ
nārāyaṇe bhagavati
katham āsīd dṛḍhā matiḥ

śrī-parīkṣit uvāca—King Parīkṣit inquired; *rajaḥ*—of the mode of passion; *tamaḥ*—and of the mode of ignorance; *sva-bhāvasya*—having a nature; *brahman*—O learned *brāhmaṇa; vṛtrasya*—of Vṛtrāsura; *pāpmanaḥ*—who was supposedly sinful; *nārāyaṇe*—in Lord Nārāyaṇa; *bhagavati*—the Supreme Personality of Godhead; *katham*—how; *āsīt*—was there; *dṛḍhā*—very strong; *matiḥ*—consciousness.

TRANSLATION

King Parīkṣit inquired from Śukadeva Gosvāmī: O learned brāhmaṇa, demons are generally sinful, being obsessed with the modes of passion and ignorance. How, then, could Vṛtrāsura have attained such exalted love for the Supreme Personality of Godhead, Nārāyaṇa?

PURPORT

In this material world, everyone is obsessed with the modes of passion and ignorance. However, unless one conquers these modes and comes to the platform of goodness, there is no chance of one's becoming a pure devotee. This is confirmed by Lord Kṛṣṇa Himself in *Bhagavad-gītā* (7.28):

yeṣāṁ tv anta-gataṁ pāpaṁ
janānāṁ puṇya-karmaṇām
te dvandva-moha-nirmuktā
bhajante māṁ dṛḍha-vratāḥ

"Persons who have acted piously in previous lives and in this life, whose sinful actions are completely eradicated and who are freed from the duality of delusion, engage themselves in My service with determination." Since Vṛtrāsura was among the demons, Mahārāja Parīkṣit wondered how it was possible for him to have become such an exalted devotee.

TEXT 2

देवानां शुद्धसत्त्वानामृषीणां चामलात्मनाम् ।
भक्तिर्मुकुन्दचरणे न प्रायेणोपजायते ॥ २ ॥

devānāṁ śuddha-sattvānām
ṛṣīṇāṁ cāmalātmanām
bhaktir mukunda-caraṇe
na prāyeṇopajāyate

devānām—of the demigods; *śuddha-sattvānām*—whose minds are purified; *ṛṣīṇām*—of great saintly persons; *ca*—and; *amala-ātmanām*—who have purified their existence; *bhaktiḥ*—devotional service; *mukunda-caraṇe*—to the lotus feet of Mukunda, the Lord, who can give liberation; *na*—not; *prāyeṇa*—almost always; *upajāyate*—develops.

TRANSLATION

Demigods situated in the mode of goodness and great saints cleansed of the dirt of material enjoyment hardly ever render pure devotional service at the lotus feet of Mukunda. [Therefore how could Vṛtrāsura have become such a great devotee?]

TEXT 3

रजोभिः समसंख्याताः पार्थिवैरिह जन्तवः ।
तेषां ये केचनेहन्ते श्रेयो वै मनुजादयः ॥ ३ ॥

rajobhiḥ sama-saṅkhyātāḥ
pārthivair iha jantavaḥ
teṣāṁ ye kecanehante
śreyo vai manujādayaḥ

rajobhiḥ—with the atoms; *sama-saṅkhyātāḥ*—having the same numerical strength; *pārthivaiḥ*—of the earth; *iha*—in this world; *jantavaḥ*—the living entities; *teṣām*—of them; *ye*—those who; *kecana*—

some; *īhante*—act; *śreyaḥ*—for religious principles; *vai*—indeed; *manuja-ādayaḥ*—the human beings and so on.

TRANSLATION

In this material world there are as many living entities as atoms. Among these living entities, a very few are human beings, and among them, few are interested in following religious principles.

TEXT 4

प्रायो मुमुक्षवस्तेषां केचनैव द्विजोत्तम ।
मुमुक्षूणां सहस्रेषु कश्चिन्मुच्येत सिध्यति ॥ ४ ॥

prāyo mumukṣavas teṣāṁ
kecanaiva dvijottama
mumukṣūṇāṁ sahasreṣu
kaścin mucyeta sidhyati

prāyaḥ—almost always; *mumukṣavaḥ*—persons interested in liberation; *teṣām*—of them; *kecana*—some; *eva*—indeed; *dvija-uttama*—O best of the *brāhmaṇas; mumukṣūṇām*—of those who desire to be liberated; *sahasreṣu*—in many thousands; *kaścit*—someone; *mucyeta*—may be actually liberated; *sidhyati*—someone is perfect.

TRANSLATION

O best of the brāhmaṇas, Śukadeva Gosvāmī, out of many persons who follow religious principles, only a few desire liberation from the material world. Among many thousands who desire liberation, one may actually achieve liberation, giving up material attachment to society, friendship, love, country, home, wife and children. And among many thousands of such liberated persons, one who can understand the true meaning of liberation is very rare.

PURPORT

There are four classes of men, namely *karmīs, jñānīs, yogīs* and *bhaktas.* This statement pertains especially to *karmīs* and *jñānīs.* A *karmī* tries to be happy within this material world by changing from one body to another. His objective is bodily comfort, either in this planet or in another. When such a person becomes a *jñānī*, however, he aspires for liberation from material bondage. Among many such persons who aspire for liberation, one may actually be liberated during his life. Such a person gives up his attachment for society, friendship, love, country, family, wife and children. Among many such persons, who are in the *vānaprastha* stage, one may understand the value of becoming a *sannyāsī*, completely accepting the renounced order of life.

TEXT 5

मुक्तानामपि सिद्धानां नारायणपरायणः ।
सुदुर्लभः प्रशान्तात्मा कोटिष्वपि महामुने ॥ ५ ॥

muktānām api siddhānāṁ
nārāyaṇa-parāyaṇaḥ
sudurlabhaḥ praśāntātmā
koṭiṣv api mahā-mune

muktānām—of those who are liberated during this life (who are unattached to the bodily comforts of society, friendship and love); *api*—even; *siddhānām*—who are perfect (because they understand the insignificance of bodily comforts); *nārāyaṇa-parāyaṇaḥ*—a person who has concluded that Nārāyaṇa is the Supreme; *su-durlabhaḥ*—very rarely found; *praśānta*—fully pacified; *ātmā*—whose mind; *koṭiṣu*—out of millions and trillions;* *api*—even; *mahā-mune*—O great sage.

TRANSLATION

O great sage, among many millions who are liberated and perfect in knowledge of liberation, one may be a devotee of Lord Nārāyaṇa, or Kṛṣṇa. Such devotees, who are fully peaceful, are extremely rare.

PURPORT

Śrīla Viśvanātha Cakravartī Ṭhākura gives the following purport to this verse. Simply desiring *mukti*, or liberation, is insufficient; one must

*The word *koṭi* means ten million. Its plural means millions and trillions.

become factually liberated. When one understands the futility of the materialistic way of life, one becomes advanced in knowledge, and therefore he situates himself in the *vānaprastha* order, unattached to family, wife and children. One should then further progress to the platform of *sannyāsa*, the actual renounced order, never to fall again and be afflicted by materialistic life. Even though one desires to be liberated, this does not mean he is liberated. Only rarely is someone liberated. Indeed, although many men take *sannyāsa* to become liberated, because of their imperfections they again become attached to women, material activities, social welfare work and so on.

Jñānīs, yogīs and *karmīs* devoid of devotional service are called offenders. Śrī Caitanya Mahāprabhu says, *māyāvādī kṛṣṇe aparādhī:* one who thinks that everything is *māyā* instead of thinking that everything is Kṛṣṇa is called an *aparādhī,* or offender. Although the Māyāvādīs, impersonalists, are offenders at the lotus feet of Kṛṣṇa, they may nonetheless be counted among the *siddhas,* those who have realized the self. They may be considered nearer to spiritual perfection because at least they have realized what spiritual life is. If such a person becomes *nārāyaṇa-parāyaṇa,* a devotee of Lord Nārāyaṇa, he is better than a *jīvan-mukta,* one who is liberated or perfect. This requires higher intelligence.

There are two kinds of *jñānīs.* One is inclined to devotional service and the other to impersonal realization. Impersonalists generally undergo great endeavor for no tangible benefit, and therefore it is said that they are husking paddy that has no grain (*sthūla-tuṣāvaghātinaḥ*). The other class of *jñānīs,* whose *jñāna* is mixed with *bhakti,* are also of two kinds—those who are devoted to the so-called false form of the Supreme Personality of Godhead and those who understand the Supreme Personality of Godhead as *sac-cid-ānanda-vigraha,* the actual spiritual form. The Māyāvādī devotees worship Nārāyaṇa or Viṣṇu with the idea that Viṣṇu has accepted a form of *māyā* and that the ultimate truth is actually impersonal. The pure devotee, however, never thinks that Viṣṇu has accepted a body of *māyā;* instead, he knows perfectly well that the original Absolute Truth is the Supreme Person. Such a devotee is actually situated in knowledge. He never merges in the Brahman effulgence. As stated in *Śrīmad-Bhāgavatam* (10.2.32):

ye 'nye 'ravindākṣa vimukta-māninas
tvayy asta-bhāvād aviśuddha-buddhayaḥ
āruhya kṛcchreṇa paraṁ padaṁ tataḥ
patanty adho 'nādṛta-yuṣmad-aṅghrayaḥ

"O Lord, the intelligence of those who think themselves liberated but who have no devotion is impure. Even though they rise to the highest point of liberation by dint of severe penances and austerities, they are sure to fall down again into material existence, for they do not take shelter at Your lotus feet." Evidence of this same point is also given in *Bhagavad-gītā* (9.11), wherein the Lord says:

avajānanti māṁ mūḍhā
mānuṣīṁ tanum āśritam
paraṁ bhāvam ajānanto
mama bhūta-maheśvaram

"Fools deride Me when I descend in the human form. They do not know My transcendental nature and My supreme dominion over all that be." When rascals (*mūḍhas*) see that Kṛṣṇa acts exactly like a human being, they deride the transcendental form of the Lord because they do not know the *paraṁ bhāvam*, His transcendental form and activities. Such persons are further described in *Bhagavad-gītā* (9.12) as follows:

moghāśā mogha-karmāṇo
mogha-jñānā vicetasaḥ
rākṣasīm āsurīṁ caiva
prakṛtiṁ mohinīṁ śritāḥ

"Those who are thus bewildered are attracted by demoniac and atheistic views. In that deluded condition, their hopes for liberation, their fruitive activities and their culture of knowledge are all defeated." Such persons do not know that Kṛṣṇa's body is not material. There is no distinction between Kṛṣṇa's body and His soul, but because less intelligent men see Kṛṣṇa as a human being, they deride Him. They cannot imagine how a person like Kṛṣṇa could be the origin of everything (*govindam ādi-*

puruṣaṁ tam ahaṁ bhajāmi). Such persons are described as *moghāśāḥ*, baffled in their hopes. Whatever they desire for the future will be baffled. Even if they apparently engage in devotional service, they are described as *moghāśāḥ* because they ultimately desire to merge into the Brahman effulgence.

Those who aspire to be elevated to the heavenly planets by devotional service will also be frustrated, because this is not the result of devotional service. However, they are also given a chance to engage in devotional service and be purified. As stated in *Śrīmad-Bhāgavatam* (1.2.17):

śṛṇvatāṁ sva-kathāḥ kṛṣṇaḥ
puṇya-śravaṇa-kīrtanaḥ
hṛdy antaḥ-stho hy abhadrāṇi
vidhunoti suhṛt satām

"Śrī Kṛṣṇa, the Personality of Godhead, who is the Paramātmā [Supersoul] in everyone's heart and the benefactor of the truthful devotee, cleanses desire for material enjoyment from the heart of the devotee who relishes His messages, which are in themselves virtuous when properly heard and chanted."

Unless the dirt within the core of one's heart is cleansed away, one cannot become a pure devotee. Therefore the word *sudurlabhaḥ* ("very rarely found") is used in this verse. Not only among hundreds and thousands, but among millions of perfectly liberated souls, a pure devotee is hardly ever found. Therefore the words *koṭiṣv api* are used herein. Śrīla Madhvācārya gives the following quotations from the *Tantra Bhāgavata:*

nava-koṭyas tu devānām
ṛṣayaḥ sapta-koṭayaḥ
nārāyaṇāyanāḥ sarve
ye kecit tat-parāyaṇāḥ

"There are ninety million demigods and seventy million sages, who are all called *nārāyaṇāyana*, devotees of Lord Nārāyaṇa. Among them, only a few are called *nārāyaṇa-parāyaṇa*."

nārāyaṇāyanā devā
ṛṣy-ādyās tat-parāyaṇāḥ
brahmādyāḥ kecanaiva syuḥ
siddho yogya-sukhaṁ labhan

The difference between the *siddhas* and *nārāyaṇa-parāyaṇas* is that direct devotees are called *nārāyaṇa-parāyaṇas* whereas those who perform various types of mystic *yoga* are called *siddhas.*

TEXT 6

वृत्रस्तु स कथं पापः सर्वलोकोपतापनः ।
इत्थं दृढमतिः कृष्ण आसीत् संग्राम उल्बणे ॥ ६ ॥

vṛtras tu sa kathaṁ pāpaḥ
sarva-lokopatāpanaḥ
itthaṁ dṛḍha-matiḥ kṛṣṇa
āsīt saṅgrāma ulbaṇe

vṛtraḥ—Vṛtrāsura; *tu*—but; *saḥ*—he; *katham*—how; *pāpaḥ*—although sinful (getting the body of a demon); *sarva-loka*—of all the three worlds; *upatāpanaḥ*—the cause of suffering; *ittham*—such; *dṛḍha-matiḥ*—firmly fixed intelligence; *kṛṣṇe*—in Kṛṣṇa; *āsīt*—there was; *saṅgrāme ulbaṇe*—in the great blazing fire of battle.

TRANSLATION

Vṛtrāsura was situated in the blazing fire of battle and was an infamous, sinful demon, always engaged in giving troubles and anxieties to others. How could such a demon become so greatly Kṛṣṇa conscious?

PURPORT

It has been described that a *nārāyaṇa-parāyaṇa,* a pure devotee, is rarely found even among millions and millions of persons. Therefore Parīkṣit Mahārāja was surprised that Vṛtrāsura, whose purpose was to give trouble and anxiety to others, was one of these devotees, even on a battlefield. What was the reason for Vṛtrāsura's advancement?

TEXT 7

अत्र नः संशयो भूयाञ्छ्रोतुं कौतूहलं प्रभो ।
यः पौरुषेण समरे सहस्राक्षमतोषयत् ॥ ७ ॥

atra naḥ saṁśayo bhūyāñ
chrotuṁ kautūhalaṁ prabho
yaḥ pauruṣeṇa samare
sahasrākṣam atoṣayat

atra—in this connection; *naḥ*—our; *saṁśayaḥ*—doubt; *bhūyān*—great; *śrotum*—to hear; *kautūhalam*—eagerness; *prabho*—O my lord; *yaḥ*—he who; *pauruṣeṇa*—by bravery and strength; *samare*—in battle; *sahasra-akṣam*—Lord Indra, who has one thousand eyes; *atoṣayat*—pleased.

TRANSLATION

My dear lord, Śukadeva Gosvāmī, although Vṛtrāsura was a sinful demon, he showed the prowess of a most exalted kṣatriya and satisfied Lord Indra in battle. How could such a demon be a great devotee of Lord Kṛṣṇa? These contradictions have caused me great doubt, and they have made me eager to hear of this from you.

TEXT 8

श्रीसूत उवाच
परीक्षितोऽथ संप्रश्नं भगवान् बादरायणिः ।
निशम्य श्रद्दधानस्य प्रतिनन्द्य वचोऽब्रवीत् ॥ ८ ॥

śrī-sūta uvāca
parīkṣito 'tha sampraśnaṁ
bhagavān bādarāyaṇiḥ
niśamya śraddadhānasya
pratinandya vaco 'bravīt

śrī-sūtaḥ uvāca—Śrī Sūta Gosvāmī said; *parīkṣitaḥ*—of Mahārāja Parīkṣit; *atha*—thus; *sampraśnam*—the perfect question; *bhagavān*—

the most powerful; *bādarāyaṇiḥ*—Śukadeva Gosvāmī, the son of Vyāsadeva; *niśamya*—hearing; *śraddadhānasya*—of his disciple, who was so faithful in understanding the truth; *pratinandya*—congratulating; *vacaḥ*—words; *abravīt*—spoke.

TRANSLATION

Śrī Sūta Gosvāmī said: After hearing Mahārāja Parīkṣit's very intelligent question, Śukadeva Gosvāmī, the most powerful sage, began answering his disciple with great affection.

TEXT 9

श्रीशुक उवाच
शृणुष्वावहितो राजन्नितिहासमिमं यथा ।
श्रुतं द्वैपायनमुखान्नारदाद्देवलादपि ॥ ९ ॥

śrī-śuka uvāca
śṛṇuṣvāvahito rājann
itihāsam imaṁ yathā
śrutaṁ dvaipāyana-mukhān
nāradād devalād api

śrī-śukaḥ uvāca—Śrī Śukadeva Gosvāmī said; *śṛṇuṣva*—please hear; *avahitaḥ*—with great attention; *rājan*—O King; *itihāsam*—history; *imam*—this; *yathā*—just as; *śrutam*—heard; *dvaipāyana*—of Vyāsadeva; *mukhāt*—from the mouth; *nāradāt*—from Nārada; *devalāt*—from Devala Ṛṣi; *api*—also.

TRANSLATION

Śrī Śukadeva Gosvāmī said: O King, I shall speak to you the same history I have heard from the mouths of Vyāsadeva, Nārada and Devala. Please listen with attention.

TEXT 10

आसीद्राजा सार्वभौमः शूरसेनेषु वै नृप ।
चित्रकेतुरिति ख्यातो यस्यासीत् कामधुङ्मही ॥१०॥

āsīd rājā sārvabhaumaḥ
śūraseneṣu vai nṛpa
citraketur iti khyāto
yasyāsīt kāmadhuṁ mahī

āsīt—there was; *rājā*—one king; *sārva-bhaumaḥ*—an emperor of the entire surface of the globe; *śūraseneṣu*—in the country known as Śūrasena; *vai*—indeed; *nṛpa*—O King; *citraketuḥ*—Citraketu; *iti*—thus; *khyātaḥ*—celebrated; *yasya*—of whom; *āsīt*—was; *kāma-dhuk*—supplying all the necessities; *mahī*—the earth.

TRANSLATION

O King Parīkṣit, in the province of Śūrasena there was a king named Citraketu, who ruled the entire earth. During his reign, the earth produced all the necessities for life.

PURPORT

Here the most significant statement is that the earth completely produced all the necessities of life during the time of King Citraketu. As stated in the *Īśopaniṣad* (Mantra 1):

īśāvāsyam idaṁ sarvaṁ
yat kiñca jagatyāṁ jagat
tena tyaktena bhuñjīthā
mā gṛdhaḥ kasya svid dhanam

"Everything animate or inanimate that is within the universe is controlled and owned by the Lord. One should therefore accept only those things necessary for himself, which are set aside as his quota, and one should not accept other things, knowing well to whom they belong." Kṛṣṇa, the supreme controller, has created the material world, which is completely perfect and free from scarcity. The Lord supplies the necessities of all living entities. These necessities come from the earth, and thus the earth is the source of supply. When there is a good ruler, that source produces the necessities of life abundantly. However, when there is not such a good ruler, there will be scarcity. This is the significance of the word *kāmadhuk*. Elsewhere in *Śrīmad-Bhāgavatam*

(1.10.4) it is said, *kāmaṁ vavarṣa parjanyaḥ sarva-kāma-dughā mahī:* "During the reign of Mahārāja Yudhiṣṭhira, the clouds showered all the water that people needed, and the earth produced all the necessities of men in profusion." We have experience that in some seasons the rains produce abundance and in other seasons there is scarcity. We have no control over the earth's productiveness, for it is naturally under the full control of the Supreme Personality of Godhead. By His order, the Lord can make the earth produce sufficiently or insufficiently. If a pious king rules the earth according to the śāstric injunctions, there will naturally be regular rainfall and sufficient produce to provide for all men. There will be no question of exploitation, for everyone will have enough. Black-marketeering and other corrupt dealings will then automatically stop. Simply ruling the land cannot solve man's problems unless the leader has spiritual capabilities. He must be like Mahārāja Yudhiṣṭhira, Parīkṣit Mahārāja or Rāmacandra. Then all the inhabitants of the land will be extremely happy.

TEXT 11

तस्य भार्यासहस्राणां सहस्राणि दशाभवन् ।
सान्तानिकश्चापि नृपो न लेभे तासु सन्ततिम्॥११॥

tasya bhāryā-sahasrāṇāṁ
sahasrāṇi daśābhavan
sāntānikaś cāpi nṛpo
na lebhe tāsu santatim

tasya—of him (King Citraketu); *bhāryā*—of wives; *sahasrāṇām*—of thousands; *sahasrāṇi*—thousands; *daśa*—ten; *abhavan*—there were; *sāntānikaḥ*—quite capable of begetting sons; *ca*—and; *api*—although; *nṛpaḥ*—the King; *na*—not; *lebhe*—obtained; *tāsu*—in them; *santatim*—a son.

TRANSLATION

This Citraketu had ten million wives, but although he was capable of producing children, he did not receive a child from any of them. By chance, all the wives were barren.

TEXT 12

रूपौदार्यवयोजन्मविद्यैश्वर्यश्रियादिभिः ।
सम्पन्नस्य गुणैः सर्वैश्चिन्ता वन्ध्यापतेरभूत् ॥१२॥

rūpaudārya-vayo-janma-
vidyaiśvarya-śriyādibhiḥ
sampannasya guṇaiḥ sarvaiś
cintā bandhyā-pater abhūt

rūpa—with beauty; *audārya*—magnanimity; *vayaḥ*—youth; *janma*—aristocratic birth; *vidyā*—education; *aiśvarya*—opulence; *śriya-ādibhiḥ*—wealth and so on; *sampannasya*—endowed; *guṇaiḥ*—with good qualities; *sarvaiḥ*—all; *cintā*—anxiety; *bandhyā-pateḥ*—of Citraketu, the husband of so many sterile wives; *abhūt*—there was.

TRANSLATION

Citraketu, the husband of these millions of wives, was endowed with a beautiful form, magnanimity and youth. He was born in a high family, he had a complete education, and he was wealthy and opulent. Nevertheless, in spite of being endowed with all these assets, he was full of anxiety because he did not have a son.

PURPORT

It appears that the King first married one wife, but she could not bear a child. Then he married a second, a third, a fourth and so on, but none of the wives could bear children. In spite of the material assets of *janmaiśvarya-śruta-śrī*—birth in an aristocratic family with full opulence, wealth, education and beauty—he was very much aggrieved because in spite of having so many wives, he had no son. Certainly his grief was natural. *Gṛhastha* life does not mean having a wife and no children. Cāṇakya Paṇḍita says, *putra-hīnaṁ gṛhaṁ śūnyam:* if a family man has no son, his home is no better than a desert. The King was certainly most unhappy that he could not get a son, and this is why he had married so many times. *Kṣatriyas* especially are allowed to marry more than one wife, and this King did so. Nonetheless, he had no issue.

TEXT 13

न तस्य संपदः सर्वा महिष्यो वामलोचनाः ।
सार्वभौमस्य भूश्चेयमभवन् प्रीतिहेतवः ॥१३॥

na tasya sampadaḥ sarvā
mahiṣyo vāma-locanāḥ
sārvabhaumasya bhūś ceyam
abhavan prīti-hetavaḥ

na—not; *tasya*—of him (Citraketu); *sampadaḥ*—the great opulences; *sarvāḥ*—all; *mahiṣyaḥ*—the queens; *vāma-locanāḥ*—having very attractive eyes; *sārva-bhaumasya*—of the emperor; *bhūḥ*—land; *ca*—also; *iyam*—this; *abhavan*—were; *prīti-hetavaḥ*—sources of pleasure.

TRANSLATION

His queens all had beautiful faces and attractive eyes, yet neither his opulences, his hundreds and thousands of queens, nor the lands of which he was the supreme proprietor were sources of happiness for him.

TEXT 14

तस्यैकदा तु भवनमङ्गिरा भगवानृषिः ।
लोकाननुचरन्नेतानुपागच्छद्यदृच्छया ॥१४॥

tasyaikadā tu bhavanam
aṅgirā bhagavān ṛṣiḥ
lokān anucarann etān
upāgacchad yadṛcchayā

tasya—of him; *ekadā*—once upon a time; *tu*—but; *bhavanam*—to the palace; *aṅgirāḥ*—Aṅgirā; *bhagavān*—very powerful; *ṛṣiḥ*—sage; *lokān*—planets; *anucaran*—traveling around; *etān*—these; *upāgacchat*—came; *yadṛcchayā*—suddenly.

TRANSLATION

Once upon a time, when the powerful sage named Aṅgirā was traveling all over the universe without engagement, by his sweet will he came to the palace of King Citraketu.

TEXT 15

तं पूजयित्वा विधिवत्प्रत्युत्थानार्हणादिभिः ।
कृतातिथ्यमुपासीदत्सुखासीनं समाहितः ॥१५॥

taṁ pūjayitvā vidhivat
pratyutthānārhaṇādibhiḥ
kṛtātithyam upāsīdat
sukhāsīnaṁ samāhitaḥ

tam—him; *pūjayitvā*—after worshiping; *vidhi-vat*—according to the rules and regulations for receiving exalted guests; *pratyutthāna*—by standing from the throne; *arhaṇa-ādibhiḥ*—offering worship and so on; *kṛta-atithyam*—who was given hospitality; *upāsīdat*—sat down near; *sukha-āsīnam*—who was seated very comfortably; *samāhitaḥ*—controlling his mind and senses.

TRANSLATION

Citraketu immediately stood up from his throne and offered him worship. He offered drinking water and eatables and in this way performed his duty as a host to a great guest. When the ṛṣi was seated very comfortably, the King, restraining his mind and senses, sat on the ground at the side of the ṛṣi's feet.

TEXT 16

महर्षिस्तमुपासीनं प्रश्रयावनतं क्षितौ ।
प्रतिपूज्य महाराज समाभाष्येदमब्रवीत् ॥१६॥

maharṣis tam upāsīnaṁ
praśrayāvanataṁ kṣitau

pratipūjya mahārāja
samābhāṣyedam abravīt

mahā-ṛṣiḥ—the great sage; *tam*—unto him (the King); *upāsīnam*—sitting near; *praśraya-avanatam*—bowing in humility; *kṣitau*—on the ground; *pratipūjya*—congratulating; *mahārāja*—O King Parīkṣit; *samābhāṣya*—addressing; *idam*—this; *abravīt*—said.

TRANSLATION

O King Parīkṣit, when Citraketu, bent low in humility, was seated at the lotus feet of the great sage, the sage congratulated him for his humility and hospitality. The sage addressed him in the following words.

TEXT 17

अङ्गिरा उवाच

अपि तेऽनामयं स्वस्ति प्रकृतीनां तथात्मनः ।
यथा प्रकृतिभिर्गुप्तः पुमान् राजा च सप्तभिः ॥१७॥

aṅgirā uvāca
api te 'nāmayaṁ svasti
prakṛtīnāṁ tathātmanaḥ
yathā prakṛtibhir guptaḥ
pumān rājā ca saptabhiḥ

aṅgirāḥ uvāca—the great sage Aṅgirā said; *api*—whether; *te*—of you; *anāmayam*—health; *svasti*—auspiciousness; *prakṛtīnām*—of your royal elements (associates and paraphernalia); *tathā*—as well as; *ātmanaḥ*—of your own body, mind and soul; *yathā*—like; *prakṛtibhiḥ*—by the elements of material nature; *guptaḥ*—protected; *pumān*—the living being; *rājā*—the king; *ca*—also; *saptabhiḥ*—by seven.

TRANSLATION

The great sage Aṅgirā said: My dear King, I hope that your body and mind and your royal associates and paraphernalia are well.

When the seven properties of material nature [the total material energy, the ego and the five objects of sense gratification] are in proper order, the living entity within the material elements is happy. Without these seven elements one cannot exist. Similarly, a king is always protected by seven elements—his instructor (svāmī or guru), his ministers, his kingdom, his fort, his treasury, his royal order and his friends.

PURPORT

As it is quoted by Śrīdhara Svāmī in his *Bhāgavatam* commentary:

svāmy-amātyau janapadā
durga-draviṇa-sañcayāḥ
daṇḍo mitraṁ ca tasyaitāḥ
sapta-prakṛtayo matāḥ

A king is not alone. He first has his spiritual master, the supreme guide. Then come his ministers, his kingdom, his fortifications, his treasury, his system of law and order, and his friends or allies. If these seven are properly maintained, the king is happy. Similarly, as explained in *Bhagavad-gītā* (*dehino 'smin yathā dehe*), the living entity, the soul, is within the material covering of the *mahat-tattva*, ego and *pañca-tanmātrā*, the five objects of sense gratification. When these seven are in proper order, the living entity is in a mood of pleasure. Generally when the associates of the king are quiet and obedient, the king can be happy. Therefore the great sage Aṅgirā Ṛṣi inquired about the King's personal health and the good fortune of his seven associates. When we inquire from a friend whether everything is well, we are concerned not only with his personal self but also with his family, his source of income, and his assistants or servants. All of them must be well, and then a person can be happy.

TEXT 18

आत्मानं प्रकृतिष्वद्धा निधाय श्रेय आप्नुयात् ।
राज्ञा तथा प्रकृतयो नरदेवाहिताधयः ॥१८॥

ātmānaṁ prakṛtiṣv addhā
nidhāya śreya āpnuyāt
rājñā tathā prakṛtayo
naradevāhitādhayaḥ

ātmānam—himself; *prakṛtiṣu*—under these seven royal elements; *addhā*—directly; *nidhāya*—placing; *śreyaḥ*—ultimate happiness; *āpnuyāt*—may obtain; *rājñā*—by the king; *tathā*—so also; *prakṛtayaḥ*—the dependent royal elements; *nara-deva*—O King; *āhita-adhayaḥ*—offering wealth and other items.

TRANSLATION

O King, O lord of humanity, when a king directly depends upon his associates and follows their instructions, he is happy. Similarly, when his associates offer their gifts and activities to the king and follow his orders, they are also happy.

PURPORT

The actual happiness of a king and his dependents is described in this verse. A king should not simply give orders to his dependents because he is supreme; sometimes he must follow their instructions. Similarly, the dependents should depend on the king. This mutual dependence will make everyone happy.

TEXT 19

अपि दाराः प्रजामात्या भृत्याः श्रेण्योऽथ मन्त्रिणः ।
पौरा जानपदा भूपा आत्मजा वशवर्तिनः ॥१९॥

api dārāḥ prajāmātyā
bhṛtyāḥ śreṇyo 'tha mantriṇaḥ
paurā jānapadā bhūpā
ātmajā vaśa-vartinaḥ

api—whether; *dārāḥ*—wives; *prajā*—citizens; *amātyāḥ*—and secretaries; *bhṛtyāḥ*—servants; *śreṇyaḥ*—merchants; *atha*—as well as;

mantriṇaḥ—ministers; *paurāḥ*—inmates of the palace; *jānapadāḥ*—the provincial governors; *bhūpāḥ*—landholders; *ātma-jāḥ*—sons; *vaśa-vartinaḥ*—under your full control.

TRANSLATION

O King, are your wives, citizens, secretaries and servants and the merchants who sell spices and oil under your control? Are you also in full control of ministers, the inhabitants of your palace, your provincial governors, your sons and your other dependents?

PURPORT

The master or king and his subordinates should be interdependent. Through cooperation, both of them can be happy.

TEXT 20

यस्यात्मानुवशश्चेत्स्यात्सर्वे तद्वशगा इमे ।
लोकाः सपाला यच्छन्ति सर्वे बलिमतन्द्रिताः ॥२०॥

yasyātmānuvaśaś cet syāt
sarve tad-vaśagā ime
lokāḥ sapālā yacchanti
sarve balim atandritāḥ

yasya—of whom; *ātmā*—mind; *anuvaśaḥ*—under control; *cet*—if; *syāt*—may be; *sarve*—all; *tat-vaśa-gāḥ*—under the control of him; *ime*—these; *lokāḥ*—the worlds; *sa-pālāḥ*—with their governors; *yacchanti*—offer; *sarve*—all; *balim*—contribution; *atandritāḥ*—becoming free from laziness.

TRANSLATION

If the king's mind is fully controlled, all his family members and governmental officers are subordinate to him. His provincial governors present taxes on time, without resistance, and what to speak of lesser servants?

PURPORT

Aṅgirā Ṛṣi asked the King whether his mind was also under control. This is most essential for happiness.

TEXT 21

आत्मनः प्रीयते नात्मा परतः स्वत एव वा ।
लक्षयेऽलब्धकामं त्वां चिन्तया शबलं मुखम् ॥२१॥

ātmanaḥ prīyate nātmā
parataḥ svata eva vā
lakṣaye 'labdha-kāmaṁ tvāṁ
cintayā śabalaṁ mukham

ātmanaḥ—of you; *prīyate*—is pleased; *na*—not; *ātmā*—the mind; *parataḥ*—due to other causes; *svataḥ*—due to yourself; *eva*—indeed; *vā*—or; *lakṣaye*—I can see; *alabdha-kāmam*—not achieving your desired goals; *tvām*—you; *cintayā*—by anxiety; *śabalam*—pale; *mukham*—face.

TRANSLATION

O King Citraketu, I can observe that your mind is not pleased. You seem not to have achieved your desired goal. Is this because of you yourself, or has it been caused by others? Your pale face reflects your deep anxiety.

TEXT 22

एवं विकल्पितो राजन् विदुषा मुनिनापि सः ।
प्रश्रयावनतोऽभ्याह प्रजाकामस्ततो मुनिम् ॥२२॥

evaṁ vikalpito rājan
viduṣā munināpi saḥ
praśrayāvanato 'bhyāha
prajā-kāmas tato munim

evam—thus; *vikalpitaḥ*—questioned; *rājan*—O King Parīkṣit; *viduṣā*—greatly learned; *muninā*—by the philosopher; *api*—although; *saḥ*—he (King Citraketu); *praśraya-avanataḥ*—being bent low due to humility; *abhyāha*—replied; *prajā-kāmaḥ*—desiring offspring; *tataḥ*—thereafter; *munim*—to the great sage.

TRANSLATION

Śukadeva Gosvāmī said: O King Parīkṣit, although the great sage Aṅgirā knew everything, he inquired from the King in this way. Thus King Citraketu, desiring a son, bent low in great humility and spoke to the great sage as follows.

PURPORT

Since the face is the index to the mind, a saintly person can study the condition of one's mind by seeing his face. When Aṅgirā Ṛṣi remarked about the King's discolored face, King Citraketu explained the cause of his anxiety as follows.

TEXT 23

चित्रकेतुरुवाच
भगवन् किं न विदितं तपोज्ञानसमाधिभिः ।
योगिनां ध्वस्तपापानां बहिरन्तः शरीरिषु ॥२३॥

citraketur uvāca
bhagavan kiṁ na viditaṁ
tapo-jñāna-samādhibhiḥ
yogināṁ dhvasta-pāpānāṁ
bahir antaḥ śarīriṣu

citraketuḥ uvāca—King Citraketu replied; *bhagavan*—O most powerful sage; *kim*—what; *na*—not; *viditam*—is understood; *tapaḥ*—by austerity; *jñāna*—knowledge; *samādhibhiḥ*—and by *samādhi* (trance, transcendental meditation); *yoginām*—by the great *yogīs* or devotees; *dhvasta-pāpānām*—who are fully freed from all sinful reactions; *bahiḥ*—externally; *antaḥ*—internally; *śarīriṣu*—in conditioned souls, who have material bodies.

TRANSLATION

King Citraketu said: O great lord Aṅgirā, because of austerity, knowledge and transcendental samādhi, you are freed from all the reactions of sinful life. Therefore, as a perfect yogī, you can understand everything external and internal regarding embodied, conditioned souls like us.

TEXT 24

तथापि पृच्छतो ब्रूयां ब्रह्मन्नात्मनि चिन्तितम् ।
भवतो विदुषश्चापि चोदितस्त्वदनुज्ञया ॥२४॥

tathāpi pṛcchato brūyāṁ
brahmann ātmani cintitam
bhavato viduṣaś cāpi
coditas tvad-anujñayā

tathāpi—still; *pṛcchataḥ*—asking; *brūyām*—let me speak; *brahman*—O great *brāhmaṇa; ātmani*—in the mind; *cintitam*—anxiety; *bhavataḥ*—to you; *viduṣaḥ*—who know everything; *ca*—and; *api*—although; *coditaḥ*—being inspired; *tvat*—your; *anujñayā*—by the order.

TRANSLATION

O great soul, you are aware of everything, yet you are asking me why I am full of anxiety. Therefore, in response to your order, let me disclose the cause.

TEXT 25

लोकपालैरपि प्रार्थ्याः साम्राज्यैश्वर्यसम्पदः ।
न नन्दयन्त्यप्रजं मां क्षुत्तृट्कामामिवापरे ॥२५॥

loka-pālair api prārthyāḥ
sāmrājyaiśvarya-sampadaḥ
na nandayanty aprajaṁ māṁ
kṣut-tṛṭ-kāmam ivāpare

loka-pālaiḥ—by great demigods; *api*—even; *prārthyāḥ*—desirable; *sāmrājya*—a great empire; *aiśvarya*—material opulence; *sampadaḥ*—possessions; *na nandayanti*—do not give pleasure; *aprajam*—because of having no son; *mām*—unto me; *kṣut*—hunger; *tṛṭ*—thirst; *kāmam*—desiring to satisfy; *iva*—like; *apare*—other enjoyable sense objects.

TRANSLATION

As a person aggrieved by hunger and thirst is not pleased by the external gratification of flower garlands or sandalwood pulp, I am not pleased with my empire, opulence or possessions, which are desirable even for great demigods, because I have no son.

TEXT 26

ततः पाहि महाभाग पूर्वैः सह गतं तमः ।
यथा तरेम दुष्पारं प्रजया तद् विधेहि नः ॥२६॥

tataḥ pāhi mahā-bhāga
pūrvaiḥ saha gataṁ tamaḥ
yathā tarema duṣpāraṁ
prajayā tad vidhehi naḥ

tataḥ—therefore, because of this; *pāhi*—kindly save; *mahā-bhāga*—O great sage; *pūrvaiḥ saha*—along with my forefathers; *gatam*—gone; *tamaḥ*—to darkness; *yathā*—so that; *tarema*—we can cross; *duṣpāram*—very difficult to cross; *prajayā*—by getting a son; *tat*—that; *vidhehi*—kindly do; *naḥ*—for us.

TRANSLATION

Therefore, O great sage, please save me and my forefathers, who are descending to the darkness of hell because I have no progeny. Kindly do something so that I may have a son to deliver us from hellish conditions.

PURPORT

According to Vedic civilization, one gets married simply to have a son, who is needed to offer oblations to his forefathers. King Citraketu responsibly desired to beget a child so that he and his forefathers might be delivered from the darkest regions. He was concerned with how to get *piṇḍa*, oblations, in the next life, not only for himself but also for his forefathers. Therefore he requested Aṅgirā Ṛṣi to favor him by doing something that could help him get a son.

TEXT 27

श्रीशुक उवाच
इत्यर्थितः स भगवान् कृपालुर्ब्रह्मणः सुतः ।
श्रपयित्वा चरुं त्वाष्ट्रं त्वष्टारमयजद् विभुः ॥२७॥

śrī-śuka uvāca
ity arthitaḥ sa bhagavān
kṛpālur brahmaṇaḥ sutaḥ
śrapayitvā caruṁ tvāṣṭraṁ
tvaṣṭāram ayajad vibhuḥ

śrī-śukaḥ uvāca—Śrī Śukadeva Gosvāmī said; *iti*—thus; *arthitaḥ*—being requested; *saḥ*—he (Aṅgirā Ṛṣi); *bhagavān*—the most powerful; *kṛpāluḥ*—being very merciful; *brahmaṇaḥ*—of Lord Brahmā; *sutaḥ*—a son (born of Lord Brahmā's mind); *śrapayitvā*—after causing to cook; *carum*—a specific oblation of sweetrice; *tvāṣṭram*—meant for the demigod known as Tvaṣṭā; *tvaṣṭāram*—Tvaṣṭā; *ayajat*—he worshiped; *vibhuḥ*—the great sage.

TRANSLATION

In response to the request of Mahārāja Citraketu, Aṅgirā Ṛṣi, who was born of Lord Brahmā's mind, was very merciful toward him. Because the sage was a greatly powerful personality, he performed a sacrifice by offering oblations of sweetrice to Tvaṣṭā.

TEXT 28

ज्येष्ठा श्रेष्ठा च या राज्ञो महिषीणां च भारत ।
नाम्ना कृतद्युतिस्तस्यै यज्ञोच्छिष्टमदाद् द्विजः ॥२८॥

jyeṣṭhā śreṣṭhā ca yā rājño
mahiṣīṇāṁ ca bhārata
nāmnā kṛtadyutis tasyai
yajñocchiṣṭam adād dvijaḥ

jyeṣṭhā—the senior; *śreṣṭhā*—the most perfect; *ca*—and; *yā*—she who; *rājñaḥ*—of the King; *mahiṣīṇām*—among all the queens; *ca*—also; *bhārata*—O Mahārāja Parīkṣit, the best of the Bhāratas; *nāmnā*—by name; *kṛtadyutiḥ*—Kṛtadyuti; *tasyai*—unto her; *yajña*—of the sacrifice; *ucchiṣṭam*—the remnants of food; *adāt*—delivered; *dvijaḥ*—the great sage (Aṅgirā).

TRANSLATION

O Parīkṣit Mahārāja, best of the Bhāratas, the remnants of the food offered in the yajña were given by the great sage Aṅgirā to the first and most perfect among Citraketu's millions of queens, whose name was Kṛtadyuti.

TEXT 29

अथाह नृपतिं राजन् भवितैकस्तवात्मजः ।
हर्षशोकप्रदस्तुभ्यमिति ब्रह्मसुतो ययौ ॥२९॥

athāha nṛpatiṁ rājan
bhavitaikas tavātmajaḥ
harṣa-śoka-pradas tubhyam
iti brahma-suto yayau

atha—thereafter; *āha*—said; *nṛpatim*—unto the King; *rājan*—O King Citraketu; *bhavitā*—there will be; *ekaḥ*—one; *tava*—your; *ātmajaḥ*—son; *harṣa-śoka*—jubilation and lamentation; *pradaḥ*—who will give; *tubhyam*—unto you; *iti*—thus; *brahma-sutaḥ*—Aṅgirā Ṛṣi, the son of Lord Brahmā; *yayau*—left.

TRANSLATION

Thereafter, the great sage told the King, "O great King, now you will have a son who will be the cause of both jubilation and

lamentation." The sage then left, without waiting for Citraketu's response.

PURPORT

The word *harṣa* means "jubilation," and *śoka* means "lamentation." The King was overwhelmed with joy when he understood that he would have a son. Because of his great jubilation, he could not actually understand the statement of the sage Aṅgirā. He accepted it to mean that there would certainly be jubilation because of the birth of his future son, but that he would be the King's only son and, being very proud of his great wealth and empire, would not be very obedient to his father. Thus the King was satisfied, thinking, "Let there be a son. It does not matter if he is not very obedient." In Bengal there is a proverb that instead of having no maternal uncle, it is better to have a maternal uncle who is blind. The King accepted this philosophy, thinking that a disobedient son would be better than no son at all. The great sage Cāṇakya Paṇḍita says:

ko 'rthaḥ putreṇa jātena
yo na vidvān na dhārmikaḥ
kāṇena cakṣuṣā kiṁ vā
cakṣuḥ pīḍaiva kevalam

"What is the use of a son who is neither a learned scholar nor a devotee? Such a son is like a blind, diseased eye, which always causes suffering." Nevertheless, the material world is so polluted that one wants to have a son even though he is useless. This attitude was represented in the history of King Citraketu.

TEXT 30

सापि तत्प्राशनादेव चित्रकेतोरधारयत् ।
गर्भं कृतद्युतिर्देवी कृत्तिकाग्नेरिवात्मजम् ॥३०॥

sāpi tat-prāśanād eva
citraketor adhārayat
garbhaṁ kṛtadyutir devī
kṛttikāgner ivātmajam

sā—she; *api*—even; *tat-prāśanāt*—by eating the remnants of food from the great sacrifice; *eva*—indeed; *citraketoḥ*—from King Citraketu; *adhārayat*—bore; *garbham*—pregnancy; *kṛtadyutiḥ*—Queen Kṛtadyuti; *devī*—the goddess; *kṛttikā*—Kṛttikā; *agneḥ*—from Agni; *iva*—as; *ātma-jam*—a son.

TRANSLATION

As Kṛttikādevī, after receiving the semen of Lord Śiva from Agni, conceived a child named Skanda [Kārttikeya], Kṛtadyuti, having received semen from Citraketu, became pregnant after eating remnants of food from the yajña performed by Aṅgirā.

TEXT 31

तस्या अनुदिनं गर्भः शुक्लपक्ष इवोडुपः ।
ववृधे शूरसेनेशतेजसा शनकैर्नृप ॥३१॥

tasyā anudinaṁ garbhaḥ
śukla-pakṣa ivoḍupaḥ
vavṛdhe śūraseneśa-
tejasā śanakaïr nṛpa

tasyāḥ—her; *anudinam*—day after day; *garbhaḥ*—embryo; *śukla-pakṣe*—during the fortnight of the waxing moon; *iva*—like; *uḍupaḥ*—the moon; *vavṛdhe*—gradually developed; *śūrasena-īśa*—of the King of Śūrasena; *tejasā*—by the semen; *śanakaiḥ*—little by little; *nṛpa*—O King Parīkṣit.

TRANSLATION

After receiving semen from Mahārāja Citraketu, the King of Śūrasena, Queen Kṛtadyuti gradually developed in her pregnancy, O King Parīkṣit, just as the moon develops during the bright fortnight.

TEXT 32

अथ काल उपावृत्ते कुमारः समजायत ।
जनयन् शूरसेनानां शृण्वतां परमां मुदम् ॥३२॥

atha kāla upāvṛtte
kumāraḥ samajāyata
janayan śūrasenānāṁ
śṛṇvatāṁ paramāṁ mudam

atha—thereafter; *kāle upāvṛtte*—in due course of time; *kumāraḥ*—the son; *samajāyata*—took birth; *janayan*—creating; *śūrasenānām*—of the inhabitants of Śūrasena; *śṛṇvatām*—hearing; *paramām*—the highest; *mudam*—delight.

TRANSLATION

Thereafter, in due course of time, a son was born to the King. Hearing news of this, all the inhabitants of the state of Śūrasena were extremely pleased.

TEXT 33

हृष्टो राजा कुमारस्य स्नातः शुचिरलंकृतः ।
वाचयित्वाशिषो विप्रैः कारयामास जातकम् ॥३३॥

hṛṣṭo rājā kumārasya
snātaḥ śucir alaṅkṛtaḥ
vācayitvāśiṣo vipraiḥ
kārayām āsa jātakam

hṛṣṭaḥ—very happy; *rājā*—the King; *kumārasya*—of his newly born son; *snātaḥ*—having bathed; *śuciḥ*—being purified; *alaṅkṛtaḥ*—being decorated with ornaments; *vācayitvā*—having caused to be spoken; *āśiṣaḥ*—words of benediction; *vipraiḥ*—by learned *brāhmaṇas; kārayām āsa*—caused to be performed; *jātakam*—the birth ceremony.

TRANSLATION

King Citraketu was especially pleased. After purifying himself by bathing and by decorating himself with ornaments, he engaged learned brāhmaṇas in offering benedictions to the child and performing the birth ceremony.

TEXT 34

तेभ्यो हिरण्यं रजतं वासांस्याभरणानि च ।
ग्रामान् हयान् गजान् प्रादाद् धेनूनामर्बुदानि षट् ॥३४॥

tebhyo hiraṇyaṁ rajataṁ
vāsāṁsy ābharaṇāni ca
grāmān hayān gajān prādād
dhenūnām arbudāni ṣaṭ

tebhyaḥ—unto them (the learned *brāhmaṇas*); *hiraṇyam*—gold; *rajatam*—silver; *vāsāṁsi*—garments; *ābharaṇāni*—ornaments; *ca*—also; *grāmān*—villages; *hayān*—horses; *gajān*—elephants; *prādāt*—gave in charity; *dhenūnām*—of cows; *arbudāni*—groups of one hundred million; *ṣaṭ*—six.

TRANSLATION

Unto the brāhmaṇas who took part in the ritualistic ceremony the King gave charity of gold, silver, garments, ornaments, villages, horses and elephants, as well as sixty crores of cows [six hundred million cows].

TEXT 35

ववर्ष कामानन्येषां पर्जन्य इव देहिनाम् ।
धन्यं यशस्यमायुष्यं कुमारस्य महामनाः ॥३५॥

vavarṣa kāmān anyeṣāṁ
parjanya iva dehinām
dhanyaṁ yaśasyam āyuṣyaṁ
kumārasya mahā-manāḥ

vavarṣa—showered, gave in charity; *kāmān*—all desirable things; *anyeṣām*—of others; *parjanyaḥ*—a cloud; *iva*—like; *dehinām*—of all living entities; *dhanyam*—with the desire for an increase of opulence; *yaśasyam*—an increase of reputation; *āyuṣyam*—and an increase of the duration of life; *kumārasya*—of the newly born child; *mahā-manāḥ*—the beneficent King Citraketu.

TRANSLATION

As a cloud indiscriminately pours water on the earth, the beneficent King Citraketu, to increase the reputation, opulence and longevity of his son, distributed like rainfall all desirable things to everyone.

TEXT 36

कृच्छ्रलब्धेऽथ राजर्षेस्तनयेऽनुदिनं पितुः ।
यथा निःस्वस्य कृच्छ्राप्ते धने स्नेहोऽन्ववर्धत ॥३६॥

kṛcchra-labdhe 'tha rājarṣes
tanaye 'nudinaṁ pituḥ
yathā niḥsvasya kṛcchrāpte
dhane sneho 'nvavardhata

kṛcchra—with great difficulty; *labdhe*—gained; *atha*—thereafter; *rāja-ṛṣeḥ*—of the pious King Citraketu; *tanaye*—for the son; *anudinam*—day after day; *pituḥ*—of the father; *yathā*—exactly as; *niḥsvasya*—of a poor man; *kṛcchra-āpte*—gained after great difficulty; *dhane*—for riches; *snehaḥ*—affection; *anvavardhata*—increased.

TRANSLATION

When a poor man gets some money after great difficulty, his affection for the money increases daily. Similarly, when King Citraketu, after great difficulty, received a son, his affection for the son increased day after day.

TEXT 37

मातुस्त्वतितरां पुत्रे स्नेहो मोहसमुद्भवः ।
कृतद्युतेः सपत्नीनां प्रजाकामज्वरोऽभवत् ॥३७॥

mātus tv atitarāṁ putre
sneho moha-samudbhavaḥ
kṛtadyuteḥ sapatnīnāṁ
prajā-kāma-jvaro 'bhavat

mātuḥ—of the mother; *tu*—also; *atitarām*—excessively; *putre*—for the son; *snehaḥ*—affection; *moha*—out of ignorance; *samudbhavaḥ*—produced; *kṛtadyuteḥ*—of Kṛtadyuti; *sapatnīnām*—of the co-wives; *prajā-kāma*—of a desire to have sons; *jvaraḥ*—a fever; *abhavat*—there was.

TRANSLATION

The mother's attraction and attention to the son, like that of the child's father, excessively increased. The other wives, seeing Kṛtadyuti's son, were very much agitated, as if by high fevers, with a desire to have sons.

TEXT 38

चित्रकेतोरतिप्रीतिर्यथा दारे प्रजावति ।
न तथान्येषु सञ्जज्ञे बालं लालयतोऽन्वहम् ॥३८॥

citraketor atiprītir
yathā dāre prajāvati
na tathānyeṣu sañjajñe
bālaṁ lālayato 'nvaham

citraketoḥ—of King Citraketu; *atiprītiḥ*—excessive attraction; *yathā*—just as; *dāre*—unto the wife; *prajā-vati*—who begot a son; *na*—not; *tathā*—like that; *anyeṣu*—unto the others; *sañjajñe*—arose; *bālam*—the son; *lālayataḥ*—taking care of; *anvaham*—constantly.

TRANSLATION

As King Citraketu fostered his son very carefully, his affection for Queen Kṛtadyuti increased, but gradually he lost affection for the other wives, who had no sons.

TEXT 39

ताः पर्यतप्यन्नात्मानं गर्हयन्त्योऽभ्यसूयया ।
आनपत्येन दुःखेन राज्ञश्चानादरेण च ॥३९॥

tāḥ paryatapyann ātmānaṁ
garhayantyo 'bhyasūyayā
ānapatyena duḥkhena
rājñaś cānādareṇa ca

tāḥ—they (the queens who did not have sons); *paryatapyan*—lamented; *ātmānam*—themselves; *garhayantyaḥ*—condemning; *abhyasūyayā*—out of envy; *ānapatyena*—due to being without sons; *duḥkhena*—by unhappiness; *rājñaḥ*—of the King; *ca*—also; *anādareṇa*—due to negligence; *ca*—also.

TRANSLATION

The other queens were extremely unhappy due to their being sonless. Because of the King's negligence toward them, they condemned themselves in envy and lamented.

TEXT 40

धिगप्रजां स्त्रियं पापां पत्युश्चागृहसम्मताम् ।
सुप्रजाभिः सपत्नीभिर्दासीमिव तिरस्कृताम् ॥४०॥

dhig aprajāṁ striyaṁ pāpāṁ
patyuś cāgṛha-sammatām
suprajābhiḥ sapatnībhir
dāsīm iva tiraskṛtām

dhik—all condemnation; *aprajām*—without a son; *striyam*—upon a woman; *pāpām*—full of sinful activities; *patyuḥ*—by the husband; *ca*—also; *a-gṛha-sammatām*—who is not honored at home; *su-prajābhiḥ*—who have sons; *sapatnībhiḥ*—by co-wives; *dāsīm*—a maidservant; *iva*—exactly like; *tiraskṛtām*—dishonored.

TRANSLATION

A wife who has no sons is neglected at home by her husband and dishonored by her co-wives exactly like a maidservant. Certainly such a woman is condemned in every respect because of her sinful life.

PURPORT

As stated by Cāṇakya Paṇḍita:

mātā yasya gṛhe nāsti
bhāryā cāpriya-vādinī
araṇyaṁ tena gantavyaṁ
yathāraṇyaṁ tathā gṛham

"A person who has no mother at home and whose wife does not speak sweetly should go to the forest. For such a person, living at home and living in the forest are equal." Similarly, for a woman who has no son, who is not cared for by her husband and whose co-wives neglect her, treating her like a maidservant, to go to the forest is better than to remain at home.

TEXT 41

दासीनां को नु सन्तापः स्वामिनः परिचर्यया ।
अभीक्ष्णं लब्धमानानां दास्या दासीव दुर्भगाः ॥४१॥

dāsīnāṁ ko nu santāpaḥ
svāminaḥ paricaryayā
abhīkṣṇaṁ labdha-mānānāṁ
dāsyā dāsīva durbhagāḥ

dāsīnām—of the maidservants; *kaḥ*—what; *nu*—indeed; *santāpaḥ*—lamentation; *svāminaḥ*—unto the husband; *paricaryayā*—by rendering service; *abhīkṣṇam*—constantly; *labdha-mānānām*—honored; *dāsyāḥ*—of the maidservant; *dāsī iva*—like a maidservant; *durbhagāḥ*—most unfortunate.

TRANSLATION

Even maidservants who are constantly engaged in rendering service to the husband are honored by the husband, and thus they have nothing for which to lament. Our position, however, is that

we are maidservants of the maidservant. Therefore we are most unfortunate.

TEXT 42

एवं सन्दह्यमानानां सपत्न्याः पुत्रसम्पदा ।
राज्ञोऽसम्मतवृत्तीनां विद्वेषो बलवानभूत् ॥४२॥

evaṁ sandahyamānānāṁ
sapatnyāḥ putra-sampadā
rājño 'sammata-vṛttīnāṁ
vidveṣo balavān abhūt

evam—thus; *sandahyamānānām*—of the queens, who were constantly burning in lamentation; *sapatnyāḥ*—of the co-wife Kṛtadyuti; *putra-sampadā*—due to the opulence of a son; *rājñaḥ*—by the King; *asammata-vṛttīnām*—not being very much favored; *vidveṣaḥ*—envy; *balavān*—very strong; *abhūt*—became.

TRANSLATION

Śrī Śukadeva Gosvāmī continued: Being neglected by their husband and seeing Kṛtadyuti's opulence in possessing a son, Kṛtadyuti's co-wives always burned in envy, which became extremely strong.

TEXT 43

विद्वेषनष्टमतयः स्त्रियो दारुणचेतसः ।
गरं ददुः कुमाराय दुर्मर्षा नृपतिं प्रति ॥४३॥

vidveṣa-naṣṭa-matayaḥ
striyo dāruṇa-cetasaḥ
garaṁ daduḥ kumārāya
durmarṣā nṛpatiṁ prati

vidveṣa-naṣṭa-matayaḥ—whose intelligence was lost in envy; *striyaḥ*—the women; *dāruṇa-cetasaḥ*—being very hardhearted;

garam—poison; *daduḥ*—administered; *kumārāya*—unto the boy; *durmarṣāḥ*—being intolerant; *nṛpatim*—the King; *prati*—upon.

TRANSLATION

As their envy increased, they lost their intelligence. Being extremely hardhearted and unable to tolerate the King's neglect, they finally administered poison to the son.

TEXT 44

कृतद्युतिरजानन्ती सपत्नीनामघं महत् ।
सुप्त एवेति सञ्चिन्त्य निरीक्ष्य व्यचरद् गृहे ॥४४॥

kṛtadyutir ajānantī
sapatnīnām aghaṁ mahat
supta eveti sañcintya
nirīkṣya vyacarad gṛhe

kṛtadyutiḥ—Queen Kṛtadyuti; *ajānantī*—being unaware of; *sapatnīnām*—of her co-wives; *agham*—sinful act; *mahat*—very great; *suptaḥ*—sleeping; *eva*—indeed; *iti*—thus; *sañcintya*—thinking; *nirīkṣya*—looking at; *vyacarat*—was walking; *gṛhe*—at home.

TRANSLATION

Unaware of the poison administered by her co-wives, Queen Kṛtadyuti walked within the house, thinking that her son was sleeping deeply. She did not understand that he was dead.

TEXT 45

शयानं सुचिरं बालमुपधार्य मनीषिणी ।
पुत्रमानय मे भद्रे इति धात्रीमचोदयत् ॥४५॥

śayānaṁ suciraṁ bālam
upadhārya manīṣiṇī
putram ānaya me bhadre
iti dhātrīm acodayat

śayānam—lying down; *su-ciram*—for a long time; *bālam*—the son; *upadhārya*—thinking; *manīṣiṇī*—very intelligent; *putram*—the son; *ānaya*—bring; *me*—unto me; *bhadre*—O gentle friend; *iti*—thus; *dhātrīm*—unto the nurse; *acodayat*—gave the order.

TRANSLATION

Thinking that her child had been sleeping for a long time, Queen Kṛtadyuti, who was certainly very intelligent, ordered the nurse, "My dear friend, please bring my son here."

TEXT 46

सा शयानमुपव्रज्य दृष्ट्वा चोत्तारलोचनम् ।
प्राणेन्द्रियात्मभिस्त्यक्तं हतास्मीत्यपतद्भुवि ।।४६।।

sā śayānam upavrajya
dṛṣṭvā cottāra-locanam
prāṇendriyātmabhis tyaktaṁ
hatāsmīty apatad bhuvi

sā—she (the maidservant); *śayānam*—lying down; *upavrajya*—going to; *dṛṣṭvā*—seeing; *ca*—also; *uttāra-locanam*—his eyes turned upward (as are those of a dead body); *prāṇa-indriya-ātmabhiḥ*—by the life force, senses and mind; *tyaktam*—abandoned; *hatā asmi*—now I am doomed; *iti*—thus; *apatat*—fell down; *bhuvi*—on the ground.

TRANSLATION

When the maidservant approached the child, who was lying down, she saw that his eyes were turned upward. There were no signs of life, all his senses having stopped, and she could understand that the child was dead. Seeing this, she immediately cried, "Now I am doomed," and fell to the ground.

TEXT 47

तस्यास्तदाकर्ण्य भृशातुरं स्वरं
घ्नन्त्याः कराभ्यामुर उच्चकैरपि ।

प्रविश्य राज्ञी त्वरयात्मजान्तिकं
दद‍र्श बालं सहसा मृतं सुतम् ॥४७॥

tasyās tadākarṇya bhṛśāturaṁ svaraṁ
ghnantyāḥ karābhyām ura uccakair api
praviśya rājñī tvarayātmajāntikaṁ
dadarśa bālaṁ sahasā mṛtaṁ sutam

tasyāḥ—of her (the maidservant); *tadā*—at that time; *ākarṇya*—hearing; *bhṛśa-āturam*—highly regretful and agitated; *svaram*—voice; *ghnantyāḥ*—striking; *karābhyām*—with the hands; *uraḥ*—the chest; *uccakaiḥ*—loudly; *api*—also; *praviśya*—entering; *rājñī*—the Queen; *tvarayā*—hastily; *ātmaja-antikam*—near her son; *dadarśa*—she saw; *bālam*—the child; *sahasā*—suddenly; *mṛtam*—dead; *sutam*—son.

TRANSLATION

In great agitation, the maidservant struck her breast with both hands and cried loudly in regretful words. Hearing her loud voice, the Queen immediately came, and when she approached her son, she saw that he was suddenly dead.

TEXT 48

पपात भूमौ परिवृद्धया शुचा
मुमोह विभ्रष्टशिरोरुहाम्बरा ॥४८॥

papāta bhūmau parivṛddhayā śucā
mumoha vibhraṣṭa-śiroruhāmbarā

papāta—fell down; *bhūmau*—on the ground; *parivṛddhayā*—highly increased; *śucā*—out of lamentation; *mumoha*—she became unconscious; *vibhraṣṭa*—scattered; *śiroruha*—hair; *ambarā*—and dress.

TRANSLATION

In great lamentation, her hair and dress in disarray, the Queen fell to the ground unconscious.

TEXT 49

ततो नृपान्तःपुरवर्तिनो जना
नराश्च नार्यश्च निशम्य रोदनम् ।
आगत्य तुल्यव्यसनाः सुदुःखिता-
स्ताश्च व्यलीकं रुरुदुः कृतागसः ॥४९॥

tato nṛpāntaḥpura-vartino janā
narāś ca nāryaś ca niśamya rodanam
āgatya tulya-vyasanāḥ suduḥkhitās
tāś ca vyalīkaṁ ruruduḥ kṛtāgasaḥ

tataḥ—thereafter; *nṛpa*—O King; *antaḥpura-vartinaḥ*—the inhabitants of the palace; *janāḥ*—all the people; *narāḥ*—the men; *ca*—and; *nāryaḥ*—the women; *ca*—also; *niśamya*—hearing; *rodanam*—loud crying; *āgatya*—coming; *tulya-vyasanāḥ*—being equally aggrieved; *suduḥkhitāḥ*—very greatly lamenting; *tāḥ*—they; *ca*—and; *vyalīkam*—pretentiously; *ruruduḥ*—cried; *kṛta-āgasaḥ*—who had committed the offense (by giving the poison).

TRANSLATION

O King Parīkṣit, hearing the loud crying, all the inhabitants of the palace came, both men and women. Being equally aggrieved, they also began to cry. The queens who had administered the poison also cried pretentiously, knowing full well their offense.

TEXTS 50–51

श्रुत्वा मृतं पुत्रमलक्षितान्तकं
विनष्टदृष्टिः प्रपतन् स्खलन् पथि ।
स्नेहानुबन्धैधितया शुचा भृशं
विमूर्च्छितोऽनुप्रकृतिर्द्विजैर्वृतः ॥५०॥
पपात बालस्य स पादमूले
मृतस्य विस्रस्तशिरोरुहाम्बरः ।

दीर्घं श्वसन् बाष्पकलोपरोधतो
निरुद्धकण्ठो न शशाक भाषितुम् ॥५१॥

śrutvā mṛtaṁ putram alakṣitāntakaṁ
vinaṣṭa-dṛṣṭiḥ prapatan skhalan pathi
snehānubandhaidhitayā śucā bhṛśaṁ
vimūrcchito 'nuprakṛtir dvijair vṛtaḥ

papāta bālasya sa pāda-mūle
mṛtasya visrasta-śiroruhāmbaraḥ
dīrghaṁ śvasan bāṣpa-kaloparodhato
niruddha-kaṇṭho na śaśāka bhāṣitum

śrutvā—hearing; *mṛtam*—dead; *putram*—the son; *alakṣita-antakam*—the cause of death being unknown; *vinaṣṭa-dṛṣṭiḥ*—unable to see properly; *prapatan*—constantly falling down; *skhalan*—slipping; *pathi*—on the road; *sneha-anubandha*—because of affection; *edhitayā*—increasing; *śucā*—by lamentation; *bhṛśam*—greatly; *vimūrcchitaḥ*—becoming unconscious; *anuprakṛtiḥ*—followed by ministers and other officers; *dvijaiḥ*—by learned *brāhmaṇas; vṛtaḥ*—surrounded; *papāta*—fell down; *bālasya*—of the boy; *saḥ*—he (the King); *pāda-mūle*—at the feet; *mṛtasya*—of the dead body; *visrasta*—scattered; *śiroruha*—hair; *ambaraḥ*—and dress; *dīrgham*—long; *śvasan*—breathing; *bāṣpa-kalā-uparodhataḥ*—due to crying with tearful eyes; *niruddha-kaṇṭhaḥ*—having a choked voice; *na*—not; *śaśāka*—was able; *bhāṣitum*—to speak.

TRANSLATION

When King Citraketu heard of his son's death from unknown causes, he became almost blind. Because of his great affection for his son, his lamentation grew like a blazing fire, and as he went to see the dead child, he kept slipping and falling on the ground. Surrounded by his ministers and other officers and the learned brāhmaṇas present, the King approached and fell unconscious at the child's feet, his hair and dress scattered. When the King, breathing heavily, regained consciousness, his eyes were tearful, and he could not speak.

TEXT 52

पतिं निरीक्ष्योरुशुचार्पितं तदा
मृतं च बालं सुतमेकसन्ततिम् ।
जनस्य राज्ञी प्रकृतेश्च हृद्रुजं
सती दधाना विललाप चित्रधा ॥५२॥

patiṁ nirīkṣyoru-śucārpitaṁ tadā
mṛtaṁ ca bālaṁ sutam eka-santatim
janasya rājñī prakṛteś ca hṛd-rujaṁ
satī dadhānā vilalāpa citradhā

patim—the husband; *nirīkṣya*—by seeing; *uru*—greatly; *śuca*—with lamentation; *arpitam*—pained; *tadā*—at that time; *mṛtam*—dead; *ca*—and; *bālam*—the child; *sutam*—the son; *eka-santatim*—the only son in the family; *janasya*—of all the other people gathered there; *rājñī*—the Queen; *prakṛteḥ ca*—as well as of the officers and ministers; *hṛt-rujam*—the pains within the core of the heart; *satī dadhānā*—increasing; *vilalāpa*—lamented; *citradhā*—in varieties of ways.

TRANSLATION

When the Queen saw her husband, King Citraketu, merged in great lamentation and saw the dead child, who was the only son in the family, she lamented in various ways. This increased the pain in the cores of the hearts of all the inhabitants of the palace, the ministers and all the brāhmaṇas.

TEXT 53

स्तनद्वयं कुङ्कुमपङ्कमण्डितं
निषिञ्चती साञ्जनबाष्पबिन्दुभिः ।
विकीर्य केशान् विगलत्स्रजः सुतं
शुशोच चित्रं कुररीव सुस्वरम् ॥५३॥

stana-dvayaṁ kuṅkuma-paṅka-maṇḍitaṁ
niṣiñcatī sāñjana-bāṣpa-bindubhiḥ

vikīrya keśān vigalat-srajaḥ sutaṁ
śuśoca citraṁ kurarīva susvaram

stana-dvayam—her two breasts; *kuṅkuma*—with *kuṅkuma* powder (which is generally sprayed on the breasts of women); *paṅka*—ointment; *maṇḍitam*—decorated; *niṣiñcatī*—moistening; *sa-añjana*—mixed with the eye ointment; *bāṣpa*—of tears; *bindubhiḥ*—by drops; *vikīrya*—scattering; *keśān*—hair; *vigalat*—was falling down; *srajaḥ*—on which the flower garland; *sutam*—for her son; *śuśoca*—lamented; *citram*—variegated; *kurarī iva*—like a *kurarī* bird; *su-svaram*—in a very sweet voice.

TRANSLATION

The garland of flowers decorating the Queen's head fell, and her hair scattered. Falling tears melted the collyrium on her eyes and moistened her breasts, which were covered with kuṅkuma powder. As she lamented the loss of her son, her loud crying resembled the sweet sound of a kurarī bird.

TEXT 54

अहो विधातस्त्वमतीव बालिशो
यस्त्वात्मसृष्टचप्रतिरूपमीहसे ।
परे नु जीवत्यपरस्य या मृति-
र्विपर्ययश्चेत्त्वमसि ध्रुवः परः ॥५४॥

aho vidhātas tvam atīva bāliśo
yas tv ātma-sṛṣṭy-apratirūpam īhase
pare nu jīvaty aparasya yā mṛtir
viparyayaś cet tvam asi dhruvaḥ paraḥ

aho—alas (in great lamentation); *vidhātaḥ*—O Providence; *tvam*—You; *atīva*—very much; *bāliśaḥ*—inexperienced; *yaḥ*—who; *tu*—indeed; *ātma-sṛṣṭi*—of Your own creation; *apratirūpam*—just the opposite; *īhase*—You are performing and desiring; *pare*—while the father or the elder; *nu*—indeed; *jīvati*—is living; *aparasya*—of one who was born later; *yā*—which; *mṛtiḥ*—death; *viparyayaḥ*—contradictory; *cet*—if; *tvam*—You; *asi*—are; *dhruvaḥ*—indeed; *paraḥ*—an enemy.

TRANSLATION

Alas, O Providence, O Creator, You are certainly inexperienced in creation, for during the lifetime of a father You have caused the death of his son, thus acting in opposition to Your creative laws. If You are determined to contradict these laws, You are certainly the enemy of living entities and are never merciful.

PURPORT

This is the way a conditioned soul condemns the supreme creator when he meets reverses. Sometimes he accuses the Supreme Personality of Godhead of being crooked because some people are happy and some are not. Here the Queen blames supreme providence for her son's death. Following the creative laws, a father should die first and then his son. If the creative laws are changed according to the whims of providence, then providence certainly should not be considered merciful, but must be considered inimical to the created being. Actually it is not the creator, but the conditioned soul who is inexperienced. He does not know how the subtle laws of fruitive activity work, and without knowledge of these laws of nature, he ignorantly criticizes the Supreme Personality of Godhead.

TEXT 55

न हि क्रमश्चेदिह मृत्युजन्मनोः
शरीरिणामस्तु तदात्मकर्मभिः ।
यः स्नेहपाशो निजसर्गवृद्धये
स्वयं कृतस्ते तमिमं विवृश्चसि ॥५५॥

na hi kramaś ced iha mṛtyu-janmanoḥ
śarīriṇām astu tad ātma-karmabhiḥ
yaḥ sneha-pāśo nija-sarga-vṛddhaye
svayaṁ kṛtas te tam imaṁ vivṛścasi

na—not; *hi*—indeed; *kramaḥ*—chronological order; *cet*—if; *iha*—in this material world; *mṛtyu*—of death; *janmanoḥ*—and of birth; *śarīriṇām*—of the conditioned souls, who have accepted material bodies; *astu*—let it be; *tat*—that; *ātma-karmabhiḥ*—by the results of one's *karma* (fruitive activities); *yaḥ*—that which; *sneha-pāśaḥ*—bondage of affection; *nija-sarga*—Your own creation; *vṛddhaye*—to increase; *svayam*—personally; *kṛtaḥ*—made; *te*—by You; *tam*—that; *imam*—this; *vivṛścasi*—you are cutting.

TRANSLATION

My Lord, You may say that there is no law that a father must die in the lifetime of his son and that a son must be born in the lifetime of his father, since everyone lives and dies according to his own fruitive activity. However, if fruitive activity is so strong that birth and death depend upon it, there is no need of a controller, or God. Again, if You say that a controller is needed because the material energy does not have the power to act, one may answer that if the bonds of affection You have created are disturbed by fruitive action, no one will raise children with affection; instead, everyone will cruelly neglect his children. Since You have cut the bonds of affection that compel a parent to raise his child, You appear inexperienced and unintelligent.

PURPORT

As stated in the *Brahma-saṁhitā, karmāṇi nirdahati kintu ca bhakti-bhājām:* one who has taken to Kṛṣṇa consciousness, devotional service, is not affected by the results of *karma.* In this verse, *karma* has been stressed on the basis of *karma-mīmāṁsā* philosophy, which says that one must act according to his *karma* and that a supreme controller must give the results of *karma.* The subtle laws of *karma,* which are controlled by the Supreme, cannot be understood by ordinary conditioned souls. Therefore Kṛṣṇa says that one who can understand Him and how He is acting, controlling everything by subtle laws, immediately becomes freed by His grace. That is the statement of *Brahma-saṁhitā* (*karmāṇi nirdahati kintu ca bhakti-bhājām*). One should take to devotional service without reservations and surrender everything to the supreme will of the Lord. That will make one happy in this life and the next.

TEXT 56

त्वं तात नार्हसि च मां कृपणामनाथां
त्यक्तुं विचक्ष्व पितरं तव शोकतप्तम् ।
अञ्जस्तरेम भवताप्रजदुस्तरं यद्
ध्वान्तं न याह्यकरुणेन यमेन दूरम् ॥५६॥

tvaṁ tāta nārhasi ca māṁ kṛpaṇām anāthāṁ
tyaktuṁ vicakṣva pitaraṁ tava śoka-taptam
añjas tarema bhavatāpraja-dustaraṁ yad
dhvāntaṁ na yāhy akaruṇena yamena dūram

tvam—you; *tāta*—my dear son; *na*—not; *arhasi*—ought; *ca*—and; *mām*—me; *kṛpaṇām*—very poor; *anāthām*—without a protector; *tyaktum*—to give up; *vicakṣva*—look; *pitaram*—at the father; *tava*—your; *śoka-taptam*—affected by so much lamentation; *ajñaḥ*—easily; *tarema*—we can cross; *bhavatā*—by you; *apraja-dustaram*—very difficult to cross for one without a son; *yat*—which; *dhvāntam*—the kingdom of darkness; *na yāhi*—do not go away; *akaruṇena*—merciless; *yamena*—with Yamarāja; *dūram*—any further.

TRANSLATION

My dear son, I am helpless and very much aggrieved. You should not give up my company. Just look at your lamenting father. We are helpless because without a son we shall have to suffer the distress of going to the darkest hellish regions. You are the only hope by which we can get out of these dark regions. Therefore I request you not to go any further with the merciless Yama.

PURPORT

According to the Vedic injunctions, one must accept a wife just to beget a son who can deliver one from the clutches of Yamarāja. Unless one has a son to offer oblations to the *pitās*, or forefathers, one must suffer in Yamarāja's kingdom. King Citraketu was very much aggrieved, thinking that because his son was going away with Yamarāja, he himself would again suffer. The subtle laws exist for the *karmīs;* if one becomes a devotee, he has no more obligations to the laws of *karma.*

TEXT 57

उत्तिष्ठ तात त इमे शिशवो वयस्या-
स्त्वामाह्वयन्ति नृपनन्दन संविहर्तुम् ।
सुप्तश्चिरं ह्यशनया च भवान् परीतो
भुङ्क्ष्व स्तनं पिब शुचो हर नः स्वकानाम् ॥५७॥

uttiṣṭha tāta ta ime śiśavo vayasyās
tvām āhvayanti nṛpa-nandana saṁvihartum
suptaś ciraṁ hy aśanayā ca bhavān parīto
bhuṅkṣva stanaṁ piba śuco hara naḥ svakānām

uttiṣṭha—kindly get up; *tāta*—my dear son; *te*—they; *ime*—all these; *śiśavaḥ*—children; *vayasyāḥ*—playmates; *tvām*—you; *āhvayanti*—are calling; *nṛpa-nandana*—O son of the King; *saṁvihartum*—to play with; *suptaḥ*—you have slept; *ciram*—for a long time; *hi*—indeed; *aśanayā*—by hunger; *ca*—also; *bhavān*—you; *parītaḥ*—overcome; *bhuṅkṣva*—please eat; *stanam*—at the breast (of your mother); *piba*—drink; *śucaḥ*—lamentation; *hara*—just dissipate; *naḥ*—of us; *svakānām*—your relatives.

TRANSLATION

My dear son, you have slept a long time. Now please get up. Your playmates are calling you to play. Since you must be very hungry, please get up and suck my breast and dissipate our lamentation.

TEXT 58

नाहं तनूज ददृशे हतमङ्गला ते
मुग्धस्मितं मुदितवीक्षणमाननाब्जम् ।
किं वा गतोऽस्यपुनरन्वयमन्यलोकं
नीतोऽघृणेन न शृणोमि कला गिरस्ते ॥५८॥

nāhaṁ tanūja dadṛśe hata-maṅgalā te
mugdha-smitaṁ mudita-vīkṣaṇam ānanābjam
kiṁ vā gato 'sy apunar-anvayam anya-lokaṁ
nīto 'ghṛṇena na śṛṇomi kalā giras te

na—not; *aham*—I; *tanū-ja*—my dear son (born of my body); *dadṛśe*—saw; *hata-maṅgalā*—because of my being the most unfortunate; *te*—your; *mugdha-smitam*—with charming smiling; *mudita-vīkṣaṇam*—with closed eyes; *ānana-abjam*—lotus face; *kiṁ vā*—whether; *gataḥ*—gone away; *asi*—you are; *a-punaḥ-anvayam*—from which one does not return; *anya-lokam*—to another planet, or the planet of Yamarāja; *nītaḥ*—having been taken away; *aghṛṇena*—by the cruel Yamarāja; *na*—not; *śṛṇomi*—I can hear; *kalāḥ*—very pleasing; *giraḥ*—utterances; *te*—your.

TRANSLATION

My dear son, I am certainly most unfortunate, for I can no longer see your mild smiling. You have closed your eyes forever. I therefore conclude that you have been taken from this planet to another, from which you will not return. My dear son, I can no longer hear your pleasing voice.

TEXT 59

श्रीशुक उवाच
विलपन्त्या मृतं पुत्रमिति चित्रविलापनैः ।
चित्रकेतुर्भृशं तप्तो मुक्तकण्ठो रुरोद ह ॥५९॥

śrī-śuka uvāca
vilapantyā mṛtaṁ putram
iti citra-vilāpanaiḥ
citraketur bhṛśaṁ tapto
mukta-kaṇṭho ruroda ha

śrī-śukaḥ uvāca—Śrī Śukadeva Gosvāmī said; *vilapantyā*—with the woman who was lamenting; *mṛtam*—dead; *putram*—for the son; *iti*—thus; *citra-vilāpanaiḥ*—with various lamentations; *citraketuḥ*—King

Citraketu; *bhṛśam*—very much; *taptaḥ*—aggrieved; *mukta-kaṇṭhaḥ*—loudly; *ruroda*—cried; *ha*—indeed.

TRANSLATION

Śrī Śukadeva Gosvāmī continued: Accompanied by his wife, who was thus lamenting for her dead son, King Citraketu began crying loudly with an open mouth, being greatly aggrieved.

TEXT 60

तयोर्विलपतोः सर्वे दम्पत्योस्तदनुव्रताः ।
रुरुदुः स्म नरा नार्यः सर्वमासीदचेतनम् ॥६०॥

tayor vilapatoḥ sarve
dampatyos tad-anuvratāḥ
ruruduḥ sma narā nāryaḥ
sarvam āsīd acetanam

tayoḥ—while the two of them; *vilapatoḥ*—were lamenting; *sarve*—all; *dam-patyoḥ*—the King, along with his wife; *tat-anuvratāḥ*—their followers; *ruruduḥ*—cried loudly; *sma*—indeed; *narāḥ*—the male members; *nāryaḥ*—the female members; *sarvam*—the whole kingdom; *āsīt*—became; *acetanam*—almost unconscious.

TRANSLATION

As the King and Queen lamented, all their male and female followers joined them in crying. Because of the sudden accident, all the citizens of the kingdom were almost unconscious.

TEXT 61

एवं कश्मलमापन्नं नष्टसंज्ञमनायकम् ।
ज्ञात्वाङ्गिरा नाम ऋषिराजगाम सनारदः ॥६१॥

evaṁ kaśmalam āpannaṁ
naṣṭa-saṁjñam anāyakam

jñātvāṅgirā nāma ṛṣir
ājagāma sanāradaḥ

evam—thus; *kaśmalam*—misery; *āpannam*—having gotten; *naṣṭa*—lost; *saṁjñam*—consciousness; *anāyakam*—without help; *jñātvā*—knowing; *aṅgirāḥ*—Aṅgirā; *nāma*—named; *ṛṣiḥ*—the saintly person; *ājagāma*—came; *sa-nāradaḥ*—with Nārada Muni.

TRANSLATION

When the great sage Aṅgirā understood that the King was almost dead in an ocean of lamentation, he went there with Nārada Ṛṣi.

Thus end the Bhaktivedanta purports of the Sixth Canto, Fourteenth Chapter, of the Śrīmad-Bhāgavatam, *entitled "King Citraketu's Lamentation."*

CHAPTER FIFTEEN

The Saints Nārada and Aṅgirā Instruct King Citraketu

In this chapter, Aṅgirā Ṛṣi, along with Nārada, consoles Citraketu as far as possible. Aṅgirā and Nārada Ṛṣi came to relieve the King from excessive lamentation by instructing him about the spiritual significance of life.

The great saints Aṅgirā and Nārada explained that the relationship between father and son is not factual; it is simply a representation of the illusory energy. The relationship did not exist before, nor will it stay in the future. By the arrangement of time, the relationship exists only in the present. One should not lament for temporary relationships. The entire cosmic manifestation is temporary; although not unreal, it is not factual. By the direction of the Supreme Personality of Godhead, everything created in the material world is transient. By a temporary arrangement, a father begets a child, or a living entity becomes the child of a so-called father. This temporary arrangement is made by the Supreme Lord. Neither the father nor the son exists independently.

As the King listened to the great sages, he was relieved from his false lamentation, and then he inquired about their identity. The great sages presented who they were and instructed that all sufferings are due to the bodily conception of life. When one understands his spiritual identity and surrenders to the Supreme Personality of Godhead, the supreme spiritual person, one becomes actually happy. When one searches for happiness in matter, one must certainly lament for bodily relationships. Self-realization means spiritual realization of one's relationship with Kṛṣṇa. Such realization ends one's miserable material life.

TEXT 1

श्रीशुक उवाच

ऊचतुर्मृतकोपान्ते पतितं मृतकोपमम् ।
शोकाभिभूतं राजानं बोधयन्तौ सदुक्तिभिः ॥ १ ॥

śrī-śuka uvāca
ūcatur mṛtakopānte
patitaṁ mṛtakopamam
śokābhibhūtaṁ rājānaṁ
bodhayantau sad-uktibhiḥ

śrī-śukaḥ uvāca—Śrī Śukadeva Gosvāmī said; *ūcatuḥ*—they spoke; *mṛtaka*—the dead body; *upānte*—near; *patitam*—fallen; *mṛtaka-upamam*—exactly like another dead body; *śoka-abhibhūtam*—very much aggrieved by lamentation; *rājānam*—to the King; *bodhayantau*—giving instruction; *sat-uktibhiḥ*—by instructions that are factual, not temporary.

TRANSLATION

Śrī Śukadeva Gosvāmī said: While King Citraketu, overcome by lamentation, lay like a dead body at the side of the dead body of his son, the two great sages Nārada and Aṅgirā instructed him about spiritual consciousness as follows.

TEXT 2

कोऽयं स्यात् तव राजेन्द्र भवान् यमनुशोचति ।
त्वं चास्य कतमः सृष्टौ पुरेदानीमतः परम् ॥ २ ॥

ko 'yaṁ syāt tava rājendra
bhavān yam anuśocati
tvaṁ cāsya katamaḥ sṛṣṭau
puredānīm ataḥ param

kaḥ—who; *ayam*—this; *syāt*—is; *tava*—to you; *rāja-indra*—O best of kings; *bhavān*—Your Lordship; *yam*—whom; *anuśocati*—laments over; *tvam*—you; *ca*—and; *asya*—to him (the dead boy); *katamaḥ*—who; *sṛṣṭau*—in the birth; *purā*—previously; *idānīm*—at this time, at the present; *ataḥ param*—and hereafter, in the future.

TRANSLATION

O King, what relationship does the dead body for which you lament have with you, and what relationship do you have with

him? You may say that you are now related as father and son, but do you think this relationship existed before? Does it truly exist now? Will it continue in the future?

PURPORT

The instructions given by Nārada and Aṅgirā Muni are the true spiritual instructions for the illusioned conditioned soul. This world is temporary, but because of our previous *karma* we come here and accept bodies, creating temporary relationships in terms of society, friendship, love, nationality and community, which are all finished at death. These temporary relationships did not exist in the past, nor will they exist in the future. Therefore at the present moment the so-called relationships are illusions.

TEXT 3

यथा प्रयान्ति संयान्ति स्रोतोवेगेन बालुकाः ।
संयुज्यन्ते वियुज्यन्ते तथा कालेन देहिनः ॥ ३ ॥

yathā prayānti saṁyānti
sroto-vegena bālukāḥ
saṁyujyante viyujyante
tathā kālena dehinaḥ

yathā—just as; *prayānti*—move apart; *saṁyānti*—come together; *srotaḥ-vegena*—by the force of waves; *bālukāḥ*—the small particles of sand; *saṁyujyante*—they are united; *viyujyante*—they are separated; *tathā*—similarly; *kālena*—by time; *dehinaḥ*—the living entities who have accepted material bodies.

TRANSLATION

O King, as small particles of sand sometimes come together and are sometimes separated due to the force of the waves, the living entities who have accepted material bodies sometimes come together and are sometimes separated by the force of time.

PURPORT

The misunderstanding of the conditioned soul is the bodily conception of life. The body is material, but within the body is the soul. This is spiritual understanding. Unfortunately, one who is in ignorance, under the spell of material illusion, accepts the body to be the self. He cannot understand that the body is matter. Like small particles of sand, bodies come together and are separated by the force of time, and people falsely lament for unification and separation. Unless one knows this, there is no question of happiness. Therefore in *Bhagavad-gītā* (2.13) this is the first instruction given by the Lord:

dehino 'smin yathā dehe
kaumāraṁ yauvanaṁ jarā
tathā dehāntara-prāptir
dhīras tatra na muhyati

"As the embodied soul continually passes, in this body, from boyhood to youth to old age, the soul similarly passes into another body at death. The self-realized soul is not bewildered by such a change." We are not the body; we are spiritual beings trapped in the body. Our real interest lies in understanding this simple fact. Then we can make further spiritual progress. Otherwise, if we remain in the bodily conception of life, our miserable material existence will continue forever. Political adjustments, social welfare work, medical assistance and the other programs we have manufactured for peace and happiness will never endure. We shall have to undergo the sufferings of material life one after another. Therefore material life is said to be *duḥkhālayam aśāśvatam;* it is a reservoir of miserable conditions.

TEXT 4

यथा धानासु वै धाना भवन्ति न भवन्ति च ।
एवं भूतानि भूतेषु चोदितानीशमायया ॥ ४ ॥

yathā dhānāsu vai dhānā
bhavanti na bhavanti ca
evaṁ bhūtāni bhūteṣu
coditānīśa-māyayā

yathā—just as; *dhānāsu*—through seeds of paddy; *vai*—indeed; *dhānāḥ*—grains; *bhavanti*—are generated; *na*—not; *bhavanti*—are generated; *ca*—also; *evam*—in this way; *bhūtāni*—the living entities; *bhūteṣu*—in other living entities; *coditāni*—impelled; *īśa-māyayā*—by the potency or power of the Supreme Personality of Godhead.

TRANSLATION

When seeds are sown in the ground, they sometimes grow into plants and sometimes do not. Sometimes the ground is not fertile, and the sowing of seeds is unproductive. Similarly, sometimes a prospective father, being impelled by the potency of the Supreme Lord, can beget a child, but sometimes conception does not take place. Therefore one should not lament over the artificial relationship of parenthood, which is ultimately controlled by the Supreme Lord.

PURPORT

Mahārāja Citraketu was actually not destined to get a son. Therefore although he married hundreds and thousands of wives, all of them proved barren, and he could not beget even one child. When Aṅgirā Ṛṣi came to see the King, the King requested the great sage to enable him to have at least one son. Because of the blessing of Aṅgirā Ṛṣi, a child was sent by the grace of *māyā*, but the child was not to live for long. Therefore in the beginning Aṅgirā Ṛṣi told the King that he would beget a child who would cause jubilation and lamentation.

King Citraketu was not destined to get a child by providence, or the will of the Supreme. Just as sterile grain cannot produce more grain, a sterile person, by the will of the Supreme Lord, cannot beget a child. Sometimes a child is born even to an impotent father and sterile mother, and sometimes a potent father and fertile mother are childless. Indeed, sometimes a child is born despite contraceptive methods, and therefore the parents kill the child in the womb. In the present age, killing children in the womb has become a common practice. Why? When contraceptive methods are taken, why don't they act? Why is a child sometimes produced so that the father and mother have to kill it in the womb? We must conclude that our arrangement of so-called scientific knowledge cannot determine what will take place; what is enacted actually depends on the supreme will. It is by the supreme will that we are situated in certain conditions in terms of family, community and personality. These are all arrangements of the Supreme Lord according to our desires under the spell of *māyā*, illusion. In devotional life, therefore, one should not desire anything, since everything depends on the Supreme Personality of Godhead. As stated in *Bhakti-rasāmṛta-sindhu* (1.1.11):

anyābhilāṣitā-śūnyaṁ
jñāna-karmādy-anāvṛtam
ānukūlyena kṛṣṇānu-
śīlanaṁ bhaktir uttamā

"One should render transcendental loving service to the Supreme Lord Kṛṣṇa favorably and without desire for material profit or gain through fruitive activities or philosophical speculation. That is called pure devotional service." One should act only to develop Kṛṣṇa consciousness. For everything else, one should fully depend upon the Supreme Person. We should not create plans that will ultimately make us frustrated.

TEXT 5

वयं च त्वं च ये चेमे तुल्यकालाश्चराचराः ।
जन्ममृत्योर्यथा पश्चात् प्राङ्नैवमधुनापि भोः ॥ ५ ॥

vayaṁ ca tvaṁ ca ye ceme
tulya-kālāś carācarāḥ
janma-mṛtyor yathā paścāt
prāṅ naivam adhunāpi bhoḥ

vayam—we (the great sages and the ministers and adherents of the King); *ca*—and; *tvam*—you; *ca*—also; *ye*—who; *ca*—also; *ime*—these; *tulya-kālāḥ*—assembled at the same time; *cara-acarāḥ*—moving and not moving; *janma*—birth; *mṛtyoḥ*—and death; *yathā*—just as; *paścāt*—after; *prāk*—before; *na*—not; *evam*—thus; *adhunā*—at present; *api*—although; *bhoḥ*—O King.

TRANSLATION

O King, both you and us—your advisers, wives and ministers—as well as everything moving and not moving throughout the entire cosmos at this time, are in a temporary situation. Before our birth this situation did not exist, and after our death it will exist no longer. Therefore our situation now is temporary, although it is not false.

PURPORT

The Māyāvādī philosophers say, *brahma satyaṁ jagan mithyā:* Brahman, the living being, is factual, but his present bodily situation is false. According to the Vaiṣṇava philosophy, however, the present situation is not false but temporary. It is like a dream. A dream does not exist before one falls asleep, nor does it continue after one awakens. The period for dreaming exists only between these two, and therefore it is false in the sense that it is impermanent. Similarly, the entire material creation, including our own creation and those of others, is impermanent. We do not lament for the situation in a dream before the dream takes place or after it is over, and so during the dream, or during a dreamlike situation, one should not accept it as factual and lament about it. This is real knowledge.

TEXT 6

भूतैर्भूतानि भूतेशः सृजत्यवति हन्ति च ।
आत्मसृष्टैरस्वतन्त्रैरनपेक्षोऽपि बालवत् ॥ ६ ॥

bhūtair bhūtāni bhūteśaḥ
sṛjaty avati hanti ca
ātma-sṛṣṭair asvatantrair
anapekṣo 'pi bālavat

bhūtaiḥ—by some living beings; *bhūtāni*—other living entities; *bhūta-īśaḥ*—the Supreme Personality of Godhead, the master of everything; *sṛjati*—creates; *avati*—maintains; *hanti*—kills; *ca*—also; *ātma-sṛṣṭaiḥ*—who are created by Him; *asvatantraiḥ*—not independent;

anapekṣaḥ—not interested (in creation); *api*—although; *bāla-vat*—like a boy.

TRANSLATION

The Supreme Personality of Godhead, the master and proprietor of everything, is certainly not interested in the temporary cosmic manifestation. Nonetheless, just as a boy at the beach creates something in which he is not interested, the Lord, keeping everything under His control, causes creation, maintenance and annihilation. He creates by engaging a father to beget a son, He maintains by engaging a government or king to see to the public's welfare, and He annihilates through agents for killing, such as snakes. The agents for creation, maintenance and annihilation have no independent potency, but because of the spell of the illusory energy, one thinks himself the creator, maintainer and annihilator.

PURPORT

No one can independently create, maintain or annihilate. *Bhagavad-gītā* (3.27) therefore says:

prakṛteḥ kriyamāṇāni
guṇaiḥ karmāṇi sarvaśaḥ
ahaṅkāra-vimūḍhātmā
kartāham iti manyate

"The bewildered spirit soul, under the influence of the three modes of material nature, thinks himself the doer of activities that are in actuality carried out by nature." *Prakṛti,* material nature, as directed by the Supreme Personality of Godhead, induces all living entities to create, maintain or annihilate according to the modes of nature. But the living entity, without knowledge of the Supreme Person and His agent the material energy, thinks that he is the doer. In fact, he is not at all the doer. As an agent of the supreme doer, the Supreme Lord, one should abide by the Lord's orders. The present chaotic conditions of the world are due to the ignorance of leaders who forget that they have been appointed to act by the Supreme Personality of Godhead. Because they have been appointed by the Lord, their duty is to consult the Lord and act accordingly.

The book for consultation is *Bhagavad-gītā*, in which the Supreme Lord gives directions. Therefore those who are engaged in creation, maintenance and annihilation should consult the Supreme Person, who has appointed them, and should act accordingly. Then everyone will be satisfied, and there will be no disturbances.

TEXT 7

देहेन देहिनो राजन् देहाद्देहोऽभिजायते ।
बीजादेव यथा बीजं देह्यर्थ इव शाश्वतः ॥ ७ ॥

dehena dehino rājan
dehād deho 'bhijāyate
bījād eva yathā bījaṁ
dehy artha iva śāśvataḥ

dehena—by the body; *dehinaḥ*—of the father possessing a material body; *rājan*—O King; *dehāt*—from the body (of the mother); *dehaḥ*—another body; *abhijāyate*—takes birth; *bījāt*—from one seed; *eva*—indeed; *yathā*—just as; *bījam*—another seed; *dehī*—a person who has accepted a material body; *arthaḥ*—the material elements; *iva*—like; *śāśvataḥ*—eternal.

TRANSLATION

As from one seed another seed is generated, O King, so from one body [the body of the father], through another body [the body of the mother], a third body is generated [the body of a son]. As the elements of the material body are eternal, the living entity who appears through these material elements is also eternal.

PURPORT

From *Bhagavad-gītā* we understand that there are two energies, namely the superior energy and inferior energy. Inferior energy consists of the five gross and three subtle material elements. The living entity, who represents the superior energy, appears in different types of bodies through these elements by the manipulation or supervision of the material energy. Actually both the material and spiritual energies—matter and spirit—exist eternally as potencies of the Supreme Personality of Godhead. The potent entity is the Supreme Person. Since the spiritual energy, the living being, who is part and parcel of the Supreme Lord, desires to enjoy this material world, the Lord gives him a chance to accept different types of material bodies and enjoy or suffer in different material conditions. Factually, the spiritual energy, the living entity who desires to enjoy material things, is manipulated by the Supreme Lord. The so-called father and mother have nothing to do with the living entity. As a result of his own choice and *karma*, the living being takes different bodies through the agency of so-called fathers and mothers.

TEXT 8

देहदेहिविभागोऽयमविवेककृतः पुरा ।
जातिव्यक्तिविभागोऽयं यथा वस्तुनि कल्पितः ॥८॥

deha-dehi-vibhāgo 'yam
aviveka-kṛtaḥ purā
jāti-vyakti-vibhāgo 'yaṁ
yathā vastuni kalpitaḥ

deha—of this body; *dehi*—and the proprietor of the body; *vibhāgaḥ*—the division; *ayam*—this; *aviveka*—from ignorance; *kṛtaḥ*—made; *purā*—from time immemorial; *jāti*—of the class or caste; *vyakti*—and the individual; *vibhāgaḥ*—division; *ayam*—this; *yathā*—just as; *vastuni*—in the original object; *kalpitaḥ*—imagined.

TRANSLATION

Divisions of generalization and specification, such as nationality and individuality, are the imaginations of persons who are not advanced in knowledge.

PURPORT

Actually there are two energies—material and spiritual. Both of them are ever-existing because they are emanations from the eternal truth, the Supreme Lord. Because the individual soul, the individual living entity, has desired to act in forgetfulness of his original identity since time immemorial, he is accepting different positions in material bodies and being designated according to many divisions of nationality, community, society, species and so on.

TEXT 9

श्रीशुक उवाच
एवमाश्वासितो राजा चित्रकेतुर्द्विजोक्तिभिः ।
विमृज्य पाणिना वक्त्रमाधिम्लानमभाषत ॥ ९ ॥

śrī-śuka uvāca
evam āśvāsito rājā
citraketur dvijoktibhiḥ
vimṛjya pāṇinā vaktram
ādhi-mlānam abhāṣata

śrī-śukaḥ uvāca—Śrī Śukadeva Gosvāmī said; *evam*—thus; *āśvāsitaḥ*—being enlightened or given hope; *rājā*—the King; *citraketuḥ*—Citraketu; *dvija-uktibhiḥ*—by the instructions of the great *brāhmaṇas* (Nārada and Aṅgirā Ṛṣi); *vimṛjya*—wiping off; *pāṇinā*—by the hand; *vaktram*—his face; *ādhi-mlānam*—shriveled due to lamentation; *abhāṣata*—spoke intelligently.

TRANSLATION

Śrī Śukadeva Gosvāmī continued: Thus enlightened by the instructions of Nārada and Aṅgirā, King Citraketu became hopeful with knowledge. Wiping his shriveled face with his hand, the King began to speak.

TEXT 10

श्रीराजोवाच
कौ युवां ज्ञानसम्पन्नौ महिष्ठौ च महीयसाम् ।
अवधूतेन वेषेण गूढाविह समागतौ ॥१०॥

śrī-rājovāca
kau yuvāṁ jñāna-sampannau
mahiṣṭhau ca mahīyasām

avadhūtena veṣeṇa
gūḍhāv iha samāgatau

śrī-rājā uvāca—King Citraketu said; *kau*—who; *yuvām*—you two; *jñāna-sampannau*—fully developed in knowledge; *mahiṣṭhau*—the greatest; *ca*—also; *mahīyasām*—among other great personalities; *avadhūtena*—of the liberated wandering mendicants; *veṣeṇa*—by the dress; *gūḍhau*—disguised; *iha*—in this place; *samāgatau*—arrived.

TRANSLATION

King Citraketu said: You have both come here dressed like avadhūtas, liberated persons, just to cover your identities, but I see that of all men, you are the most elevated in awareness. You know everything as it is. Therefore you are the greatest of all great personalities.

TEXT 11

चरन्ति ह्यवनौ कामं ब्राह्मणा भगवत्प्रियाः ।
मादृशां ग्राम्यबुद्धीनां बोधायोन्मत्तलिङ्गिनः ॥११॥

caranti hy avanau kāmaṁ
brāhmaṇā bhagavat-priyāḥ
mādṛśāṁ grāmya-buddhīnāṁ
bodhāyonmatta-liṅginaḥ

caranti—wander; *hi*—indeed; *avanau*—on the surface of the world; *kāmam*—according to desire; *brāhmaṇāḥ*—the *brāhmaṇas; bhagavat-priyāḥ*—who are also Vaiṣṇavas, very dear to the Personality of Godhead; *mā-dṛśām*—of those like me; *grāmya-buddhīnām*—who are obsessed with temporary material consciousness; *bodhāya*—for the awakening; *unmatta-liṅginaḥ*—who dress as if madmen.

TRANSLATION

Brāhmaṇas who are exalted to the position of Vaiṣṇavas, the most dear servants of Kṛṣṇa, sometimes dress like madmen. Just to

benefit materialists like us, who are always attached to sense gratification, and just to dissipate our ignorance, these Vaiṣṇavas wander on the surface of the globe according to their desire.

TEXTS 12–15

कुमारो नारद ऋभुरङ्गिरा देवलोऽसितः ।
अपान्तरतमा व्यासो मार्कण्डेयोऽथ गौतमः ॥१२॥
वसिष्ठो भगवान् रामः कपिलो बादरायणिः ।
दुर्वासा याज्ञवल्क्यश्च जातुकर्णस्तथारुणिः ॥१३॥
रोमशश्च्यवनो दत्त आसुरिः सपतञ्जलिः ।
ऋषिर्वेदशिरा धौम्यो मुनिः पञ्चशिखस्तथा ॥१४॥
हिरण्यनाभः कौशल्यः श्रुतदेव ऋतध्वजः ।
एते परे च सिद्धेशाश्चरन्ति ज्ञानहेतवः ॥१५॥

kumāro nārada ṛbhur
aṅgirā devalo 'sitaḥ
apāntaratamā vyāso
mārkaṇḍeyo 'tha gautamaḥ

vasiṣṭho bhagavān rāmaḥ
kapilo bādarāyaṇiḥ
durvāsā yājñavalkyaś ca
jātukarṇas tathāruṇiḥ

romaśaś cyavano datta
āsuriḥ sapatañjaliḥ
ṛṣir veda-śirā dhaumyo
muniḥ pañcaśikhas tathā

hiraṇyanābhaḥ kauśalyaḥ
śrutadeva ṛtadhvajaḥ
ete pare ca siddheśāś
caranti jñāna-hetavaḥ

kumāraḥ—Sanat-kumāra; *nāradaḥ*—Nārada Muni; *ṛbhuḥ*—Ṛbhu; *aṅgirāḥ*—Aṅgirā; *devalaḥ*—Devala; *asitaḥ*—Asita; *apāntaratamāḥ*—Vyāsa's previous name, Apāntaratamā; *vyāsaḥ*—Vyāsa; *mārkaṇḍeyaḥ*—Mārkaṇḍeya; *atha*—and; *gautamaḥ*—Gautama; *vasiṣṭhaḥ*—Vasiṣṭha; *bhagavān rāmaḥ*—Lord Paraśurāma; *kapilaḥ*—Kapila; *bādarāyaṇiḥ*—Śukadeva Gosvāmī; *durvāsāḥ*—Durvāsā; *yājñavalkyaḥ*—Yājñavalkya; *ca*—also; *jātukarṇaḥ*—Jātukarṇa; *tathā*—as well as; *aruṇiḥ*—Aruṇi; *romaśaḥ*—Romaśa; *cyavanaḥ*—Cyavana; *dattaḥ*—Dattātreya; *āsuriḥ*—Āsuri; *sa-patañjaliḥ*—with Patañjali Ṛṣi; *ṛṣiḥ*—the sage; *veda-śirāḥ*—the head of the *Vedas;* *dhaumyaḥ*—Dhaumya; *muniḥ*—the sage; *pañcaśikhaḥ*—Pañcaśikha; *tathā*—so also; *hiraṇyanābhaḥ*—Hiraṇyanābha; *kauśalyaḥ*—Kauśalya; *śrutadevaḥ*—Śrutadeva; *ṛtadhvajaḥ*—Ṛtadhvaja; *ete*—all of these; *pare*—others; *ca*—and; *siddha-īśāḥ*—the masters of mystic power; *caranti*—wander; *jñāna-hetavaḥ*—very learned persons who preach all over the world.

TRANSLATION

O great souls, I have heard that among the great and perfect persons wandering the surface of the earth to instruct knowledge to people covered by ignorance are Sanat-kumāra, Nārada, Ṛbhu, Aṅgirā, Devala, Asita, Apāntaratamā [Vyāsadeva], Mārkaṇḍeya, Gautama, Vasiṣṭha, Bhagavān Paraśurāma, Kapila, Śukadeva, Durvāsā, Yājñavalkya, Jātukarṇa and Aruṇi. Others are Romaśa, Cyavana, Dattātreya, Āsuri, Patañjali, the great sage Dhaumya who is like the head of the Vedas, the sage Pañcaśikha, Hiraṇyanābha, Kauśalya, Śrutadeva and Ṛtadhvaja. You must certainly be among them.

PURPORT

The word *jñāna-hetavaḥ* is very significant because great personalities like those listed in these verses wander on the surface of the globe not to mislead the populace, but to distribute real knowledge. Without this knowledge, human life is wasted. The human form of life is meant for realization of one's relationship with Kṛṣṇa, or God. One who lacks this knowledge is categorized among the animals. The Lord Himself says in *Bhagavad-gītā* (7.15):

na māṁ duṣkṛtino mūḍhāḥ
prapadyante narādhamāḥ
māyayāpahṛta-jñānā
āsuraṁ bhāvam āśritāḥ

"Those miscreants who are grossly foolish, lowest among mankind, whose knowledge is stolen by illusion, and who partake of the atheistic nature of demons, do not surrender unto Me."

Ignorance is the bodily conception of life (*yasyātma-buddhiḥ kuṇape tri-dhātuke... sa eva go-kharaḥ*). Practically everyone throughout the universe, especially on this planet, Bhūrloka, thinks that there is no separate existence of the body and soul and therefore no need of self-realization. But that is not a fact. Therefore all the *brāhmaṇas* listed here, being devotees, travel all over the world to awaken Kṛṣṇa consciousness in the hearts of such foolish materialists.

The *ācāryas* mentioned in these verses are described in the *Mahābhārata*. The word *pañcaśikha* is also important. One who is liberated from the conceptions of *annamaya, prāṇamaya, manomaya, vijñānamaya* and *ānandamaya* and who is perfectly aware of the subtle coverings of the soul is called *pañcaśikha*. According to the statements of the *Mahābhārata* (*Śānti-parva*, Chapters 218–219), an *ācārya* named Pañcaśikha took birth in the family of Mahārāja Janaka, the ruler of Mithila. The Sāṅkhya philosophers accept Pañcaśikhācārya as one of them. Real knowledge pertains to the living entity dwelling within the body. Unfortunately, because of ignorance, the living entity identifies himself with the body and therefore feels pleasure and pain.

TEXT 16

तस्माद्युवां ग्राम्यपशोर्मम मूढधियः प्रभू ।
अन्धे तमसि मग्नस्य ज्ञानदीप उदीर्यताम् ॥१६॥

tasmād yuvāṁ grāmya-paśor
mama mūḍha-dhiyaḥ prabhū
andhe tamasi magnasya
jñāna-dīpa udīryatām

tasmāt—therefore; *yuvām*—both of you; *grāmya-paśoḥ*—of an animal like a hog, pig or dog; *mama*—me; *mūḍha-dhiyaḥ*—who am very foolish (due to having no spiritual knowledge); *prabhū*—O my two lords; *andhe*—in blind; *tamasi*—darkness; *magnasya*—of one who is absorbed; *jñāna-dīpaḥ*—the torchlight of knowledge; *udīryatām*—let it be ignited.

TRANSLATION

Because you are great personalities, you can give me real knowledge. I am as foolish as a village animal like a pig or dog because I am merged in the darkness of ignorance. Therefore, please ignite the torch of knowledge to save me.

PURPORT

This is the way to receive knowledge. One must submit oneself at the lotus feet of great personalities who can actually deliver transcendental knowledge. It is therefore said, *tasmād guruṁ prapadyeta jijñāsuḥ śreya uttamam:* "One who is inquisitive to understand the highest goal and benefit of life must approach a bona fide spiritual master and surrender unto him." Only one who is actually eager to receive knowledge to eradicate the darkness of ignorance is eligible to approach a *guru,* or spiritual master. The *guru* should not be approached for material benefits. One should not approach a *guru* just to cure some disease or receive some miraculous benefit. This is not the way to approach the *guru. Tad-vijñānārtham:* one should approach the *guru* to understand the transcendental science of spiritual life. Unfortunately, in this age of Kali there are many bogus *gurus* who display magic to their disciples, and many foolish disciples want to see such magic for material benefits. These disciples are not interested in pursuing spiritual life to save themselves from the darkness of ignorance. It is said:

oṁ ajñāna-timirāndhasya
jñānāñjana-śalākayā
cakṣur unmīlitaṁ yena
tasmai śrī-gurave namaḥ

"I was born in the darkest ignorance, and my spiritual master opened my eyes with the torch of knowledge. I offer my respectful obeisances unto him." This gives the definition of the *guru.* Everyone is in the darkness of ignorance. Therefore everyone needs to be enlightened with transcendental knowledge. One who enlightens his disciple and saves him from rotting in the darkness of ignorance in this material world is a true *guru.*

TEXT 17

श्रीअङ्गिरा उवाच
अहं ते पुत्रकामस्य पुत्रदोऽस्म्यङ्गिरा नृप ।
एष ब्रह्मसुतः साक्षान्नारदो भगवानृषिः ॥१७॥

śrī-aṅgirā uvāca
ahaṁ te putra-kāmasya
putrado 'smy aṅgirā nṛpa
eṣa brahma-sutaḥ sākṣān
nārado bhagavān ṛṣiḥ

śrī-aṅgirāḥ uvāca—the great sage Aṅgirā said; *aham*—I; *te*—of you; *putra-kāmasya*—desiring to have a son; *putra-daḥ*—the giver of the son; *asmi*—am; *aṅgirāḥ*—Aṅgirā Ṛṣi; *nṛpa*—O King; *eṣaḥ*—this; *brahma-sutaḥ*—the son of Lord Brahmā; *sākṣāt*—directly; *nāradaḥ*—Nārada Muni; *bhagavān*—the most powerful; *ṛṣiḥ*—sage.

TRANSLATION

Aṅgirā said: My dear King, when you desired to have a son, I approached you. Indeed, I am the same Aṅgirā Ṛṣi who gave you this son. As for this ṛṣi, he is the great sage Nārada, the direct son of Lord Brahmā.

TEXTS 18–19

इत्थं त्वां पुत्रशोकेन मग्नं तमसि दुस्तरे ।
अतदर्हमनुस्मृत्य महापुरुषगोचरम् ॥१८॥
अनुग्रहाय भवतः प्राप्तावावामिह प्रभो ।
ब्रह्मण्यो भगवद्भक्तो नावासादितुमर्हसि ॥१९॥

itthaṁ tvāṁ putra-śokena
magnaṁ tamasi dustare
atad-arham anusmṛtya
mahāpuruṣa-gocaram

anugrahāya bhavataḥ
prāptāv āvām iha prabho
brahmaṇyo bhagavad-bhakto
nāvāsāditum arhasi

ittham—in this way; *tvām*—you; *putra-śokena*—because of grief at the death of your son; *magnam*—merged; *tamasi*—in darkness; *dustare*—insurmountable; *a-tat-arham*—unsuitable for a person like you; *anusmṛtya*—remembering; *mahā-puruṣa*—the Supreme Personality of Godhead; *gocaram*—who are advanced in understanding; *anugrahāya*—just to show favor; *bhavataḥ*—toward you; *prāptau*—arrived; *āvām*—we two; *iha*—in this place; *prabho*—O King; *brahmaṇyaḥ*—one who is situated in the Supreme Absolute Truth; *bhagavat-bhaktaḥ*—an advanced devotee of the Supreme Personality of Godhead; *na*—not; *avāsāditum*—to lament; *arhasi*—you deserve.

TRANSLATION

My dear King, you are an advanced devotee of the Supreme Personality of Godhead. To be absorbed in lamentation for the loss of something material is unsuitable for a person like you. Therefore we have both come to relieve you from this false lamentation, which is due to your being merged in the darkness of ignorance. For those who are advanced in spiritual knowledge to be affected by material loss and gain is not at all desirable.

PURPORT

Several words in this verse are very important. The word *mahā-puruṣa* refers to advanced devotees and also to the Supreme Personality of Godhead. *Mahā* means "the supreme," and *puruṣa* means "person." One who always engages in the service of the Supreme Lord is called *mahā-pauruṣika.* Śukadeva Gosvāmī and Mahārāja Parīkṣit are sometimes addressed as *mahā-pauruṣika.* A devotee should always aspire to engage in the service of advanced devotees. As Śrīla Narottama dāsa Ṭhākura has sung:

tāṅdera caraṇa sevi bhakta-sane vāsa
janame janame haya, ei abhilāṣa

A devotee should always aspire to live in the association of advanced devotees and engage in the service of the Lord through the *paramparā* system. One should serve the mission of Śrī Caitanya Mahāprabhu through the instructions of the great Gosvāmīs of Vṛndāvana. This is called *tāṅdera caraṇa sevi.* While serving the lotus feet of the Gosvāmīs, one should live in the association of devotees (*bhakta-sane vāsa*). This is the business of a devotee. A devotee should not aspire for material profit or lament for material loss. When Aṅgirā Ṛṣi and Nārada saw that Mahārāja Citraketu, an advanced devotee, had fallen in the darkness of ignorance and was lamenting for the material body of his son, by their causeless mercy they came to advise him so that he could be saved from this ignorance.

Another significant word is *brahmaṇya.* The Supreme Personality of Godhead is sometimes addressed by the prayer *namo brahmaṇya-devāya,* which offers obeisances unto the Lord because He is served by the devotees. Therefore this verse states, *brahmaṇyo bhagavad-bhakto nāvāsāditum arhasi.* This is the symptom of an advanced devotee. *Brahma-bhūtaḥ prasannātmā.* For a devotee—an advanced, self-realized soul—there is no cause for material jubilation or lamentation. He is always transcendental to conditional life.

TEXT 20

तदैव ते परं ज्ञानं ददामि गृहमागतः ।
ज्ञात्वान्याभिनिवेशं ते पुत्रमेव ददाम्यहम् ॥२०॥

tadaiva te paraṁ jñānaṁ
dadāmi gṛham āgataḥ
jñātvānyābhiniveśaṁ te
putram eva dadāmy aham

tadā—then; *eva*—indeed; *te*—unto you; *param*—transcendental; *jñānam*—knowledge; *dadāmi*—I would have delivered; *gṛham*—to your home; *āgataḥ*—came; *jñātvā*—knowing; *anya-abhiniveśam*—absorption in something else (in material things); *te*—your; *putram*—a son; *eva*—only; *dadāmi*—gave; *aham*—I.

TRANSLATION

When I first came to your home, I could have given you the supreme transcendental knowledge, but when I saw that your mind was absorbed in material things, I gave you only a son, who caused you jubilation and lamentation.

TEXTS 21–23

अधुना पुत्रिणां तापो भवतैवानुभूयते ।
एवं दारा गृहा रायो विविधैश्वर्यसम्पदः ॥२१॥
शब्दादयश्च विषयाश्चला राज्यविभूतयः ।
मही राज्यं बलं कोषो भृत्यामात्यसुहृज्जनाः ॥२२॥
सर्वेऽपि शूरसेनेमे शोकमोहभयार्तिदाः ।
गन्धर्वनगरप्रख्याः स्वप्नमायामनोरथाः ॥२३॥

adhunā putriṇāṁ tāpo
bhavataivānubhūyate
evaṁ dārā gṛhā rāyo
vividhaiśvarya-sampadaḥ

śabdādayaś ca viṣayāś
calā rājya-vibhūtayaḥ
mahī rājyaṁ balaṁ koṣo
bhṛtyāmātya-suhṛj-janāḥ

sarve 'pi śūraseneme
śoka-moha-bhayārtidāḥ
gandharva-nagara-prakhyāḥ
svapna-māyā-manorathāḥ

adhunā—at the present moment; *putriṇām*—of persons who have children; *tāpaḥ*—the tribulation; *bhavatā*—by you; *eva*—indeed; *anubhūyate*—is experienced; *evam*—in this way; *dārāḥ*—good wife; *gṛhāḥ*—residence; *rāyaḥ*—riches; *vividha*—various; *aiśvarya*—opulences; *sampadaḥ*—prosperities; *śabda-ādayaḥ*—sound and so on; *ca*—and; *viṣayāḥ*—the objects of sense gratification; *calāḥ*—temporary; *rājya*—of the kingdom; *vibhūtayaḥ*—opulences; *mahī*—land; *rājyam*—kingdom; *balam*—strength; *koṣaḥ*—treasury; *bhṛtya*—servants; *amātya*—ministers; *suhṛt-janāḥ*—allies; *sarve*—all; *api*—indeed; *śūrasena*—O King of Śūrasena; *ime*—these; *śoka*—of lamentation; *moha*—of illusion; *bhaya*—of fear; *arti*—and distress; *dāḥ*—givers; *gandharva-nagara-prakhyāḥ*—headed by the illusory sight of a *gandharva-nagara,* a big palace within the forest; *svapna*—dreams; *māyā*—illusions; *manorathāḥ*—and concoctions of the mind.

TRANSLATION

My dear King, now you are actually experiencing the misery of a person who has sons and daughters. O King, owner of the state of Śūrasena, one's wife, his house, the opulence of his kingdom, and his various other opulences and objects of sense perception are all the same in that they are temporary. One's kingdom, military power, treasury, servants, ministers, friends and relatives are all causes of fear, illusion, lamentation and distress. They are like a gandharva-nagara, a nonexistent palace that one imagines to exist in the forest. Because they are impermanent, they are no better than illusions, dreams and mental concoctions.

PURPORT

This verse describes the entanglement of material existence. In material existence, the living entity possesses many things—the material body, children, wife and so on (*dehāpatya-kalatrādiṣu*). One may think that these will give him protection, but that is impossible. In spite of all these possessions, the spirit soul has to give up his present situation and accept another. The next situation may be unfavorable, but even if it is favorable, one must give it up and again accept another body. In this way, one's tribulation in material existence continues. A sane man should be perfectly aware that these things will never be able to give him happiness. One must be situated in his spiritual identity and eternally serve the Supreme Personality of Godhead as a devotee. Aṅgirā Ṛṣi and Nārada Muni gave this instruction to Mahārāja Citraketu.

TEXT 24

दृश्यमाना विनार्थेन न दृश्यन्ते मनोभवाः ।
कर्मभिर्ध्यायतो नानाकर्माणि मनसोऽभवन् ॥२४॥

dṛśyamānā vinārthena
na dṛśyante manobhavāḥ
karmabhir dhyāyato nānā-
karmāṇi manaso 'bhavan

dṛśyamānāḥ—being perceived; *vinā*—without; *arthena*—substance or reality; *na*—not; *dṛśyante*—are seen; *manobhavāḥ*—creations of mental concoction; *karmabhiḥ*—by fruitive activities; *dhyāyataḥ*—meditating upon; *nānā*—various; *karmāṇi*—fruitive activities; *manasaḥ*—from the mind; *abhavan*—appear.

TRANSLATION

These visible objects like wife, children and property are like dreams and mental concoctions. Actually what we see has no permanent existence. It is sometimes seen and sometimes not. Only because of our past actions do we create such mental concoctions, and because of these concoctions, we perform further activities.

PURPORT

Everything material is a mental concoction because it is sometimes visible and sometimes not. At night when we dream of tigers and snakes, they are not actually present, but we are afraid because we are affected by what we envision in our dreams. Everything material is like a dream because it actually has no permanent existence.

Śrīla Viśvanātha Cakravartī Ṭhākura writes as follows in his commentary: *arthena vyāghra-sarpādinā vinaiva dṛśyamānāḥ svapnādi-bhaṅge sati na dṛśyante tad evaṁ dārādayo 'vāstava-vastu-bhūtāḥ svapnādayo 'vastu-bhūtāś ca sarve manobhavāḥ mano-vāsanā janyatvān manobhavāḥ.* At night one dreams of tigers and snakes, and while dreaming he actually sees them, but as soon as the dream is broken they no longer exist. Similarly, the material world is a creation of our mental concoctions. We have come to this material world to enjoy material resources, and by mental concoction we discover many, many objects of enjoyment because our minds are absorbed in material things. This is why we receive various bodies. According to our mental concoctions we work in various ways, desiring various achievements, and by nature and the order of the Supreme Personality of Godhead (*karmaṇā daiva-netreṇa*) we get the advantages we desire. Thus we become more and more involved with material concoctions. This is the reason for our suffering in the material world. By one kind of activity we create another, and they are all products of our mental concoctions.

TEXT 25

अयं हि देहिनो देहो द्रव्यज्ञानक्रियात्मकः ।
देहिनो विविधक्लेशसन्तापकृदुदाहृतः ॥२५॥

ayaṁ hi dehino deho
dravya-jñāna-kriyātmakaḥ
dehino vividha-kleśa-
santāpa-kṛd udāhṛtaḥ

ayam—this; *hi*—certainly; *dehinaḥ*—of the living entity; *dehaḥ*—body; *dravya-jñāna-kriyā-ātmakaḥ*—consisting of the material elements, the senses for acquiring knowledge, and the acting senses; *dehinaḥ*—of the living entity; *vividha*—various; *kleśa*—sufferings; *santāpa*—and of pains; *kṛt*—the cause; *udāhṛtaḥ*—is declared.

TRANSLATION

The living entity in the bodily conception of life is absorbed in the body, which is a combination of the physical elements, the five senses for gathering knowledge, and the five senses of action, along with the mind. Through the mind the living entity suffers

three kinds of tribulations—adhibhautika, adhidaivika and adhyātmika. Therefore this body is a source of all miseries.

PURPORT

In the Fifth Canto (5.5.4), while instructing his sons, Ṛṣabhadeva said, *asann api kleśada āsa dehaḥ:* the body, although temporary, is the cause of all the miseries of material existence. As already discussed in the previous verse, the entire material creation is based on mental concoction. The mind sometimes induces us to think that if we purchase an automobile we can enjoy the physical elements, such as earth, water, air and fire, combined in forms of iron, plastic, petrol and so on. Working with the five material elements (*pañca-bhūtas*), as well as with our five knowledge-gathering senses like the eyes, ears and tongue and our five active senses like the hands and legs, we become involved in the material condition. Thus we are subjected to the tribulations known as *adhyātmika, adhidaivika* and *adhibhautika.* The mind is the center because the mind creates all these things. As soon as the material object is struck, however, the mind is affected, and we suffer. For example, with the material elements, the working senses and the knowledge-gathering senses we create a very nice car, and when the car is accidentally smashed in a collision, the mind suffers, and through the mind the living entity suffers.

The fact is that the living entity, while concocting with the mind, creates the material condition. Because matter is destructible, through the material condition the living entity suffers. Otherwise, the living entity is detached from all material conditions. When one comes to the Brahman platform, the platform of spiritual life, fully understanding that he is a spiritual soul (*ahaṁ brahmāsmi*), he is no longer affected by lamentation or hankering. As the Lord says in *Bhagavad-gītā* (18.54):

brahma-bhūtaḥ prasannātmā
na śocati na kāṅkṣati

"One who is thus transcendentally situated at once realizes the Supreme Brahman and becomes fully joyful. He never laments nor desires to have anything." Elsewhere in *Bhagavad-gītā* (15.7) the Lord says:

mamaivāṁśo jīva-loke
jīva-bhūtaḥ sanātanaḥ
manaḥ-ṣaṣṭhānīndriyāṇi
prakṛti-sthāni karṣati

"The living entities in this conditioned world are My eternal fragmental parts. Due to conditioned life, they are struggling very hard with the six senses, which include the mind." The living entity is actually part and parcel of the Supreme Personality of Godhead and is unaffected by material conditions, but because the mind (*manaḥ*) is affected, the senses are affected, and the living entity struggles for existence within this material world.

TEXT 26

तस्मात् स्वस्थेन मनसा विमृश्य गतिमात्मनः ।
द्वैते ध्रुवार्थविश्रम्भं त्यजोपशममाविश ॥२६॥

tasmāt svasthena manasā
vimṛśya gatim ātmanaḥ
dvaite dhruvārtha-viśrambhaṁ
tyajopaśamam āviśa

tasmāt—therefore; *svasthena*—with a careful; *manasā*—mind; *vimṛśya*—considering; *gatim*—real position; *ātmanaḥ*—of yourself; *dvaite*—in the duality; *dhruva*—as permanent; *artha*—object; *viśrambham*—belief; *tyaja*—give up; *upaśamam*—a peaceful condition; *āviśa*—take to.

TRANSLATION

Therefore, O King Citraketu, carefully consider the position of the ātmā. In other words, try to understand who you are—whether body, mind or soul. Consider where you have come from, where you are going after giving up this body, and why you are under the control of material lamentation. Try to understand your real position in this way, and then you will be able to give up your unnecessary attachment. You will also be able to give up the belief

that this material world, or anything not directly in touch with service to Kṛṣṇa, is eternal. Thus you will obtain peace.

PURPORT

The Kṛṣṇa consciousness movement is factually endeavoring to bring human society to a sober condition. Because of a misdirected civilization, people are jumping in materialistic life like cats and dogs, performing all sorts of abominable, sinful actions and becoming increasingly entangled. The Kṛṣṇa consciousness movement includes self-realization because one is first directed by Lord Kṛṣṇa to understand that one is not the body but the owner of the body. When one understands this simple fact, he can direct himself toward the goal of life. Because people are not educated in terms of the goal of life, they are working like madmen and becoming more and more attached to the material atmosphere. The misguided man accepts the material condition as everlasting. One must give up his faith in material things and give up attachment for them. Then one will be sober and peaceful.

TEXT 27

श्रीनारद उवाच
एतां मन्त्रोपनिषदं प्रतीच्छ प्रयतो मम ।
यां धारयन् सप्तरात्राद् द्रष्टा सङ्कर्षणं विभुम् ॥२७॥

śrī-nārada uvāca
etāṁ mantropaniṣadaṁ
pratīccha prayato mama
yāṁ dhārayan sapta-rātrād
draṣṭā saṅkarṣaṇaṁ vibhum

śrī-nāradaḥ uvāca—Śrī Nārada Muni said; *etām*—this; *mantra-upaniṣadam*—*Upaniṣad* in the form of a *mantra* by which one can achieve the highest goal of life; *pratīccha*—accept; *prayataḥ*—with great attention (after finishing the funeral ceremony of your dead son); *mama*—from me; *yām*—which; *dhārayan*—accepting; *sapta-rātrāt*—after seven nights; *draṣṭā*—you will see; *saṅkarṣaṇam*—the Supreme Personality of Godhead, Saṅkarṣaṇa; *vibhum*—the Lord.

TRANSLATION

The great sage Nārada continued: My dear King, attentively receive from me a mantra, which is most auspicious. After accepting it from me, in seven nights you will be able to see the Lord face to face.

TEXT 28

यत्पादमूलमुपसृत्य नरेन्द्र पूर्वे
शर्वादयो भ्रममिमं द्वितयं विसृज्य ।
सद्यस्तदीयमतुलानधिकं महित्वं
प्रापुर्भवानपि परं नचिरादुपैति ॥२८॥

yat-pāda-mūlam upasṛtya narendra pūrve
śarvādayo bhramam imaṁ dvitayaṁ visṛjya
sadyas tadīyam atulānadhikaṁ mahitvaṁ
prāpur bhavān api paraṁ na cirād upaiti

yat-pāda-mūlam—the lotus feet of whom (Lord Saṅkarṣaṇa); *upasṛtya*—obtaining shelter at; *nara-indra*—O King; *pūrve*—formerly; *śarva-ādayaḥ*—great demigods like Lord Mahādeva; *bhramam*—illusion; *imam*—this; *dvitayam*—consisting of duality; *visṛjya*—giving up; *sadyaḥ*—immediately; *tadīyam*—His; *atula*—unequaled; *anadhikam*—unsurpassed; *mahitvam*—glories; *prāpuḥ*—achieved; *bhavān*—yourself; *api*—also; *param*—the supreme abode; *na*—not; *cirāt*—after a long time; *upaiti*—will obtain.

TRANSLATION

My dear King, in former days Lord Śiva and other demigods took shelter of the lotus feet of Saṅkarṣaṇa. Thus they immediately got free from the illusion of duality and achieved unequaled and unsurpassed glories in spiritual life. You will very soon attain that very same position.

Thus end the Bhaktivedanta purports of the Sixth Canto, Fifteenth Chapter, of the Śrīmad-Bhāgavatam, *entitled "The Saints Nārada and Aṅgirā Instruct King Citraketu."*

CHAPTER SIXTEEN

King Citraketu Meets the Supreme Lord

As related in this chapter, Citraketu was able to talk with his dead son and hear from him the truth of life. When Citraketu was appeased, the great sage Nārada gave him a *mantra,* and by chanting this *mantra* Citraketu found shelter at the lotus feet of Saṅkarṣaṇa.

The living entity is eternal. Thus he has neither birth nor death (*na hanyate hanyamāne śarīre*). According to the reactions of one's fruitive activities, one takes birth in various species of life among the birds, beasts, trees, human beings, demigods and so on, thus rotating through various bodies. For a certain period of time, one receives a particular type of body as a son or father in a false relationship. All our relationships in this material world with friends, relatives or enemies consist of duality, in which one feels happy and distressed on the basis of illusion. The living entity is actually a spiritual soul who is part and parcel of God and has nothing to do with relationships in the world of duality. Therefore Nārada Muni advised Citraketu not to lament for his so-called dead son.

After hearing instructions from their dead child, Citraketu and his wife could understand that all relationships in this material world are causes of misery. The queens who had administered poison to the son of Kṛtadyuti were very much ashamed. They atoned for the sinful act of killing a child and gave up their aspiration to have sons. Thereafter, Nārada Muni chanted prayers to Nārāyaṇa, who exists as *catur-vyūha,* and instructed Citraketu about the Supreme Lord, who creates, maintains and annihilates everything and who is the master of the material nature. After instructing King Citraketu in this way, he returned to Brahmaloka. These instructions about the Absolute Truth are called the *mahā-vidyā.* After being initiated by Nārada Muni, King Citraketu chanted the *mahā-vidyā,* and after one week he attained the presence of Lord Saṅkarṣaṇa, who was surrounded by the four Kumāras. The Lord was nicely dressed in bluish garments, with a helmet and ornaments of gold. His face appeared very happy. In the presence of Lord Saṅkarṣaṇa, Citraketu offered his obeisances and began to offer prayers.

In his prayers, Citraketu said that millions of universes rest in the pores of Saṅkarṣaṇa, who is limitless, having no beginning and end. The Lord is well known to the devotees for His eternity. The difference between worshiping the Lord and worshiping the demigods is that the worshiper of the Lord also becomes eternal, whereas whatever benedictions one can get from the demigods are impermanent. Unless one becomes a devotee, one cannot understand the Supreme Personality of Godhead.

After Citraketu finished his prayers, the unlimited Supreme Lord explained knowledge of Himself to Citraketu.

TEXT 1

श्रीबादरायणिरुवाच
अथ देवऋषी राजन् सम्परेतं नृपात्मजम् ।
दर्शयित्वेति होवाच ज्ञातीनामनुशोचताम् ॥ १ ॥

śrī-bādarāyaṇir uvāca
atha deva-ṛṣī rājan
samparetaṁ nṛpātmajam
darśayitveti hovāca
jñātīnām anuśocatām

śrī-bādarāyaṇiḥ uvāca—Śrī Śukadeva Gosvāmī said; *atha*—thus; *deva-ṛṣiḥ*—the great sage Nārada; *rājan*—O King; *samparetam*—dead; *nṛpa-ātmajam*—the son of the King; *darśayitvā*—making visible; *iti*—thus; *ha*—indeed; *uvāca*—explained; *jñātīnām*—to all the relatives; *anuśocatām*—who were lamenting.

TRANSLATION

Śrī Śukadeva Gosvāmī said: My dear King Parīkṣit, by his mystic power the great sage Nārada brought the dead son into the vision of all the lamenting relatives and then spoke as follows.

TEXT 2

श्रीनारद उवाच
जीवात्मन् पश्य भद्रं ते मातरं पितरं च ते ।
सुहृदो बान्धवास्तप्ताः शुचा त्वत्कृतया भृशम् ॥ २ ॥

śrī-nārada uvāca
jīvātman paśya bhadraṁ te
mātaraṁ pitaraṁ ca te
suhṛdo bāndhavās taptāḥ
śucā tvat-kṛtayā bhṛśam

śrī-nāradaḥ uvāca—Śrī Nārada Muni said; *jīva-ātman*—O living entity; *paśya*—just see; *bhadram*—good fortune; *te*—unto you; *mātaram*—the mother; *pitaram*—the father; *ca*—and; *te*—of you; *suhṛdaḥ*—friends; *bāndhavāḥ*—relatives; *taptāḥ*—aggrieved; *śucā*—by lamentation; *tvat-kṛtayā*—because of you; *bhṛśam*—very greatly.

TRANSLATION

Śrī Nārada Muni said: O living entity, all good fortune unto you. Just see your father and mother. All your friends and relatives are overwhelmed with grief because of your passing away.

TEXT 3

कलेवरं स्वमाविश्य शेषमायुः सुहृद्वृतः ।
भुङ्क्ष्व भोगान् पितृप्रत्तानधितिष्ठ नृपासनम् ॥ ३ ॥

kalevaraṁ svam āviśya
śeṣam āyuḥ suhṛd-vṛtaḥ
bhuṅkṣva bhogān pitṛ-prattān
adhitiṣṭha nṛpāsanam

kalevaram—body; *svam*—your own; *āviśya*—entering; *śeṣam*—the balance; *āyuḥ*—duration of life; *suhṛt-vṛtaḥ*—surrounded by your friends and relatives; *bhuṅkṣva*—just enjoy; *bhogān*—all enjoyable opulences; *pitṛ*—by your father; *prattān*—awarded; *adhitiṣṭha*—accept; *nṛpa-āsanam*—the throne of the king.

TRANSLATION

Because you died untimely, the balance of your lifetime still remains. Therefore you may reenter your body and enjoy the remainder of your life, surrounded by your friends and relatives. Accept the royal throne and all the opulences given by your father.

TEXT 4

जीव उवाच
कस्मिञ्जन्मन्यमी मह्यं पितरो मातरोऽभवन् ।
कर्मभिर्भ्राम्यमाणस्य देवतिर्यङ्नृयोनिषु ॥ ४ ॥

jīva uvāca
kasmiñ janmany amī mahyaṁ
pitaro mātaro 'bhavan
karmabhir bhrāmyamāṇasya
deva-tiryaṅ-nṛ-yoniṣu

jīvaḥ uvāca—the living entity said; *kasmin*—in which; *janmani*—birth; *amī*—all those; *mahyam*—to me; *pitaraḥ*—fathers; *mātaraḥ*—mothers; *abhavan*—were; *karmabhiḥ*—by the results of fruitive action; *bhrāmyamāṇasya*—who am wandering; *deva-tiryak*—of the demigods and the lower animals; *nṛ*—and of the human species; *yoniṣu*—in the wombs.

TRANSLATION

By the mystic power of Nārada Muni, the living entity reentered his dead body for a short time and spoke in reply to Nārada Muni's request. He said: According to the results of my fruitive activities, I, the living being, transmigrate from one body to another, sometimes going to the species of the demigods, sometimes to the species of lower animals, sometimes among the vegetables, and sometimes to the human species. Therefore, in which birth were these my mother and father? No one is actually my mother and father. How can I accept these two people as my parents?

PURPORT

Here it is made clear that the living being enters a material body that is like a machine created by the five gross elements of material nature (earth, water, fire, air and sky) and the three subtle elements (mind, intelligence and ego). As confirmed in *Bhagavad-gītā*, there are two separate identities, called the inferior and superior natures, which both belong to the Supreme Personality of Godhead. According to the results of a living entity's fruitive actions, he is forced to enter the material elements in different types of bodies.

This time the living entity was supposed to have been the son of Mahārāja Citraketu and Queen Kṛtadyuti because according to the laws of nature he had entered a body made by the King and Queen. Actually, however, he was not their son. The living entity is the son of the Supreme Personality of Godhead, and because he wants to enjoy this material world, the Supreme Lord gives him a chance to enter various bodies. The living entity has no true relationship with the material body he gets from his material father and mother. He is part and parcel of the Supreme Lord, but he is allowed to go through different bodies. The body created by the so-called father and mother actually has nothing to do with its so-called creators. Therefore the living entity flatly denied that Mahārāja Citraketu and his wife were his father and mother.

TEXT 5

बन्धुज्ञात्यरिमध्यस्थमित्रोदासीनविद्विषः ।
सर्व एव हि सर्वेषां भवन्ति क्रमशो मिथः ॥ ५ ॥

bandhu-jñāty-ari-madhyastha-
mitrodāsīna-vidviṣaḥ
sarva eva hi sarveṣāṁ
bhavanti kramaśo mithaḥ

bandhu—friends; *jñāti*—family members; *ari*—enemies; *madhya-stha*—neutrals; *mitra*—well-wishers; *udāsīna*—indifferent; *vidviṣaḥ*—or envious persons; *sarve*—all; *eva*—indeed; *hi*—certainly; *sarveṣām*—of all; *bhavanti*—become; *kramaśaḥ*—gradually; *mithaḥ*—of one another.

TRANSLATION

In this material world, which advances like a river that carries away the living entity, all people become friends, relatives and enemies in due course of time. They also act neutrally, they mediate, they despise one another, and they act in many other relationships. Nonetheless, despite these various transactions, no one is permanently related.

PURPORT

It is our practical experience in this material world that the same person who is one's friend today becomes one's enemy tomorrow. Our relationships as friends or enemies, family men or outsiders, are actually the results of our different dealings. Citraketu Mahārāja was lamenting for his son, who was now dead, but he could have considered the situation otherwise. "This living entity," he could have thought, "was my enemy in my last life, and now, having appeared as my son, he is prematurely leaving just to give me pain and agony." Why should he not consider his dead son his former enemy and instead of lamenting be jubilant because of an enemy's death? As stated in *Bhagavad-gītā* (3.27), *prakṛteḥ kriyamāṇāni guṇaiḥ karmāṇi sarvaśaḥ:* factually everything is happening because of our association with the modes of material nature. Therefore one who is my friend today in association with the mode of goodness may be my enemy tomorrow in association with the modes of passion and ignorance. As the modes of material nature work, in illusion we accept others as friends, enemies, sons or fathers in terms of the reactions of different dealings under different conditions.

TEXT 6

यथा वस्तूनि पण्यानि हेमादीनि ततस्ततः ।
पर्यटन्ति नरेष्वेवं जीवो योनिषु कर्तृषु ॥ ६ ॥

yathā vastūni paṇyāni
hemādīni tatas tataḥ
paryaṭanti nareṣv evaṁ
jīvo yoniṣu kartṛṣu

yathā—just as; *vastūni*—commodities; *paṇyāni*—meant for trading; *hema-ādīni*—such as gold; *tataḥ tataḥ*—from here to there; *paryaṭanti*—move about; *nareṣu*—among men; *evam*—in this way; *jīvaḥ*—the living entity; *yoniṣu*—in different species of life; *kartṛṣu*—in different material fathers.

TRANSLATION

Just as gold and other commodities are continually transferred from one place to another in due course of purchase and sale, so the living entity, as a result of his fruitive activities, wanders throughout the entire universe, being injected into various bodies in different species of life by one kind of father after another.

PURPORT

It has already been explained that Citraketu's son was his enemy in a past life and had now appeared as his son just to give him more severe pain. Indeed, the untimely death of the son caused severe lamentation for the father. One may put forward the argument, "If the King's son was his enemy, how could the King have so much affection for him?" In answer, the example is given that when someone's wealth falls into the hands of his enemy, the money becomes the enemy's friend. Then the enemy can use it for his own purposes. Indeed, he can even use it to harm its previous owner. Therefore the money belongs neither to the one party nor to the other. The money is always money, but in different situations it can be used as an enemy or a friend.

As explained in *Bhagavad-gītā,* it is not by any father or mother that the living entity is given his birth. The living entity is a completely separate identity from the so-called father and mother. By the laws of nature, the living entity is forced to enter the semen of a father and be injected into the womb of the mother. He is not in control of selecting what kind of father he will accept. *Prakṛteḥ kriyamāṇāni:* the laws of nature force him to go to different fathers and mothers, just like a consumer commodity that is purchased and sold. Therefore the so-called relationship of father and son is an arrangement of *prakṛti,* or nature. It has no meaning, and therefore it is called illusion.

The same living entity sometimes takes shelter of an animal father and mother and sometimes a human father and mother. Sometimes he accepts a father and mother among the birds, and sometimes he accepts a demigod father and mother. Śrī Caitanya Mahāprabhu therefore says:

brahmāṇḍa bhramite kona bhāgyavān jīva
guru-kṛṣṇa-prasāde pāya bhakti-latā-bīja

Harassed life after life by the laws of nature, the living entity wanders throughout the entire universe in different planets and different species of life. Somehow or other, if he is fortunate enough, he comes in touch with a devotee who reforms his entire life. Then the living entity goes back home, back to Godhead. Therefore it is said:

janame janame sabe pitā mātā pāya
kṛṣṇa guru nahi mile baja hari ei

In the transmigration of the soul through different bodies, everyone, in every form of life—be it human, animal, tree or demigod—gets a father and mother. This is not very difficult. The difficulty is to obtain a bona fide spiritual master and Kṛṣṇa. Therefore the duty of a human being is to capture the opportunity to come in touch with Kṛṣṇa's representative, the bona fide spiritual master. Under the guidance of the spiritual master, the spiritual father, one can return home, back to Godhead.

TEXT 7

नित्यस्यार्थस्य सम्बन्धो ह्यनित्यो दृश्यते नृषु ।
यावद्यस्य हि सम्बन्धो ममत्वं तावदेव हि ॥ ७ ॥

nityasyārthasya sambandho
hy anityo dṛśyate nṛṣu
yāvad yasya hi sambandho
mamatvaṁ tāvad eva hi

nityasya—of the eternal; *arthasya*—thing; *sambandhaḥ*—relationship; *hi*—indeed; *anityaḥ*—temporary; *dṛśyate*—is seen; *nṛṣu*—in human society; *yāvat*—as long as; *yasya*—of whom; *hi*—indeed; *sambandhaḥ*—relationship; *mamatvam*—ownership; *tāvat*—that long; *eva*—indeed; *hi*—certainly.

TRANSLATION

A few living entities are born in the human species, and others are born as animals. Although both are living entities, their relationships are impermanent. An animal may remain in the custody of a human being for some time, and then the same animal may be transferred to the possession of other human beings. As soon as the animal goes away, the former proprietor no longer has a sense of ownership. As long as the animal is in his possession he certainly has an affinity for it, but as soon as the animal is sold, the affinity is lost.

PURPORT

Aside from the fact that the soul transmigrates from one body to another, even in this life the relationships between living entities are impermanent, as exemplified in this verse. The son of Citraketu was named Harṣaśoka, or "jubilation and lamentation." The living entity is certainly eternal, but because he is covered by a temporary dress, the body, his eternity is not observed. *Dehino 'smin yathā dehe kaumāraṁ yauvanaṁ jarā:* "The embodied soul continually passes, in this body, from boyhood to youth to old age." Thus the bodily dress is impermanent. The living entity, however, is permanent. As an animal is transferred from one owner to another, the living entity who was the son of Citraketu lived as his son for some time, but as soon as he was transferred to another body, the affectionate relationship was broken. As stated in the example given in the previous verse, when one has a commodity in his hands he considers it his, but as soon as it is transferred it becomes someone else's commodity. Then one no longer has a relationship with it; he has no affection for it, nor does he lament for it.

TEXT 8

एवं योनिगतो जीवः स नित्यो निरहङ्कृतः ।
यावद्यत्रोपलभ्येत तावत्स्वत्वं हि तस्य तत् ॥ ८ ॥

evaṁ yoni-gato jīvaḥ
sa nityo nirahaṅkṛtaḥ
yāvad yatropalabhyeta
tāvat svatvaṁ hi tasya tat

evam—thus; *yoni-gataḥ*—being within a specific species of life; *jīvaḥ*—the living entity; *saḥ*—he; *nityaḥ*—eternal; *nirahaṅkṛtaḥ*—without identification with the body; *yāvat*—as long as; *yatra*—where; *upalabhyeta*—he may be found; *tāvat*—that long; *svatvam*—the concept of self; *hi*—indeed; *tasya*—of him; *tat*—that.

TRANSLATION

Even though one living entity becomes connected with another because of a relationship based on bodies that are perishable, the living entity is eternal. Actually it is the body that is born or lost, not the living entity. One should not accept that the living entity takes birth or dies. The living being actually has no relationship with so-called fathers and mothers. As long as he appears as the son of a certain father and mother as a result of his past fruitive activities, he has a connection with the body given by that father and mother. Thus he falsely accepts himself as their son and acts affectionately. After he dies, however, the relationship is finished. Under these circumstances, one should not be falsely involved with jubilation and lamentation.

PURPORT

When the living entity lives within the material body, he falsely thinks that he is the body, although actually he is not. His relationship with his body and his so-called father and mother are false, illusory conceptions. These illusions continue as long as one is not enlightened about the situation of the living entity.

TEXT 9

एष नित्योऽव्ययः सूक्ष्म एष सर्वाश्रयः स्वदृक् ।
आत्ममायागुणैर्विश्वमात्मानं सृजते प्रभुः ॥ ९ ॥

eṣa nityo 'vyayaḥ sūkṣma
eṣa sarvāśrayaḥ svadṛk
ātmamāyā-guṇair viśvam
ātmānaṁ sṛjate prabhuḥ

eṣaḥ—this living entity; *nityaḥ*—eternal; *avyayaḥ*—imperishable; *sūkṣmaḥ*—very, very fine (not seen by the material eyes); *eṣaḥ*—this living entity; *sarva-āśrayaḥ*—the cause of different types of bodies; *sva-dṛk*—self-effulgent; *ātma-māyā-guṇaiḥ*—by the Supreme Personality of Godhead's modes of material nature; *viśvam*—this material world; *ātmānam*—himself; *sṛjate*—appears; *prabhuḥ*—the master.

TRANSLATION

The living entity is eternal and imperishable because he actually has no beginning and no end. He never takes birth or dies. He is the basic principle of all types of bodies, yet he does not belong to the bodily category. The living being is so sublime that he is equal in quality to the Supreme Lord. Nonetheless, because he is extremely small, he is prone to be illusioned by the external energy, and thus he creates various bodies for himself according to his different desires.

PURPORT

In this verse the philosophy of *acintya-bhedābheda*—simultaneous oneness and difference—is described. The living entity is eternal (*nitya*) like the Supreme Personality of Godhead, but the difference is that the Supreme Lord is the greatest, no one being equal to or greater than Him, whereas the living entity is *sūkṣma*, or extremely small. The *śāstra* describes that the magnitude of the living entity is one ten-thousandth the size of the tip of a hair. The Supreme Lord is all-pervading (*aṇḍāntara-stha-paramāṇu-cayāntara-stham*). Relatively, if the living entity is accepted as the smallest, there should naturally be inquiry about the greatest. The greatest is the Supreme Personality of Godhead, and the smallest is the living entity.

Another peculiar characteristic of the *jīva* is that he becomes covered by *māyā*. *Ātmamāyā-guṇaiḥ:* he is prone to being covered by the Supreme Lord's illusory energy. The living entity is responsible for his conditional life in the material world, and therefore he is described as *prabhu* ("the master"). If he likes he can come to this material world, and if he likes he can return home, back to Godhead. Because he wanted to enjoy this material world, the Supreme Personality of Godhead gave him a material body through the agency of the material energy. As the Lord Himself says in *Bhagavad-gītā* (18.61):

īśvaraḥ sarva-bhūtānāṁ
hṛd-deśe 'rjuna tiṣṭhati
bhrāmayan sarva-bhūtāni
yantrārūḍhāni māyayā

"The Supreme Lord is situated in everyone's heart, O Arjuna, and is directing the wanderings of all living entities, who are seated as on a machine, made of the material energy." The Supreme Lord gives the living entity a chance to enjoy in this material world as he desires, but He openly expresses His own desire that the living entity give up all material aspirations, fully surrender unto Him and return home, back to Godhead.

The living entity is the smallest (*sūkṣma*). Jīva Gosvāmī says in this connection that the living entity within the body is extremely difficult for materialistic scientists to find, although we understand from authorities that the living entity is within the body. The body is different from the living entity.

TEXT 10

न ह्यस्यास्ति प्रियः कश्चिन्नाप्रियः स्वः परोऽपि वा ।
एकः सर्वधियां द्रष्टा कर्तॄणां गुणदोषयोः ॥१०॥

na hy asyāsti priyaḥ kaścin
nāpriyaḥ svaḥ paro 'pi vā
ekaḥ sarva-dhiyāṁ draṣṭā
kartṝṇāṁ guṇa-doṣayoḥ

na—not; *hi*—indeed; *asya*—to the living entity; *asti*—there is; *priyaḥ*—dear; *kaścit*—someone; *na*—not; *apriyaḥ*—not dear; *svaḥ*—own; *paraḥ*—other; *api*—also; *vā*—or; *ekaḥ*—the one; *sarva-*

dhiyām—of the varieties of intelligence; *draṣṭā*—the seer; *kartṝṇām*—of the performers; *guṇa-doṣayoḥ*—of right and wrong activities.

TRANSLATION

For this living entity, no one is dear, nor is anyone unfavorable. He makes no distinction between that which is his own and that which belongs to anyone else. He is one without a second; in other words, he is not affected by friends and enemies, well-wishers or mischief-mongers. He is only an observer, a witness, of the different qualities of men.

PURPORT

As explained in the previous verse, the living entity has the same qualities as the Supreme Personality of Godhead, but he has them in minute quantities because he is a small particle (*sūkṣma*) whereas the Supreme Lord is all-pervading and great. For the Supreme Lord there are no friends, enemies or relatives, for He is completely free from all the disqualifications of ignorance that characterize the conditioned souls. On the other hand, He is extremely kind and favorable to His devotees, and He is not at all satisfied with persons who are envious of His devotees. As the Lord Himself confirms in *Bhagavad-gītā* (9.29):

samo 'haṁ sarva-bhūteṣu
na me dveṣyo 'sti na priyaḥ
ye bhajanti tu māṁ bhaktyā
mayi te teṣu cāpy aham

"I envy no one, nor am I partial to anyone. I am equal to all. But whoever renders service unto Me in devotion is a friend, is in Me, and I am also a friend to him." The Supreme Lord has no enemy or friend, but He is inclined toward a devotee who always engages in His devotional service. Similarly, elsewhere in the *Gītā* (16.19) the Lord says:

tān ahaṁ dviṣataḥ krūrān
saṁsāreṣu narādhamān
kṣipāmy ajasram aśubhān
āsurīṣv eva yoniṣu

"Those who are envious and mischievous, who are the lowest among men, are cast by Me into the ocean of material existence, into various demoniac species of life." The Lord is extremely antagonistic toward those who are envious of His devotees. To protect His devotees, the Lord sometimes has to kill their enemies. For example, to protect Prahlāda Mahārāja, the Lord had to kill his enemy Hiraṇyakaśipu, although Hiraṇyakaśipu attained salvation because of being killed by the Lord. Since the Lord is the witness of everyone's activities, He witnesses the actions of the enemies of His devotees, and He is inclined to punish them. In other cases, however, He simply witnesses what the living entities do and gives the results of one's sinful or pious actions.

TEXT 11

नादत्त आत्मा हि गुणं न दोषं न क्रियाफलम् ।
उदासीनवदासीनः परावरदृगीश्वरः ॥११॥

nādatta ātmā hi guṇaṁ
na doṣaṁ na kriyā-phalam
udāsīnavad āsīnaḥ
parāvara-dṛg īśvaraḥ

na—not; *ādatte*—accepts; *ātmā*—the Supreme Lord; *hi*—indeed; *guṇam*—happiness; *na*—not; *doṣam*—unhappiness; *na*—nor; *kriyā-phalam*—the result of any fruitive activity; *udāsīna-vat*—exactly like a neutral man; *āsīnaḥ*—sitting (in the core of the heart); *para-avara-dṛk*—seeing the cause and effect; *īśvaraḥ*—the Supreme Lord.

TRANSLATION

The Supreme Lord [ātmā], the creator of cause and effect, does not accept the happiness and distress that result from fruitive actions. He is completely independent of having to accept a material body, and because He has no material body, He is always neutral. The living entities, being part and parcel of the Lord, possess His qualities in a minute quantity. Therefore one should not be affected by lamentation.

PURPORT

The conditioned soul has friends and enemies. He is affected by the good qualities and the faults of his position. The Supreme Lord, however, is always transcendental. Because He is the *īśvara,* the supreme controller, He is not affected by duality. It may therefore be said that He sits in the core of everyone's heart as the neutral witness of the causes and effects of one's activities, good and bad. We should also understand that *udāsīna,* neutral, does not mean that He takes no action. Rather, it means that He is not personally affected. For example, a court judge is neutral when two opposing parties appear before him, but he still takes action as the case warrants. To become completely neutral, indifferent, to material activities, we should simply seek shelter at the lotus feet of the supreme neutral person.

Mahārāja Citraketu was advised that remaining neutral in such trying circumstances as the death of one's son is impossible. Nevertheless, since the Lord knows how to adjust everything, the best course is to depend upon Him and do one's duty in devotional service to the Lord. In all circumstances, one should be undisturbed by duality. As stated in *Bhagavad-gītā* (2.47):

karmaṇy evādhikāras te
mā phaleṣu kadācana
mā karma-phala-hetur bhūr
mā te saṅgo 'stv akarmaṇi

"You have a right to perform your prescribed duty, but you are not entitled to the fruits of action. Never consider yourself to be the cause of the results of your activities, and never be attached to not doing your duty." One should execute one's devotional duty, and for the results of one's actions one should depend upon the Supreme Personality of Godhead.

TEXT 12

श्रीबादरायणिरुवाच
इत्युदीर्य गतो जीवो ज्ञातयस्तस्य ते तदा ।
विस्मिता मुमुचुः शोकं छित्त्वात्मस्नेहशृङ्खलाम् ॥१२॥

śrī-bādarāyaṇir uvāca
ity udīrya gato jīvo
jñātayas tasya te tadā
vismitā mumucuḥ śokaṁ
chittvātma-sneha-śṛṅkhalām

śrī-bādarāyaṇiḥ uvāca—Śrī Śukadeva Gosvāmī said; *iti*—in this way; *udīrya*—speaking; *gataḥ*—went; *jīvaḥ*—the living entity (who had appeared as the son of Mahārāja Citraketu); *jñātayaḥ*—the relatives and family members; *tasya*—of him; *te*—they; *tadā*—at that time; *vismitāḥ*—being astonished; *mumucuḥ*—gave up; *śokam*—lamentation; *chittvā*—cutting off; *ātma-sneha*—of affection due to a relationship; *śṛṅkhalām*—the iron shackles.

TRANSLATION

Śrī Śukadeva Gosvāmī continued: When the conditioned soul [jīva] in the form of Mahārāja Citraketu's son had spoken in this way and then left, Citraketu and the other relatives of the dead son were all astonished. Thus they cut off the shackles of their affection, which was due to their relationship with him, and gave up their lamentation.

TEXT 13

निर्हृत्य ज्ञातयो ज्ञातेर्देहं कृत्वोचिताः क्रियाः ।
तत्यजुर्दुस्त्यजं स्नेहं शोकमोहभयार्तिदम् ॥१३॥

nirhṛtya jñātayo jñāter
dehaṁ kṛtvocitāḥ kriyāḥ
tatyajur dustyajaṁ snehaṁ
śoka-moha-bhayārtidam

nirhṛtya—removing; *jñātayaḥ*—King Citraketu and all the other relatives; *jñāteḥ*—of the son; *deham*—the body; *kṛtvā*—performing; *ucitāḥ*—suitable; *kriyāḥ*—activities; *tatyajuḥ*—gave up; *dustyajam*—very difficult to give up; *sneham*—affection; *śoka*—lamentation; *moha*—illusion; *bhaya*—fear; *arti*—and distress; *dam*—giving.

TRANSLATION

After the relatives had discharged their duties by performing the proper funeral ceremonies and burning the dead child's body, they gave up the affection that leads to illusion, lamentation, fear and pain. Such affection is undoubtedly difficult to give up, but they gave it up very easily.

TEXT 14

बालघ्न्यो व्रीडितास्तत्र बालहत्याहतप्रभाः ।
बालहत्याव्रतं चेरुर्ब्राह्मणैर्यन्निरूपितम् ।
यमुनायां महाराज स्मरन्त्यो द्विजभाषितम् ॥१४॥

bāla-ghnyo vrīḍitās tatra
bāla-hatyā-hata-prabhāḥ
bāla-hatyā-vrataṁ cerur
brāhmaṇair yan nirūpitam
yamunāyāṁ mahārāja
smarantyo dvija-bhāṣitam

bāla-ghnyaḥ—the killers of the child; *vrīḍitāḥ*—being very much ashamed; *tatra*—there; *bāla-hatyā*—because of killing the child; *hata*—having lost; *prabhāḥ*—all bodily luster; *bāla-hatyā-vratam*—the atonement for killing the child; *ceruḥ*—executed; *brāhmaṇaiḥ*—by the priests; *yat*—which; *nirūpitam*—described; *yamunāyām*—at the River Yamunā; *mahā-rāja*—O King Parīkṣit; *smarantyaḥ*—remembering; *dvija-bhāṣitam*—the statement given by the *brāhmaṇa.*

TRANSLATION

Queen Kṛtyadyuti's co-wives, who had poisoned the child, were very much ashamed, and they lost all their bodily luster. While lamenting, O King, they remembered the instructions of Aṅgirā and gave up their ambition to bear children. Following the directions of the brāhmaṇas, they went to the bank of the Yamunā, where they bathed and atoned for their sinful activities.

PURPORT

In this verse the word *bāla-hatyā-hata-prabhāḥ* is to be particularly noted. The practice of killing children has existed in human society for a long time—since time immemorial—but in the days of yore it was very rarely performed. At the present moment, however, in this age of Kali, abortion—killing of the child within the womb—has become very common, and sometimes a child is even killed after birth. If a woman performs such an abominable act, she gradually loses all her bodily luster (*bāla-hatyā-hata-prabhāḥ*). It is also to be noted that the ladies who had committed the sinful act of administering poison to the child were very much ashamed, and according to the directions of the *brāhmaṇas,* they had to undergo atonement for killing the child. Any woman who has ever performed such an infamously sinful act must atone for it, but no one now is doing that. Under the circumstances, the women responsible must suffer in this life and the next. Those who are sincere souls, after hearing this incident, should refrain from such child-killing and should atone for their sinful activities by taking to Kṛṣṇa consciousness very seriously. If one chants the Hare Kṛṣṇa *mahā-mantra* without offenses, all of one's sinful actions are surely atoned for immediately, but one should not commit such deeds again, for that is an offense.

TEXT 15

स इत्थं प्रतिबुद्धात्मा चित्रकेतुर्द्विजोक्तिभिः ।
गृहान्धकूपान्निष्क्रान्तः सरःपङ्कादिव द्विपः ॥१५॥

sa ittharh pratibuddhātmā
citraketur dvijoktibhiḥ
gṛhāndha-kūpān niṣkrāntaḥ
saraḥ-paṅkād iva dvipaḥ

saḥ—he; *ittham*—in this way; *pratibuddha-ātmā*—being fully aware of spiritual knowledge; *citraketuḥ*—King Citraketu; *dvija-uktibhiḥ*—by the instructions of the perfect *brāhmaṇas* (Aṅgirā and Nārada Muni); *gṛha-andha-kūpāt*—from the dark well of family life; *niṣkrāntaḥ*—came out; *saraḥ*—of a lake or reservoir of water; *paṅkāt*—from the mud; *iva*—like; *dvipaḥ*—an elephant.

TRANSLATION

Thus enlightened by the instructions of the brāhmaṇas Aṅgirā and Nārada, King Citraketu became fully aware of spiritual knowledge. As an elephant becomes free from a muddy reservoir of water, King Citraketu came out of the dark well of family life.

TEXT 16

कालिन्द्यां विधिवत् स्नात्वा कृतपुण्यजलक्रियः ।
मौनेन संयतप्राणो ब्रह्मपुत्राववन्दत ॥१६॥

kālindyāṁ vidhivat snātvā
kṛta-puṇya-jala-kriyaḥ
maunena saṁyata-prāṇo
brahma-putrāv avandata

kālindyām—in the River Yamunā; *vidhi-vat*—according to prescribed regulations; *snātvā*—bathing; *kṛta*—performing; *puṇya*—pious; *jala-kriyaḥ*—oblations by offering water; *maunena*—with gravity; *saṁyata-prāṇaḥ*—controlling the mind and senses; *brahma-putrau*—unto the two sons of Lord Brahmā (Aṅgirā and Nārada); *avandata*—offered his prayers and obeisances.

TRANSLATION

The King bathed in the water of the Yamunā, and according to prescribed duties, he offered oblations of water to the forefathers and demigods. Very gravely controlling his senses and mind, he then offered his respects and obeisances to the sons of Lord Brahmā [Aṅgirā and Nārada].

TEXT 17

अथ तस्मै प्रपन्नाय भक्ताय प्रयतात्मने ।
भगवान्नारदः प्रीतो विद्यामेतामुवाच ह ॥१७॥

atha tasmai prapannāya
bhaktāya prayatātmane

bhagavān nāradaḥ prīto
vidyām etām uvāca ha

atha—thereafter; *tasmai*—unto him; *prapannāya*—who was surrendered; *bhaktāya*—being a devotee; *prayata-ātmane*—who was self-controlled; *bhagavān*—the most powerful; *nāradaḥ*—Nārada; *prītaḥ*—being very pleased; *vidyām*—transcendental knowledge; *etām*—this; *uvāca*—spoke; *ha*—indeed.

TRANSLATION

Thereafter, being very much pleased with Citraketu, who was a self-controlled devotee and surrendered soul, Nārada, the most powerful sage, spoke to him the following transcendental instructions.

TEXTS 18–19

ॐ नमस्तुभ्यं भगवते वासुदेवाय धीमहि ।
प्रद्युम्नायानिरुद्धाय नमः सङ्कर्षणाय च ॥१८॥
नमो विज्ञानमात्राय परमानन्दमूर्तये ।
आत्मारामाय शान्ताय निवृत्तद्वैतदृष्टये ॥१९॥

oṁ namas tubhyaṁ bhagavate
vāsudevāya dhīmahi
pradyumnāyāniruddhāya
namaḥ saṅkarṣaṇāya ca

namo vijñāna-mātrāya
paramānanda-mūrtaye
ātmārāmāya śāntāya
nivṛtta-dvaita-dṛṣṭaye

oṁ—O my Lord; *namaḥ*—obeisances; *tubhyam*—unto You; *bhagavate*—the Supreme Personality of Godhead; *vāsudevāya*—Kṛṣṇa, the son of Vasudeva; *dhīmahi*—let me meditate upon; *pradyumnāya*—unto Pradyumna; *aniruddhāya*—unto Aniruddha; *namaḥ*—respectful obeisances; *saṅkarṣaṇāya*—unto Lord Saṅkarṣaṇa; *ca*—also; *namaḥ*—all obeisances; *vijñāna-mātrāya*—unto the form full of knowledge; *parama-ānanda-mūrtaye*—full of transcendental bliss; *ātma-ārāmāya*—unto the Lord, who is self-sufficient; *śāntāya*—and free from disturbances; *nivṛtta-dvaita-dṛṣṭaye*—whose vision turns away from duality, or who is one without a second.

TRANSLATION

[Nārada gave Citraketu the following mantra.] O Lord, O Supreme Personality of Godhead, who are addressed by the oṁkāra [praṇava], I offer my respectful obeisances unto You. O Lord Vāsudeva, I meditate upon You. O Lord Pradyumna, Lord Aniruddha and Lord Saṅkarṣaṇa, I offer You my respectful obeisances. O reservoir of spiritual potency, O supreme bliss, I offer my respectful obeisances unto You, who are self-sufficient and most peaceful. O ultimate truth, one without a second, You are realized as Brahman, Paramātmā and Bhagavān and are therefore the reservoir of all knowledge. I offer my respectful obeisances unto You.

PURPORT

In *Bhagavad-gītā* Kṛṣṇa says that He is *praṇavaḥ sarva-vedeṣu*, the syllable *oṁ* in the Vedic *mantras*. In transcendental knowledge, the Lord is addressed as *praṇava, oṁkāra*, which is a symbolic representation of the Lord in sound. *Oṁ namo bhagavate vāsudevāya*. Vāsudeva, who is an expansion of Nārāyaṇa, expands Himself as Pradyumna, Aniruddha and Saṅkarṣaṇa. From Saṅkarṣaṇa comes a second Nārāyaṇa expansion, and from this Nārāyaṇa come further expansions of Vāsudeva, Pradyumna, Saṅkarṣaṇa and Aniruddha. The Saṅkarṣaṇa in this group is the original cause of the three *puruṣas*, namely Kāraṇodakaśāyī Viṣṇu, Garbhodakaśāyī Viṣṇu and Kṣīrodakaśāyī Viṣṇu. Kṣīrodakaśāyī Viṣṇu is situated in every universe in a special planet called Śvetadvīpa. This is confirmed in the *Brahma-saṁhitā: aṇḍāntara-stha*. The word *aṇḍa* means this universe. Within this universe is a planet called Śvetadvīpa, where Kṣīrodakaśāyī Viṣṇu is situated. From Him come all the incarnations within this universe.

As confirmed in the *Brahma-saṁhitā*, all these forms of the Supreme Personality of Godhead are *advaita*, nondifferent, and they are also *acyuta*, infallible; they do not fall down like the conditioned souls. The ordinary living entity is prone to falling into the clutches of *māyā*, but the Supreme Lord in His different incarnations and forms is *acyuta*, infallible. Therefore His body is different from the material body possessed by the conditioned soul.

The word *mātrā* is explained in the Medinī dictionary as follows: *mātrā karṇa-vibhūṣāyāṁ vitte māne paricchade*. The word *mātrā*, in its different imports, is used to indicate the decoration of the ear, possession, respect, and the possession of a covering. As stated in *Bhagavad-gītā* (2.14):

mātrā-sparśās tu kaunteya
śītoṣṇa-sukha-duḥkha-dāḥ
āgamāpāyino 'nityās
tāṁs titikṣasva bhārata

"O son of Kuntī, the nonpermanent appearance of happiness and distress, and their disappearance in due course, are like the appearance and disappearance of winter and summer seasons. They arise from sense perception, O scion of Bharata, and one must learn to tolerate them without being disturbed." In the conditioned state of life, the body is used as our dress, and as one needs different dresses during the summer and winter, we conditioned souls are changing bodies according to our desires. However, because the body of the Supreme Lord is full of knowledge, it needs no covering. The idea that Kṛṣṇa's body is like ours—in other words, that His body and soul are different—is a misunderstanding. There are no such differences for Kṛṣṇa, because His body is full of knowledge. Here we receive material bodies because of a lack of knowledge, but because Kṛṣṇa, Vāsudeva, is full of knowledge, there is no difference between His body and His soul. Kṛṣṇa remembers what He said forty million years ago to the sun-god, but an ordinary being cannot remember what he said the day before yesterday. This is the difference between Kṛṣṇa's body and our body. Therefore the Lord is addressed as *vijñāna-mātrāya paramānanda-mūrtaye*.

Because the Lord's body is full of knowledge, He always enjoys transcendental bliss. Indeed, His very form is *paramānanda.* This is confirmed in the *Vedānta-sūtra: ānandamayo 'bhyāsāt.* By nature the Lord is *ānandamaya.* Whenever we see Kṛṣṇa, He is always full of *ānanda* in all circumstances. No one can make Him morose. *Ātmārāmāya:* He does not need to search for external enjoyment, because He is self-sufficient. *Śāntāya:* He has no anxiety. One who has to seek pleasure from other sources is always full of anxiety. *Karmīs, jñānīs* and *yogīs* are full of anxiety because they want something, but a devotee does not want anything; he is simply satisfied in the service of the Lord, who is fully blissful.

Nivṛtta-dvaita-dṛṣṭaye: in our conditioned life our bodies have different parts, but although Kṛṣṇa apparently has different bodily parts, no part of His body is different from any other part. Kṛṣṇa can see with His eyes, and Kṛṣṇa can see without His eyes. Therefore in the *Śvetāśvatara Upaniṣad* it is said, *paśyaty acakṣuḥ.* He can see with His hands and legs. He does not need a particular bodily part to perform a particular action. *Aṅgāni yasya sakalendriya-vṛttimanti:* He can do anything He desires with any part of His body, and therefore He is called almighty.

TEXT 20

आत्मानन्दानुभूत्यैव न्यस्तशक्त्यूर्मये नमः ।
हृषीकेशाय महते नमस्तेऽनन्तमूर्तये ॥२०॥

ātmānandānubhūtyaiva
nyasta-śakty-ūrmaye namaḥ
hṛṣīkeśāya mahate
namas te 'nanta-mūrtaye

ātma-ānanda—of Your personal bliss; *anubhūtyā*—by perception; *eva*—certainly; *nyasta*—given up; *śakti-ūrmaye*—the waves of material nature; *namaḥ*—respectful obeisances; *hṛṣīkeśāya*—unto the supreme controller of the senses; *mahate*—unto the Supreme; *namaḥ*—respectful obeisances; *te*—unto You; *ananta*—unlimited; *mūrtaye*—whose expansions.

TRANSLATION

Perceiving Your personal bliss, You are always transcendental to the waves of material nature. Therefore, my Lord, I offer my respectful obeisances unto You. You are the supreme controller of the senses, and Your expansions of form are unlimited. You are the greatest, and therefore I offer my respectful obeisances unto You.

PURPORT

This verse analytically differentiates the living entity from the Supreme Lord. The form of the Lord and the form of the conditioned soul are different because the Lord is always blissful whereas the conditioned soul is always under the threefold miseries of the material world. The Supreme Lord is *sac-cid-ānanda-vigraha.* He derives *ānanda,* bliss, from His own self. The Lord's body is transcendental, spiritual, but because the conditioned soul has a material body, he has many bodily and mental troubles. The conditioned soul is always perturbed by attachment and detachment, whereas the Supreme Lord is always free from such dualities. The Lord is the supreme master of all the senses, whereas the conditioned soul is controlled by the senses. The Lord is the greatest, whereas the living entity is the smallest. The living entity is conditioned by the waves of material nature, but the Supreme Lord is transcendental to all actions and reactions. The expansions of the Supreme Lord's body are innumerable (*advaitam acyutam anādim ananta-rūpam*), but the conditioned soul is limited to only one form. From history we learn that a conditioned soul, by mystic power, can sometimes expand into eight forms, but the Lord's bodily expansions are unlimited. This means that the bodies of the Supreme Personality of Godhead have no beginning and no end, unlike the bodies of the living entities.

TEXT 21

वचस्युपरतेऽप्राप्य य एको मनसा सह ।
अनामरूपश्चिन्मात्रः सोऽव्यान्नः सदसत्परः ॥२१॥

vacasy uparate 'prāpya
ya eko manasā saha

anāma-rūpaś cin-mātraḥ
so 'vyān naḥ sad-asat-paraḥ

vacasi—when the words; *uparate*—cease; *aprāpya*—not achieving the goal; *yaḥ*—He who; *ekaḥ*—one without a second; *manasā*—the mind; *saha*—with; *anāma*—with no material name; *rūpaḥ*—or material form; *cit-mātraḥ*—totally spiritual; *saḥ*—He; *avyāt*—may kindly protect; *naḥ*—us; *sat-asat-paraḥ*—who is the cause of all causes (the supreme cause).

TRANSLATION

The words and mind of the conditioned soul cannot approach the Supreme Personality of Godhead, for material names and forms are not applicable to the Lord, who is entirely spiritual, beyond the conception of gross and subtle forms. The impersonal Brahman is another of His forms. May He, by His pleasure, protect us.

PURPORT

The impersonal Brahman, which is the effulgence of the Lord, is described in this verse.

TEXT 22

यस्मिन्निदं यतश्चेदं तिष्ठत्यप्येति जायते ।
मृण्मयेष्विव मृज्जातिस्तस्मै ते ब्रह्मणे नमः ॥२२॥

yasminn idaṁ yataś cedaṁ
tiṣṭhaty apyeti jāyate
mṛṇmayeṣv iva mṛj-jātis
tasmai te brahmaṇe namaḥ

yasmin—in whom; *idam*—this (cosmic manifestation); *yataḥ*—from whom; *ca*—also; *idam*—this (cosmic manifestation); *tiṣṭhati*—stands; *apyeti*—dissolves; *jāyate*—is born; *mṛt-mayeṣu*—in things made of earth; *iva*—like; *mṛt-jātiḥ*—birth from earth; *tasmai*—unto Him; *te*—You; *brahmaṇe*—the supreme cause; *namaḥ*—respectful obeisances.

TRANSLATION

As pots made completely of earth are situated on earth after being created and are transformed into earth again when broken, this cosmic manifestation is caused by the Supreme Brahman, situated in the Supreme Brahman, and annihilated in the same Supreme Brahman. Therefore, since the Supreme Lord is the cause of Brahman, let us offer Him our respectful obeisances.

PURPORT

The Supreme Lord is the cause of the cosmic manifestation, He maintains it after creation, and after annihilation the Lord is the reservoir of everything.

TEXT 23

यन्न स्पृशन्ति न विदुर्मनोबुद्धीन्द्रियासवः ।
अन्तर्बहिश्च विततं व्योमवत्तन्नतोऽस्म्यहम् ॥२३॥

yan na spṛśanti na vidur
mano-buddhīndriyāsavaḥ
antar bahiś ca vitataṁ
vyomavat tan nato 'smy aham

yat—whom; *na*—not; *spṛśanti*—can touch; *na*—nor; *viduḥ*—can know; *manaḥ*—the mind; *buddhi*—the intelligence; *indriya*—the senses; *asavaḥ*—the life airs; *antaḥ*—within; *bahiḥ*—outside; *ca*—also; *vitatam*—expanded; *vyoma-vat*—like the sky; *tat*—unto Him; *nataḥ*—bowed; *asmi*—am; *aham*—I.

TRANSLATION

The Supreme Brahman emanates from the Supreme Personality of Godhead and expands like the sky. Although untouched by anything material, it exists within and without. Nonetheless, the mind, intelligence, senses and living force can neither touch Him nor know Him. I offer unto Him my respectful obeisances.

TEXT 24

देहेन्द्रियप्राणमनोधियोऽमी
यदंशविद्धाः प्रचरन्ति कर्मसु ।
नैवान्यदा लौहमिवाप्रतप्तं
स्थानेषु तद् द्रष्ट्रपदेशमेति ॥२४॥

dehendriya-prāṇa-mano-dhiyo 'mī
yad-aṁśa-viddhāḥ pracaranti karmasu
naivānyadā lauham ivāprataptaṁ
sthāneṣu tad draṣṭrapadeśam eti

deha—the body; *indriya*—senses; *prāṇa*—life airs; *manaḥ*—mind; *dhiyaḥ*—and intelligence; *amī*—all those; *yat-aṁśa-viddhāḥ*—being influenced by rays of Brahman, or the Supreme Lord; *pracaranti*—they move; *karmasu*—in various activities; *na*—not; *eva*—indeed; *anyadā*—at other times; *lauham*—iron; *iva*—like; *apratapṭam*—not heated (by fire); *sthāneṣu*—in those circumstances; *tat*—that; *draṣṭr-apadeśam*—the name of a subject matter; *eti*—achieves.

TRANSLATION

As iron has the power to burn when made red-hot in the association of fire, so the body, senses, living force, mind and intelligence, although merely lumps of matter, can function in their activities when infused with a particle of consciousness by the Supreme Personality of Godhead. As iron cannot burn unless heated by fire, the bodily senses cannot act unless favored by the Supreme Brahman.

PURPORT

Red-hot iron can burn, but it cannot burn the original fire. Therefore the consciousness of the small particle of Brahman is fully dependent on the power of the Supreme Brahman. In *Bhagavad-gītā* the Lord says, *mattaḥ smṛtir jñānam apohanaṁ ca:* "From Me the conditioned soul receives memory, knowledge and forgetfulness." The power for activities comes from the Supreme Lord, and when the Lord withdraws this power, the conditioned soul no longer has energy with which to act through his various senses. The body includes five knowledge-acquiring senses, five active senses and the mind, but actually these are merely lumps of matter. For example, the brain is nothing but matter, but when electrified by the energy of the Supreme Personality of Godhead, the brain can act, just as iron can burn when made red-hot by the influence of fire. The brain can act while we are awake or even while we are dreaming, but when we are fast asleep or unconscious the brain is inactive. Since the brain is a lump of matter, it does not have independent power with which to act. It can act only when favored by the influence of the Supreme Personality of Godhead, who is Brahman or Parabrahman. This is the way to understand how the Supreme Brahman, Kṛṣṇa, is present everywhere, just as the sunshine is present because of the sun-god in the sun globe. The Supreme Lord is called Hṛṣīkeśa; He is the only conductor of the senses. Unless empowered by His energy, our senses cannot act. In other words, He is the only seer, the only worker, the only listener, and the only active principle or supreme controller.

TEXT 25

ॐ नमो भगवते महापुरुषाय महानुभावाय महाविभूतिपतये सकल-
सात्वतपरिवृढनिकरकरकमलकुड्मलोपलालितचरणारविन्दयुगल परमपरमेष्ठि
न्नमस्ते ॥ २५ ॥

oṁ namo bhagavate mahā-puruṣāya mahānubhāvāya mahā-vibhūti-pataye sakala-sātvata-parivṛḍha-nikara-kara-kamala-kuḍmalopalālita-caraṇāravinda-yugala parama-parameṣṭhin namas te.

oṁ—O Supreme Personality of Godhead; *namaḥ*—respectful obeisances; *bhagavate*—unto You, the Lord, who are full in six opulences; *mahā-puruṣāya*—the supreme enjoyer; *mahā-anubhāvāya*—the most perfect realized soul, or the Supersoul; *mahā-vibhūti-pataye*—the master of all mystic power; *sakala-sātvata-parivṛḍha*—of all the best devotees; *nikara*—of the multitude; *kara-kamala*—of the lotus hands; *kuḍmala*—by the buds; *upalālita*—served; *caraṇa-aravinda-yugala*—

whose two lotus feet; *parama*—topmost; *parame-ṣṭhin*—who are situated in the spiritual planet; *namaḥ te*—respectful obeisances unto You.

TRANSLATION

O transcendental Lord, who are situated in the topmost planet of the spiritual world, Your two lotus feet are always massaged by a multitude of the best devotees with their lotus-bud hands. You are the Supreme Personality of Godhead, complete in six opulences. You are the supreme person mentioned in the Puruṣa-sūkta prayers. You are the most perfect, self-realized master of all mystic power. Let me offer my respectful obeisances unto You.

PURPORT

It is said that the Absolute Truth is one, but is manifested in different features as Brahman, Paramātmā and Bhagavān. The previous verses described the Brahman and Paramātmā features of the Absolute Truth. Now this prayer is offered in *bhakti-yoga* to the Absolute Supreme Person. The words used in this regard are *sakala-sātvata-parivṛḍha.* The word *sātvata* means "devotees," and *sakala* means "all together." The devotees, who also have lotus feet, serve the lotus feet of the Lord with their lotus hands. The devotees may sometimes not be competent to serve the lotus feet of the Lord, and therefore the Lord is addressed as *parama-parameṣṭhin.* He is the Supreme Person, yet He is very kind to the devotees. No one is competent to serve the Lord, but even if a devotee is not competent, the merciful Lord accepts the humble attempt of the devotee.

TEXT 26

श्रीशुक उवाच

भक्तायैतां प्रपन्नाय विद्यामादिश्य नारदः ।
ययावङ्गिरसा साकं धाम स्वायम्भुवं प्रभो ॥२६॥

śrī-śuka uvāca
bhaktāyaitāṁ prapannāya
vidyām ādiśya nāradaḥ

yayāv aṅgirasā sākaṁ
dhāma svāyambhuvaṁ prabho

śrī-śukaḥ uvāca—Śrī Śukadeva Gosvāmī said; *bhaktāya*—unto the devotee; *etām*—this; *prapannāya*—unto one who fully surrendered; *vidyām*—transcendental knowledge; *ādiśya*—instructing; *nāradaḥ*—the great sage Nārada; *yayau*—left; *aṅgirasā*—the great saint Aṅgirā; *sākam*—with; *dhāma*—for the topmost planet; *svāyambhuvam*—belonging to Lord Brahmā; *prabho*—O King.

TRANSLATION

Śrī Śukadeva Gosvāmī continued: Nārada, having become the spiritual master of Citraketu, instructed him fully in this prayer because Citraketu was fully surrendered. O King Parīkṣit, Nārada then left with the great sage Aṅgirā for the topmost planet, known as Brahmaloka.

PURPORT

When Aṅgirā had first come to visit King Citraketu, he did not bring Nārada with him. However, after the death of Citraketu's son, Aṅgirā brought Nārada to instruct King Citraketu about *bhakti-yoga*. The difference was that in the beginning Citraketu was not in a temperament of renunciation, but after the death of his son, when he was overwhelmed by his great plight, he was awakened to the platform of renunciation by instructions regarding the falsity of this material world and material possessions. It is only at this stage that *bhakti-yoga* can be instructed. As long as one is attached to material enjoyment, *bhakti-yoga* cannot be understood. This is confirmed in *Bhagavad-gītā* (2.44):

bhogaiśvarya-prasaktānāṁ
tayāpahṛta-cetasām
vyavasāyātmikā buddhiḥ
samādhau na vidhīyate

"In the minds of those who are too attached to sense enjoyment and material opulence, and who are bewildered by such things, the resolute determination of devotional service to the Supreme Lord does not take place." As long as one is very much attached to material enjoyment, one cannot concentrate his mind on the subject matter of devotional service.

The Kṛṣṇa consciousness movement is progressing successfully in the Western countries at the present moment because the youth in the West have reached the stage of *vairāgya,* or renunciation. They are practically disgusted with material pleasure from material sources, and this has resulted in a population of hippies throughout the Western countries. Now if these young people are instructed about *bhakti-yoga,* Kṛṣṇa consciousness, the instructions will certainly be effective.

As soon as Citraketu understood the philosophy of *vairāgya-vidyā,* the knowledge of renunciation, he could understand the process of *bhakti-yoga.* In this regard Śrīla Sārvabhauma Bhaṭṭācārya has said, *vairāgya-vidyā-nija-bhakti-yoga. Vairāgya-vidyā* and *bhakti-yoga* are parallel lines. One is essential for understanding the other. It is also said, *bhaktiḥ pareśānubhavo viraktir anyatra ca* (*Bhāg.* 11.2.42). Advancement in devotional service, or Kṛṣṇa consciousness, is characterized by increasing renunciation of material enjoyment. Nārada Muni is the father of devotional service, and therefore, just to bestow causeless mercy upon King Citraketu, Aṅgirā brought Nārada Muni to instruct the King. These instructions were extremely effective. Anyone who follows in the footsteps of Nārada Muni is certainly a pure devotee.

TEXT 27

चित्रकेतुस्तु तां विद्यां यथा नारदभाषिताम् ।
धारयामास सप्ताहमब्भक्षः सुसमाहितः ॥२७॥

citraketus tu tāṁ vidyāṁ
yathā nārada-bhāṣitām
dhārayām āsa saptāham
ab-bhakṣaḥ susamāhitaḥ

citraketuḥ—King Citraketu; *tu*—indeed; *tām*—that; *vidyām*—transcendental knowledge; *yathā*—just as; *nārada-bhāṣitām*—instructed by the great sage Nārada; *dhārayām āsa*—chanted; *sapta-aham*—continuously for one week; *ap-bhakṣaḥ*—only drinking water; *su-samāhitaḥ*—with great attention and care.

TRANSLATION

Fasting and drinking only water, Citraketu for one week continuously chanted with great care and attention the mantra given by Nārada Muni.

TEXT 28

ततः स सप्तरात्रान्ते विद्यया धार्यमाणया ।
विद्याधराधिपत्यं च लेभेऽप्रतिहतं नृप ॥२८॥

tataḥ sa sapta-rātrānte
vidyayā dhāryamāṇayā
vidyādharādhipatyaṁ ca
lebhe 'pratihataṁ nṛpa

tataḥ—from this; *saḥ*—he; *sapta-rātra-ante*—at the end of seven nights; *vidyayā*—by the prayers; *dhāryamāṇayā*—being carefully practiced; *vidyādhara-adhipatyam*—mastership of the Vidyādharas (as an intermediate result); *ca*—also; *lebhe*—achieved; *apratihatam*—undeviated from the instructions of the spiritual master; *nṛpa*—O King Parīkṣit.

TRANSLATION

O King Parīkṣit, after only one week of repeatedly practicing the mantra received from the spiritual master, Citraketu achieved the rule of the planet of the Vidyādharas as an intermediate product of his spiritual advancement in knowledge.

PURPORT

If a devotee, after being initiated, adheres rigidly to the instructions of the spiritual master, he is naturally endowed with the material opulences of *vidyādhara-adhipatyam* and similar posts as by-products. A devotee need not practice *yoga, karma* or *jñāna* to achieve a successful result. Devotional service alone is competent to award a devotee all material power. A pure devotee, however, is never attached to material power, although he gets it very easily without personal endeavor. Citraketu received this side benefit of his devotional service, which he rigidly performed in accordance with the instructions of Nārada.

TEXT 29

ततः कतिपयाहोभिर्विद्ययेद्धमनोगतिः ।
जगाम देवदेवस्य शेषस्य चरणान्तिकम् ॥२९॥

tataḥ katipayāhobhir
vidyayeddha-mano-gatiḥ
jagāma deva-devasya
śeṣasya caraṇāntikam

tataḥ—thereafter; *katipaya-ahobhiḥ*—within a few days; *vidyayā*—by the spiritual *mantra; iddha-manaḥ-gatiḥ*—the course of his mind being enlightened; *jagāma*—went; *deva-devasya*—of the master of all other lords or demigods; *śeṣasya*—Lord Śeṣa; *caraṇa-antikam*—to the shelter of the lotus feet.

TRANSLATION

Thereafter, within a very few days, by the influence of the mantra that Citraketu had practiced, his mind became increasingly enlightened in spiritual progress, and he attained shelter at the lotus feet of Anantadeva.

PURPORT

A devotee's ultimate achievement is to take shelter of the lotus feet of the Lord in any one of the planets in the spiritual sky. As a result of rigid execution of devotional service, a devotee receives all material opulences if these are required; otherwise, the devotee is not interested in material opulences, nor does the Supreme Lord award them. When a devotee is actually engaged in the devotional service of the Lord, his apparently material opulences are not material; they are all spiritual. For example, if a devotee spends money to construct a beautiful and costly temple, the construction is not material but spiritual (*nirbandhaḥ kṛṣṇa-sambandhe yuktaṁ vairāgyam ucyate*). A devotee's mind is never diverted to the material side of the temple. The bricks, stone and wood used in the construction of the temple are spiritual, just as the Deity, although made of stone, is not stone but the Supreme Personality of Godhead Himself. The more one advances in spiritual consciousness, the more he can understand the elements of devotional service. Nothing in devotional service is material; everything is spiritual. Consequently a devotee is awarded so-called material opulence for spiritual advancement. This opulence is an aid to help the devotee advance toward the spiritual kingdom. Thus Mahārāja Citraketu remained in material opulence as a *vidyādhara-pati,* master of the Vidyādharas, and by executing devotional service he became perfect within a very few days and returned home, back to Godhead, taking shelter of the lotus feet of Lord Śeṣa, Ananta.

A *karmī's* material opulence and a devotee's material opulence are not on the same level. Śrīla Madhvācārya comments in this way:

anyāntaryāmiṇaṁ viṣṇum
upāsyānya-samīpagaḥ
bhaved yogyatayā tasya
padaṁ vā prāpnuyān naraḥ

By worshiping Lord Viṣṇu one can get whatever he desires, but a pure devotee never asks Lord Viṣṇu for any material profit. Instead he serves Lord Viṣṇu without material desires and is therefore ultimately transferred to the spiritual kingdom. In this regard, Śrīla Vīrarāghava Ācārya comments, *yatheṣṭa-gatir ity arthaḥ:* by worshiping Viṣṇu, a devotee can get whatever he likes. Mahārāja Citraketu wanted only to return home, back to Godhead, and therefore he achieved success in that way.

TEXT 30

मृणालगौरं शितिवाससं स्फुरत्-
किरीटकेयूरकटित्रकङ्कणम् ।
प्रसन्नवक्त्रारुणलोचनं वृतं
ददर्श सिद्धेश्वरमण्डलैः प्रभुम् ॥३०॥

mṛṇāla-gauraṁ śiti-vāsasaṁ sphurat-
kirīṭa-keyūra-kaṭitra-kaṅkaṇam

prasanna-vaktrāruṇa-locanaṁ vṛtaṁ
dadarśa siddheśvara-maṇḍalaiḥ prabhum

mṛṇāla-gauram—white like the fibers of a lotus; *śiti-vāsasam*—wearing garments of blue silk; *sphurat*—glittering; *kirīṭa*—helmet; *keyūra*—armlets; *kaṭitra*—belt; *kaṅkaṇam*—whose bangles; *prasanna-vaktra*—smiling face; *aruṇa-locanam*—having reddish eyes; *vṛtam*—surrounded; *dadarśa*—he saw; *siddha-īśvara-maṇḍalaiḥ*—by the most perfect devotees; *prabhum*—the Supreme Personality of Godhead.

TRANSLATION

Upon reaching the shelter of Lord Śeṣa, the Supreme Personality of Godhead, Citraketu saw that He was as white as the white fibers of a lotus flower. He was dressed in bluish garments and adorned with a brilliantly glittering helmet, armlets, belt and bangles. His face was smiling, and His eyes were reddish. He was surrounded by such exalted liberated persons as Sanat-kumāra.

TEXT 31

तद्दर्शनध्वस्तसमस्तकिल्बिषः
स्वस्थामलान्तःकरणोऽभ्ययान्मुनिः ।
प्रवृद्धभक्त्या प्रणयाश्रुलोचनः
प्रहृष्टरोमानमदादिपुरुषम् ॥३१॥

tad-darśana-dhvasta-samasta-kilbiṣaḥ
svasthāmalāntaḥkaraṇo 'bhyayān muniḥ
pravṛddha-bhaktyā praṇayāśru-locanaḥ
prahṛṣṭa-romānamad ādi-puruṣam

tat-darśana—by the sight of the Supreme Personality of Godhead; *dhvasta*—destroyed; *samasta-kilbiṣaḥ*—having all sins; *svastha*—healthy; *amala*—and pure; *antaḥkaraṇaḥ*—the core of whose heart; *abhyayāt*—approached face to face; *muniḥ*—the King, who was silent due to full mental satisfaction; *pravṛddha-bhaktyā*—with an attitude of increased devotional service; *praṇaya-aśru-locanaḥ*—with tears in his eyes because of love; *prahṛṣṭa-roma*—his hairs standing on end due to jubilation; *anamat*—offered respectful obeisances; *ādi-puruṣam*—unto the expansion of the original personality.

TRANSLATION

As soon as Mahārāja Citraketu saw the Supreme Lord, he was cleansed of all material contamination and situated in his original Kṛṣṇa consciousness, being completely purified. He became silent and grave, and because of love for the Lord, tears fell from his eyes, and his hairs stood on end. With great devotion and love, he offered his respectful obeisances unto the original Personality of Godhead.

PURPORT

The word *tad-darśana-dhvasta-samasta-kilbiṣaḥ* is very important in this verse. If one regularly sees the Supreme Personality of Godhead in the temple, one will gradually be disinfected of all material desires simply by visiting the temple and seeing the Deity. When one is freed from all the results of sinful activities, one will be purified, and with a healthy mind, completely cleansed, he will increasingly make progress in Kṛṣṇa consciousness.

TEXT 32

स उत्तमश्लोकपदाब्जविष्टरं
प्रेमाश्रुलेशैरुपमेहयन्मुहुः ।
प्रेमोपरुद्धाखिलवर्णनिर्गमो
नैवाशकत्तं प्रसमीडितुं चिरम् ॥३२॥

sa uttamaśloka-padābja-viṣṭaraṁ
premāśru-leśair upamehayan muhuḥ
premoparuddhākhila-varṇa-nirgamo
naivāśakat taṁ prasamīḍituṁ ciram

saḥ—he; *uttamaśloka*— of the Supreme Personality of Godhead; *pada-abja*—of the lotus feet; *viṣṭaram*—the resting place; *prema-aśru*—of tears of pure love; *leśaiḥ*—by drops; *upamehayan*—moistening; *muhuḥ*—again and again; *prema-uparuddha*—choked with love; *akhila*—all; *varṇa*—of the letters; *nirgamaḥ*—the coming out; *na*—not; *eva*—indeed; *aśakat*—was able; *tam*—unto Him; *prasamīḍitum*—to offer prayers; *ciram*—for a long time.

TRANSLATION

With tears of love and affection, Citraketu repeatedly moistened the resting place of the Supreme Lord's lotus feet. Because his voice was choked in ecstasy, for a considerable time he was unable to utter any of the letters of the alphabet to offer the Lord suitable prayers.

PURPORT

All the letters of the alphabet and the words constructed by those letters are meant for offering prayers to the Supreme Personality of Godhead. Mahārāja Citraketu had the opportunity to offer prayers to the Lord by composing nice verses from the letters of the alphabet, but because of his ecstasy, for a considerable time he could not join those letters to offer prayers to the Lord. As stated in *Śrīmad-Bhāgavatam* (1.5.22):

idaṁ hi puṁsas tapasaḥ śrutasya vā
sviṣṭasya sūktasya ca buddhi-dattayoḥ
avicyuto 'rthaḥ kavibhir nirūpito
yad uttamaśloka-guṇānuvarṇanam

If one has scientific, philosophical, political, economic or any other abilities and wants perfection in his knowledge, he should offer prayers to the Supreme Personality of Godhead by composing first-class poetry or engaging his talents in the service of the Lord. Citraketu wanted to do this, but he was unable because of loving ecstasy. Therefore he had to wait for a considerable time before he could offer prayers.

TEXT 33

ततः समाधाय मनो मनीषया
बभाष एतत्प्रतिलब्धवागसौ ।

नियम्य सर्वेन्द्रियबाह्यवर्तनं
जगद्गुरुं सात्वतशास्त्रविग्रहम् ॥३३॥

tataḥ samādhāya mano manīṣayā
babhāṣa etat pratilabdha-vāg asau
niyamya sarvendriya-bāhya-vartanaṁ
jagad-guruṁ sātvata-śāstra-vigraham

tataḥ—thereafter; *samādhāya*—controlling; *manaḥ*—the mind; *manīṣayā*—by his intelligence; *babhāṣa*—spoke; *etat*—this; *pratilabdha*—recovering; *vāk*—speech; *asau*—that one (King Citraketu); *niyamya*—controlling; *sarva-indriya*—of all the senses; *bāhya*—external; *vartanam*—the wandering; *jagat-gurum*—who is the spiritual master of everyone; *sātvata*—of devotional service; *śāstra*—of the holy scriptures; *vigraham*—the personified form.

TRANSLATION

Thereafter, by controlling his mind with his intelligence and thus restricting his senses from external engagements, he recovered suitable words with which to express his feelings. Thus he began offering prayers to the Lord, who is the personification of the holy scriptures [the sātvata-saṁhitās like the Brahma-saṁhitā and the Nārada-pañcarātra] and who is the spiritual master of all. He offered his prayers as follows.

PURPORT

One cannot offer prayers to the Lord with mundane words. One must become spiritually advanced by controlling the mind and senses. Then he can find suitable words to offer in prayers to the Lord. Quoting the following verse from the *Padma Purāṇa,* Śrīla Sanātana Gosvāmī forbids us to sing any song not sung by authorized devotees.

avaiṣṇava-mukhodgīrṇaṁ
pūtaṁ hari-kathāmṛtam
śravaṇaṁ naiva kartavyaṁ
sarpocchiṣṭaṁ yathā payaḥ

The words or songs of a person not fixed in Vaiṣṇava behavior, not strictly following the rules and regulations and chanting the Hare Kṛṣṇa *mantra* should not be accepted by pure devotees. The words *sātvata-śāstra-vigraham* indicate that the *sac-cid-ānanda* body of the Lord can never be accepted to be made of *māyā*. Devotees do not offer prayers to the Lord in an imaginary form. The existence of the Lord's form is supported by all Vedic literature.

TEXT 34

चित्रकेतुरुवाच
अजित जितः सममतिभिः
साधुभिर्भवान् जितात्मभिर्भवता ।
विजितास्तेऽपि च भजता-
मकामात्मनां य आत्मदोऽतिकरुणः ॥३४॥

citraketur uvāca
ajita jitaḥ sama-matibhiḥ
sādhubhir bhavān jitātmabhir bhavatā
vijitās te 'pi ca bhajatām
akāmātmanāṁ ya ātmado 'ti-karuṇaḥ

citraketuḥ uvāca—King Citraketu said; *ajita*—O my unconquerable Lord; *jitaḥ*—conquered; *sama-matibhiḥ*—by persons who have conquered the mind; *sādhubhiḥ*—the devotees; *bhavān*—Your Lordship; *jita-ātmabhiḥ*—who have completely controlled the senses; *bhavatā*—by You; *vijitāḥ*—conquered; *te*—they; *api*—also; *ca*—and; *bhajatām*—to those who always engage in Your service; *akāma-ātmanām*—with no motives for material profit; *yaḥ*—who; *ātma-daḥ*—giving Yourself; *ati-karuṇaḥ*—extremely merciful.

TRANSLATION

Citraketu said: O unconquerable Lord, although You cannot be conquered by anyone, You are certainly conquered by devotees who have control of the mind and senses. They can keep You

under their control because You are causelessly merciful to devotees who desire no material profit from You. Indeed, You give Yourself to them, and because of this You also have full control over Your devotees.

PURPORT

The Lord and the devotees both conquer. The Lord is conquered by the devotees, and the devotees are conquered by the Lord. Because of being conquered by one another, they both derive transcendental bliss from their relationship. The highest perfection of this mutual conquering is exhibited by Kṛṣṇa and the *gopīs.* The *gopīs* conquered Kṛṣṇa, and Kṛṣṇa conquered the *gopīs.* Thus whenever Kṛṣṇa played His flute, He conquered the minds of the *gopīs,* and without seeing the *gopīs* Kṛṣṇa could not be happy. Other transcendentalists, such as *jñānīs* and *yogīs,* cannot conquer the Supreme Personality of Godhead; only pure devotees can conquer Him.

Pure devotees are described as *sama-mati,* which means that they never deviate from devotional service under any circumstances. It is not that devotees worship the Supreme Lord only when happy; they worship Him even when in distress. Happiness and distress do not hamper the process of devotional service. Therefore *Śrīmad-Bhāgavatam* says that devotional service is *ahaituky apratihatā,* unmotivated and uninterrupted. When a devotee offers devotional service to the Lord without any motive (*anyābhilāṣitā-śūnyam*), his service cannot be hampered by any material condition (*apratihatā*). Thus a devotee who offers service in all conditions of life can conquer the Supreme Personality of Godhead.

A special distinction between devotees and the other transcendentalists, namely the *jñānīs* and *yogīs,* is that *jñānīs* and *yogīs* artificially try to become one with the Supreme, whereas devotees never aspire for such an impossible accomplishment. Devotees know that their position is to be eternally servants of the Supreme Lord and never to be one with Him. Therefore they are called *sama-mati* or *jitātmā.* They detest oneness with the Supreme. They have no lusty desires for oneness; instead, their desire is to be freed from all material hankering. Therefore they are called *niṣkāma,* desireless. A living entity cannot exist without desires, but desires that can never be fulfilled are called *kāma,* lusty desires.

Kāmais tais tair hṛta-jñānāḥ: because of lusty desires, nondevotees are deprived of their intelligence. Thus they are unable to conquer the Supreme Lord, whereas devotees, being freed from such unreasonable desires, can conquer the Lord. Such devotees are also conquered by the Supreme Personality of Godhead. Because they are pure, being free from all material desires, they fully surrender to the Supreme Lord, and therefore the Lord conquers them. Such devotees never aspire for liberation. They simply desire to serve the lotus feet of the Lord. Because they serve the Lord without desires for remuneration, they can conquer the mercy of the Lord. The Lord is by nature very merciful, and when He sees that His servant is working without desires for material profit, naturally He is conquered.

Devotees are always engaged in service.

sa vai manaḥ kṛṣṇa-padāravindayor
vacāṁsi vaikuṇṭha-guṇānuvarṇane

All the activities of their senses are engaged in the service of the Lord. Because of such devotion, the Lord gives Himself to His devotees as if they could use Him for any purpose they might desire. Of course, devotees have no purpose other than to serve. When a devotee fully surrenders and has no aspiration for material profit, the Lord certainly gives him all opportunities for service. This is the position of the Lord when conquered by His devotees.

TEXT 35

तव विभवः खलु भगवन्
जगदुदयस्थितिलयादीनि ।
विश्वसृजस्तेंऽशांशा-
स्तत्र मृषा स्पर्धन्ति पृथगभिमत्या ॥३५॥

tava vibhavaḥ khalu bhagavan
jagad-udaya-sthiti-layādīni
viśva-sṛjas te 'ṁśāṁśās
tatra mṛṣā spardhanti pṛthag abhimatyā

tava—Your; *vibhavaḥ*—opulences; *khalu*—indeed; *bhagavan*—O Supreme Personality of Godhead; *jagat*—of the cosmic manifestation; *udaya*—the creation; *sthiti*—maintenance; *laya-ādīni*—dissolution and so on; *viśva-sṛjaḥ*—the creators of the manifested world; *te*—they; *aṁśa-aṁśāḥ*—parts of Your plenary portion; *tatra*—in that; *mṛṣā*—in vain; *spardhanti*—rival one another; *pṛthak*—of separateness; *abhimatyā*—by a false conception.

TRANSLATION

My dear Lord, this cosmic manifestation and its creation, maintenance and annihilation are all but Your opulences. Since Lord Brahmā and the other creators are nothing but small portions of a portion of You, their partial power to create does not make them God [īśvara]. Their consciousness of themselves as separate Lords is therefore merely false prestige. It is not valid.

PURPORT

A devotee who has fully surrendered to the lotus feet of the Lord knows very well that the creative energy of the living entities, from Lord Brahmā down to the small ant, exists because the living entities are part and parcel of the Lord. In *Bhagavad-gītā* (15.7) the Lord says, *mamaivāṁśo jīva-loke jīva-bhūtaḥ sanātanaḥ:* "The living entities in this conditioned world are My eternal, fragmental parts." The living entities are nothing but very small portions of the supreme spirit, like sparks of a fire. Because they are part of the Supreme, they have a creative quality in a very minute quantity.

The so-called scientists of the modern materialistic world are proud because they have created modern facilities like great airplanes, but the credit for creating the airplanes should go to the Supreme Personality of Godhead, not to the scientists who have invented or created the so-called wonderful products. The first consideration is the intelligence of the scientist; one must be elevated by the dictation of the Supreme Lord, who says in *Bhagavad-gītā* (15.15), *mattaḥ smṛtir jñānam apohanaṁ ca:* "From Me come remembrance, knowledge and forgetfulness." Because the Supreme Lord, as Supersoul, sits within the core of every living entity's heart, the dictation by which one advances in scientific knowledge or creative faculties comes from Him. Furthermore, the ingredients to manufacture wonderful machines like airplanes are also supplied by the Lord, not by the scientists. Before the airplane was created, its ingredients already existed, having been caused by the Supreme Personality of Godhead, but when the manifested creation of the airplane is ruined, the remaining debris is a problem for the so-called creators. Another example is that the West is creating many automobiles. The ingredients for these cars are supplied, of course, by the Supreme Lord, and the intelligence for the so-called creation is also supplied by the Lord. Ultimately, when the cars are demolished, the so-called creators are faced with the problem of what to do with their ingredients. The actual creator, the original creator, is the Personality of Godhead. Only in the interim does someone create something with intelligence supplied by the Lord, and later the creation again becomes a problem. Therefore the so-called creator is not to be credited with the act of creation; the only credit goes to the Supreme Personality of Godhead. It is rightly stated herein that the credit for all the opulences of creation, maintenance and annihilation belongs to the Supreme Lord, not to the living entities.

TEXT 36

परमाणुपरममहतो-
स्त्वमाद्यन्तान्तरवर्ती त्रयविधुरः ।
आदावन्तेऽपि च सत्त्वानां
यद् ध्रुवं तदेवान्तरालेऽपि ॥३६॥

paramāṇu-parama-mahatos
tvam ādy-antāntara-vartī traya-vidhuraḥ
ādāv ante 'pi ca sattvānāṁ
yad dhruvaṁ tad evāntarāle 'pi

parama-aṇu—of the atomic particle; *parama-mahatoḥ*—and of the biggest (the result of the combination of atoms); *tvam*—You; *ādi-anta*—in both the beginning and the end; *antara*—and in the middle; *vartī*—existing; *traya-vidhuraḥ*—although without beginning, end or middle; *ādau*—in the beginning; *ante*—at the end; *api*—also; *ca*—and; *sat-*

tvānām—of all existences; *yat*—which; *dhruvam*—permanent; *tat*—that; *eva*—certainly; *antarāle*—in the middle; *api*—also.

TRANSLATION

You exist in the beginning, middle and end of everything, from the most minute particle of the cosmic manifestation—the atom—to the gigantic universes and total material energy. Nonetheless, You are eternal, having no beginning, end or middle. You are perceived to exist in these three phases, and thus You are permanent. When the cosmic manifestation does not exist, You exist as the original potency.

PURPORT

The *Brahma-saṁhitā* (5.33) says:

advaitam acyutam anādim ananta-rūpam
ādyaṁ purāṇa-puruṣaṁ nava-yauvanaṁ ca
vedeṣu durlabham adurlabham ātma-bhaktau
govindam ādi-puruṣaṁ tam ahaṁ bhajāmi

"I worship the Supreme Personality of Godhead, Govinda [Kṛṣṇa], who is the original person—absolute, infallible, without beginning, although expanded into unlimited forms, still the same original, the oldest, and the person always appearing as a fresh youth. Such eternal, blissful, all-knowing forms of the Lord cannot be understood even by the best Vedic scholars, but they are always manifest to pure, unalloyed devotees." The Supreme Personality of Godhead has no cause, for He is the cause of everything. The Lord is beyond the workings of cause and effect. He is eternally existing. In another verse the *Brahma-saṁhitā* says, *aṇḍāntara-stha-paramāṇu-cayāntara-stham:* the Lord exists within the gigantic universe and within the atom. The descent of the Lord into the atom and the universe indicates that without His presence, nothing could factually exist. Scientists say that water is a combination of hydrogen and oxygen, but when they see a vast ocean they are puzzled about where such a quantity of hydrogen and oxygen could have come from. They think that everything evolved from chemicals, but where did the chemicals come from? That they do not know. Since the Supreme Personality of Godhead is the cause of all causes, He can produce immense quantities of chemicals to create a situation for chemical evolution. We actually see that chemicals are produced from living entities. For example, a lemon tree produces many tons of citric acid. The citric acid is not the cause of the tree; rather, the tree is the cause of the acid. Similarly, the Supreme Personality of Godhead is the cause of everything. He is the cause of the tree that produces the citric acid (*bījaṁ māṁ sarva-bhūtānām*). Devotees can see that the original potencies causing the cosmic manifestation are not in chemicals but in the Supreme Personality of Godhead, for He is the cause of the chemicals.

Everything is caused or manifested by the energy of the Supreme Lord, and when everything is annihilated or dissolved, the original potency enters the body of the Supreme Lord. Therefore this verse says, *ādāv ante 'pi ca sattvānāṁ yad dhruvaṁ tad evāntarāle 'pi.* The word *dhruvam* means "permanent." The permanent reality is Kṛṣṇa, not this cosmic manifestation. As stated in *Bhagavad-gītā, aham ādir hi devānām* and *mattaḥ sarvaṁ pravartate:* Kṛṣṇa is the original cause of everything. Arjuna recognized Lord Śrī Kṛṣṇa as the original person (*puruṣaṁ śāśvataṁ divyam ādi-devam ajaṁ vibhum*), and the *Brahma-saṁhitā* describes Him as the original person (*govindam ādi-puruṣam*). He is the cause of all causes, whether at the beginning, at the end or in the middle.

TEXT 37

क्षित्यादिभिरेष किलावृतः
सप्तभिर्दशगुणोत्तरैरण्डकोशः ।
यत्र पतत्यणुकल्पः
सहाण्डकोटिकोटिभिस्तदनन्तः ॥३७॥

kṣity-ādibhir eṣa kilāvṛtaḥ
saptabhir daśa-guṇottarair aṇḍa-kośaḥ
yatra pataty aṇu-kalpaḥ
sahāṇḍa-koṭi-koṭibhis tad anantaḥ

kṣiti-ādibhiḥ—by the ingredients of the material world, headed by earth; *eṣaḥ*—this; *kila*—indeed; *āvṛtaḥ*—covered; *saptabhiḥ*—seven;

daśa-guṇa-uttaraiḥ—each ten times more than the previous one; *aṇḍa-kośaḥ*—egg-shaped universe; *yatra*—in whom; *patati*—falls; *aṇu-kalpaḥ*—like a minute atom; *saha*—with; *aṇḍa-koṭi-koṭibhiḥ*—millions of such universes; *tat*—therefore; *anantaḥ*—(You are called) unlimited.

TRANSLATION

Every universe is covered by seven layers—earth, water, fire, air, sky, the total energy and false ego—each ten times greater than the previous one. There are innumerable universes besides this one, and although they are unlimitedly large, they move about like atoms in You. Therefore You are called unlimited [ananta].

PURPORT

The *Brahma-saṁhitā* (5.48) says:

yasyaika-niśvasita-kālam athāvalambya
jīvanti loma-vilajā jagad-aṇḍa-nāthāḥ
viṣṇur mahān sa iha yasya kalā-viśeṣo
govindam ādi-puruṣaṁ tam ahaṁ bhajāmi

The origin of the material creation is Mahā-Viṣṇu, who lies in the Causal Ocean. While He sleeps in that ocean, millions of universes are generated as He exhales, and they are all annihilated when He inhales. This Mahā-Viṣṇu is a plenary portion of a portion of Viṣṇu, Govinda (*yasya kalā-viśeṣaḥ*). The word *kalā* refers to a plenary portion of a plenary portion. From Kṛṣṇa, or Govinda, comes Balarāma; from Balarāma comes Saṅkarṣaṇa; from Saṅkarṣaṇa, Nārāyaṇa; from Nārāyaṇa, the second Saṅkarṣaṇa; from the second Saṅkarṣaṇa, Mahā-Viṣṇu; from Mahā-Viṣṇu, Garbhodakaśāyī Viṣṇu; and from Garbhodakaśāyī Viṣṇu, Kṣīrodakaśāyī Viṣṇu. Kṣīrodakaśāyī Viṣṇu controls every universe. This gives an idea of the meaning of *ananta*, unlimited. What is to be said of the unlimited potency and existence of the Lord? This verse describes the coverings of the universe (*saptabhir daśa-guṇottarair aṇḍa-kośaḥ*). The first covering is earth, the second is water, the third is fire, the fourth is air, the fifth is sky, the sixth is the total material energy, and the seventh is the false ego. Beginning with the covering of earth, each covering is ten times greater than the previous one. Thus we can only imagine how great each universe is, and there are many millions of universes. As confirmed by the Lord Himself in *Bhagavad-gītā* (10.42):

athavā bahunaitena
kiṁ jñātena tavārjuna
viṣṭabhyāham idaṁ kṛtsnam
ekāṁśena sthito jagat

"But what need is there, Arjuna, for all this detailed knowledge? With a single fragment of Myself I pervade and support this entire universe." The entire material world manifests only one fourth of the Supreme Lord's energy. Therefore He is called *ananta.*

TEXT 38

विषयतृषो नरपशवो
य उपासते विभूतीर्न परं त्वाम् ।
तेषामाशिष ईश
तदनु विनश्यन्ति यथा राजकुलम् ॥३८॥

viṣaya-tṛṣo nara-paśavo
ya upāsate vibhūtīr na paraṁ tvām
teṣām āśiṣa īśa
tad anu vinaśyanti yathā rāja-kulam

viṣaya-tṛṣaḥ—eager to enjoy sense gratification; *nara-paśavaḥ*—manlike animals; *ye*—who; *upāsate*—worship very gorgeously; *vibhūtīḥ*—small particles of the Supreme Lord (the demigods); *na*—not; *param*—the Supreme; *tvām*—You; *teṣām*—of them; *āśiṣaḥ*—the benedictions; *īśa*—O supreme controller; *tat*—them (the demigods); *anu*—after; *vinaśyanti*—will be vanquished; *yathā*—just as; *rāja-kulam*—those who are supported by the government (when the government is finished).

TRANSLATION

O Lord, O Supreme, unintelligent persons who thirst for sense enjoyment and who worship various demigods are no better than

animals in the human form of life. Because of their animalistic propensities, they fail to worship Your Lordship, and instead they worship the insignificant demigods, who are but small sparks of Your glory. With the destruction of the entire universe, including the demigods, the benedictions received from the demigods also vanish, just like the nobility when a king is no longer in power.

PURPORT

Bhagavad-gītā (7.20) says, *kāmais tais tair hṛta-jñānāḥ prapadyante 'nya-devatāḥ:* "Those whose minds are distorted by material desires surrender unto the demigods." Similarly, this verse condemns worship of the demigods. We may show our respect to the demigods, but the demigods are not worshipable. The intelligence of those who worship the demigods is lost (*hṛta-jñānāḥ*) because these worshipers do not know that when the entire material cosmic manifestation is annihilated, the demigods, who are the departmental heads of that manifestation, will be vanquished. When the demigods are vanquished, the benedictions given by the demigods to unintelligent men will also be vanquished. Therefore a devotee should not hanker to obtain material opulence by worshiping the demigods, but should engage in the service of the Lord, who will satisfy all his desires.

akāmaḥ sarva-kāmo vā
mokṣa-kāma udāra-dhīḥ
tīvreṇa bhakti-yogena
yajeta puruṣaṁ param

"Whether full of all material desires, free from material desires or desiring liberation, a person who has broader intelligence must by all means worship the supreme whole, the Personality of Godhead." (*Bhāg.* 2.3.10) This is the duty of a perfect human being. One who has the shape of a human being but whose actions are nothing but those of an animal is called *nara-paśu* or *dvipada-paśu*, a two-legged animal. A human being who is not interested in Kṛṣṇa consciousness is condemned herewith as a *nara-paśu.*

TEXT 39

कामधियस्त्वयि रचिता
न परम रोहन्ति यथा करम्भबीजानि ।
ज्ञानात्मन्यगुणमये
गुणगणतोऽस्य द्वन्द्वजालानि ॥३९॥

kāma-dhiyas tvayi racitā
na parama rohanti yathā karambha-bījāni
jñānātmany aguṇamaye
guṇa-gaṇato 'sya dvandva-jālāni

kāma-dhiyaḥ—desires for sense gratification; *tvayi*—in You; *racitāḥ*—performed; *na*—not; *parama*—O Supreme Personality of Godhead; *rohanti*—do grow (produce other bodies); *yathā*—just as; *karambha-bījāni*—sterilized or fried seeds; *jñāna-ātmani*—in You, whose existence is in full knowledge; *aguṇa-maye*—who is not affected by the material qualities; *guṇa-gaṇataḥ*—from the material qualities; *asya*—of a person; *dvandva-jālāni*—the networks of duality.

TRANSLATION

O Supreme Lord, if persons obsessed with material desires for sense gratification through material opulence worship You, who are the source of all knowledge and are transcendental to material qualities, they are not subject to material rebirth, just as sterilized or fried seeds do not produce plants. Living entities are subjected to the repetition of birth and death because they are conditioned by material nature, but since You are transcendental, one who is inclined to associate with You in transcendence escapes the conditions of material nature.

PURPORT

This is confirmed in *Bhagavad-gītā* (4.9), wherein the Lord says:

janma karma ca me divyam
evaṁ yo vetti tattvataḥ

tyaktvā dehaṁ punar janma
naiti mām eti so 'rjuna

"One who knows the transcendental nature of My appearance and activities does not, upon leaving the body, take his birth again in this material world, but attains My eternal abode, O Arjuna." If one simply engages in Kṛṣṇa consciousness to understand Kṛṣṇa, he surely becomes immune to the process of repeated birth and death. As clearly stated in *Bhagavad-gītā, tyaktvā dehaṁ punar janma naiti:* such a person, simply by engaging in Kṛṣṇa consciousness or understanding the Supreme Personality of Godhead, Kṛṣṇa, becomes quite fit to return home, back to Godhead. Even those who are obsessed with material desires may also come to worship the Supreme Personality of Godhead so steadily that they go back to Godhead. The fact is that if one comes to Kṛṣṇa consciousness, although he may have many material desires, he becomes increasingly attracted to the lotus feet of Kṛṣṇa through associating with the Supreme Lord by chanting His holy name. The Supreme Lord and His holy name are identical. Thus he becomes uninterested in attachment to material enjoyment. The perfection of life is to be uninterested in material enjoyment and interested in Kṛṣṇa. If one comes to Kṛṣṇa consciousness somehow or other, even for material gain, the result is that he will be liberated. *Kāmād dveṣād bhayāt snehāt.* Whether for the satisfaction of material desires, because of the influence of envy, because of fear, because of affection or because of any other reason, if one comes to Kṛṣṇa, his life is successful.

TEXT 40

जितमजित तदा भवता
यदाह भागवतं धर्ममनवद्यम् ।
निष्किञ्चना ये मुनय
आत्मारामा यमुपासतेऽपवर्गाय ॥४०॥

jitam ajita tadā bhavatā
yadāha bhāgavataṁ dharmam anavadyam
niṣkiñcanā ye munaya
ātmārāmā yam upāsate 'pavargāya

jitam—conquered; *ajita*—O unconquerable one; *tadā*—then; *bhavatā*—by Your Lordship; *yadā*—when; *āha*—spoke; *bhāgavatam*—which helps the devotee approach the Supreme Personality of Godhead; *dharmam*—the religious process; *anavadyam*—faultless (free from contamination); *niṣkiñcanāḥ*—who have no desire to be happy with material opulences; *ye*—those who; *munayaḥ*—great philosophers and exalted sages; *ātma-ārāmāḥ*—who are self-satisfied (being completely aware of their constitutional position as eternal servants of the Lord); *yam*—whom; *upāsate*—worship; *apavargāya*—for achieving liberation from material bondage.

TRANSLATION

O unconquerable one, when You spoke about bhāgavata-dharma, which is the uncontaminated religious system for achieving the shelter of Your lotus feet, that was Your victory. Persons who have no material desires, like the Kumāras, who are self-satisfied sages, worship You to be liberated from material contamination. In other words, they accept the process of bhāgavata-dharma to achieve shelter at Your lotus feet.

PURPORT

As stated by Śrīla Rūpa Gosvāmī in *Bhakti-rasāmṛta-sindhu:*

anyābhilāṣitā-śūnyaṁ
jñāna-karmādy-anāvṛtam
ānukūlyena kṛṣṇānu-
śīlanaṁ bhaktir uttamā

"One should render transcendental loving service to the Supreme Lord Kṛṣṇa favorably and without desires for material profit or gain through fruitive activities or philosophical speculation. That is called pure devotional service."

The *Nārada-pañcarātra* also says:

sarvopādhi-vinirmuktaṁ
tat-paratvena nirmalam

hṛṣīkeṇa hṛṣīkeśa-
sevanaṁ bhaktir ucyate

"One should be free from all material designations and cleansed of all material contamination. He should be restored to his pure identity, in which he engages his senses in the service of the proprietor of the senses. That is called devotional service." This is also called *bhāgavata-dharma.* Without material aspirations, one should simply serve Kṛṣṇa, as advised in *Bhagavad-gītā, Nārada-pañcarātra* and *Śrīmad-Bhāgavatam. Bhāgavata-dharma* is the process of religion enunciated by pure devotees, direct representatives of the Supreme Personality of Godhead like Nārada, Śukadeva Gosvāmī and their humble servants in the disciplic succession. By understanding *bhāgavata-dharma,* one immediately becomes free from material contamination. Living entities, who are part and parcel of the Supreme Personality of Godhead, are loitering in this material world suffering. When they are instructed by the Lord Himself about *bhāgavata-dharma* and they adopt it, that is victory for the Lord, for He then reclaims these fallen souls. A devotee following the principles of *bhāgavata-dharma* feels very much obligated to the Supreme Personality of Godhead. He can understand the difference between life without *bhāgavata-dharma* and life with *bhāgavata-dharma* and thus he ever remains obliged to the Lord. Taking to Kṛṣṇa consciousness and bringing fallen souls to Kṛṣṇa consciousness is victory for Lord Kṛṣṇa.

sa vai puṁsāṁ paro dharmo
yato bhaktir adhokṣaje
ahaituky apratihatā
yayātmā suprasīdati

"The supreme occupation [*dharma*] for all humanity is that by which men can attain to loving devotional service unto the transcendent Lord. Such devotional service must be unmotivated and uninterrupted in order to completely satisfy the self." (*Bhāg.* 1.2.6) Therefore *Śrīmad-Bhāgavatam* is the pure transcendental process of religion.

TEXT 41

विषममतिर्न यत्र नृणां
त्वमहमिति मम तवेति च यदन्यत्र ।
विषमधिया रचितो यः
स ह्यविशुद्धः क्षयिष्णुरधर्मबहुलः ॥४१॥

viṣama-matir na yatra nṛṇāṁ
tvam aham iti mama taveti ca yad anyatra
viṣama-dhiyā racito yaḥ
sa hy aviśuddhaḥ kṣayiṣṇur adharma-bahulaḥ

viṣama—unequal (your religion, my religion; your belief, my belief); *matiḥ*—consciousness; *na*—not; *yatra*—in which; *nṛṇām*—of human society; *tvam*—you; *aham*—I; *iti*—thus; *mama*—my; *tava*—your; *iti*—thus; *ca*—also; *yat*—which; *anyatra*—elsewhere (in religious systems other than *bhāgavata-dharma*); *viṣama-dhiyā*—by this unequal intelligence; *racitaḥ*—made; *yaḥ*—that which; *saḥ*—that system of religion; *hi*—indeed; *aviśuddhaḥ*—not pure; *kṣayiṣṇuḥ*—temporary; *adharma-bahulaḥ*—full of irreligion.

TRANSLATION

Being full of contradictions, all forms of religion but bhāgavata-dharma work under conceptions of fruitive results and distinctions of "you and I" and "yours and mine." The followers of Śrīmad-Bhāgavatam have no such consciousness. They are all Kṛṣṇa conscious, thinking that they are Kṛṣṇa's and Kṛṣṇa is theirs. There are other, low-class religious systems, which are contemplated for the killing of enemies or the gain of mystic power, but such religious systems, being full of passion and envy, are impure and temporary. Because they are full of envy, they are full of irreligion.

PURPORT

Bhāgavata-dharma has no contradictions. Conceptions of "your religion" and "my religion" are completely absent from *bhāgavata-*

dharma. Bhāgavata-dharma means following the orders given by the Supreme Lord, Bhagavān, as stated in *Bhagavad-gītā: sarva-dharmān parityajya mām ekaṁ śaraṇaṁ vraja.* God is one, and God is for everyone. Therefore everyone must surrender to God. That is the pure conception of religion. Whatever God orders constitutes religion (*dharmaṁ tu sākṣād bhagavat-praṇītam*). In *bhāgavata-dharma* there is no question of "what you believe" and "what I believe." Everyone must believe in the Supreme Lord and carry out His orders. *Ānukūlyena kṛṣṇānuśīlanam:* whatever Kṛṣṇa says—whatever God says—should be directly carried out. That is *dharma,* religion.

If one is actually Kṛṣṇa conscious, he cannot have any enemies. Since his only engagement is to induce others to surrender to Kṛṣṇa, or God, how can he have enemies? If one advocates the Hindu religion, the Muslim religion, the Christian religion, this religion or that religion, there will be conflicts. History shows that the followers of religious systems without a clear conception of God have fought with one another. There are many instances of this in human history, but systems of religion that do not concentrate upon service to the Supreme are temporary and cannot last for long because they are full of envy. There are many activities directed against such religious systems, and therefore one must give up the idea of "my belief" and "your belief." Everyone should believe in God and surrender unto Him. That is *bhāgavata-dharma.*

Bhāgavata-dharma is not a concocted sectarian belief, for it entails research to find how everything is connected with Kṛṣṇa (*īśāvāsyam idaṁ sarvam*). According to the Vedic injunctions, *sarvaṁ khalv idaṁ brahma:* Brahman, the Supreme, is present in everything. *Bhāgavata-dharma* captures this presence of the Supreme. *Bhāgavata-dharma* does not consider everything in the world to be false. Because everything emanates from the Supreme, nothing can be false; everything has some use in the service of the Supreme. For example, we are now dictating into a microphone and recording on a dictating machine, and thus we are finding how the machine can be connected to the Supreme Brahman. Since we are using this machine in the service of the Lord, it is Brahman. This is the meaning of *sarvaṁ khalv idaṁ brahma.* Everything is Brahman because everything can be used for the service of the Supreme Lord. Nothing is *mithyā,* false; everything is factual.

Bhāgavata-dharma is called *sarvotkṛṣṭa,* the best of all religious systems, because those who follow *bhāgavata-dharma* are not envious of anyone. Pure *bhāgavatas,* pure devotees, invite everyone, without envy, to join the Kṛṣṇa consciousness movement. A devotee is therefore exactly like the Supreme Personality of Godhead. *Suhṛdaṁ sarva-bhūtānām:* he is the friend of all living entities. Therefore this is the best of all religious systems. Whereas so-called religions are meant for a particular type of person who believes in a particular way, such discrimination has no place in Kṛṣṇa consciousness, or *bhāgavata-dharma.* If we scrutinize the religious systems meant for worship of demigods or anyone else but the Supreme Personality of Godhead, we will find that they are full of envy and therefore impure.

TEXT 42

कः क्षेमो निजपरयोः
कियान् वार्थः स्वपरद्रुहा धर्मेण ।
स्वद्रोहात्तव कोपः
परसम्पीडया च तथाधर्मः ॥४२॥

kaḥ kṣemo nija-parayoḥ
kiyān vārthaḥ sva-para-druhā dharmeṇa
sva-drohāt tava kopaḥ
para-sampīḍayā ca tathādharmaḥ

kaḥ—what; *kṣemaḥ*—benefit; *nija*—to oneself; *parayoḥ*—and to others; *kiyān*—how much; *vā*—or; *arthaḥ*—purpose; *sva-para-druhā*—which is envious of the performer and of others; *dharmeṇa*—with the religious system; *sva-drohāt*—from being envious of one's own self; *tava*—of You; *kopaḥ*—anger; *para-sampīḍayā*—by giving pain to others; *ca*—also; *tathā*—as well as; *adharmaḥ*—irreligion.

TRANSLATION

How can a religious system that produces envy of one's self and of others be beneficial for oneself and for them? What is auspicious about following such a system? What is actually to be

gained? By causing pain to one's own self due to self-envy and by causing pain to others, one arouses Your anger and practices irreligion.

PURPORT

Any religious system but the process of *bhāgavata-dharma*—service as an eternal servant of the Supreme Personality of Godhead—is a system of envy of one's own self and of others. For example, there are many systems of religion in which animal sacrifices are recommended. Such animal sacrifices are inauspicious both for the performer and for the animal. Although one is sometimes permitted to sacrifice an animal before the goddess Kālī and eat it instead of purchasing meat from a slaughterhouse, permission to eat meat after a sacrifice in the presence of the goddess Kālī is not the order of the Supreme Personality of Godhead. It is simply a concession for the miserable person who will not give up eating meat. It is meant to restrict his desire for unrestricted meat-eating. Such a religious system is condemned. Therefore Kṛṣṇa says, *sarva-dharmān parityajya mām ekaṁ śaraṇaṁ vraja:* "Give up all other duties and surrender unto Me." That is the last word in religion.

One may argue that the sacrifice of animals is recommended in the *Vedas.* This recommendation, however, is a restriction. Without Vedic restrictions on the purchase of meat, people will purchase meat from the market, which will be overflooded with meat shops, and slaughterhouses will increase. To restrict this, sometimes the *Vedas* say that one may eat meat after sacrificing an insignificant animal like a goat before the goddess Kālī. In any case, a system of religion in which animal sacrifices are recommended is inauspicious for those who perform the sacrifices and for the animals. Envious persons who perform ostentatious animal sacrifices are condemned in *Bhagavad-gītā* (16.17) as follows:

ātma-sambhāvitāḥ stabdhā
dhana-māna-madānvitāḥ
yajante nāma-yajñais te
dambhenāvidhi-pūrvakam

"Self-complacent and always impudent, deluded by wealth and false prestige, they sometimes perform sacrifices in name only without following any rules or regulations." Sometimes animal sacrifices are performed very gorgeously with grand arrangements for worshiping the goddess Kālī, but such festivals, although performed in the name of *yajña*, are not actually *yajña*, for *yajña* means to satisfy the Supreme Personality of Godhead. Therefore it is recommended that in this age specifically, *yajñaiḥ saṅkīrtana-prāyair yajanti hi sumedhasaḥ:* those who have good intelligence satisfy the *yajña-puruṣa*, Viṣṇu, by chanting the Hare Kṛṣṇa *mantra*. Envious persons, however, are condemned by the Supreme Personality of Godhead as follows:

ahaṅkāraṁ balaṁ darpaṁ
kāmaṁ krodhaṁ ca saṁśritāḥ
māṁ ātma-para-deheṣu
pradviṣanto 'bhyasūyakāḥ

tān ahaṁ dviṣataḥ krūrān
saṁsāreṣu narādhamān
kṣipāmy ajasram aśubhān
āsurīṣv eva yoniṣu

"Bewildered by false ego, strength, pride, lust and anger, the demon becomes envious of the Supreme Personality of Godhead, who is situated in his own body and in the bodies of others, and blasphemes against the real religion. Those who are envious and mischievous, who are the lowest among men, are cast by Me into the ocean of material existence, into various demoniac species of life." (Bg. 16.18–19) These persons are condemned by the Supreme Personality of Godhead, as indicated by the words *tava kopaḥ*. A person who commits murder is envious of himself and also the person he has killed, for the result of committing murder is that he will be arrested and hanged. If one transgresses the laws of a man-made government, he may escape being killed by the state, but one cannot escape the laws of God. A killer of any animal must be killed in his next life by the same animal. This is the law of nature. One must follow the instructions of the Supreme Lord: *sarva-dharmān parityajya māṁ ekaṁ śaraṇaṁ vraja*. If one follows any other system of religion, he is subject to punishment by the Supreme Personality of Godhead in many different ways. Therefore if one follows a concocted system of religion, he is envious not only of others but also of himself. Consequently his system of religion is useless.

Śrīmad-Bhāgavatam (1.2.8) says:

dharmaḥ svanuṣṭhitaḥ puṁsāṁ
viṣvaksena-kathāsu yaḥ
notpādayed yadi ratiṁ
śrama eva hi kevalam

"Duties [*dharma*] executed by men, regardless of occupation, are only so much useless labor if they do not provoke attraction for the message of the Supreme Lord." Following a system of religion that does not awaken one's Kṛṣṇa consciousness, or God consciousness, is merely a waste of time and labor.

TEXT 43

न व्यभिचरति तवेक्षा
यया ह्यभिहितो भागवतो धर्मः ।
स्थिरचरसत्त्वकदम्बे-
ष्वपृथग्धियो यमुपासते त्वार्याः ॥४३॥

na vyabhicarati tavekṣā
yayā hy abhihito bhāgavato dharmaḥ
sthira-cara-sattva-kadambeṣv
apṛthag-dhiyo yam upāsate tv āryāḥ

na—not; *vyabhicarati*—fails; *tava*—Your; *īkṣā*—outlook; *yayā*—by which; *hi*—indeed; *abhihitaḥ*—declared; *bhāgavataḥ*—in relationship with Your instructions and activities; *dharmaḥ*—religious principle; *sthira*—nonmoving; *cara*—moving; *sattva-kadambeṣu*—among the living entities; *apṛthak-dhiyaḥ*—who do not consider distinctions; *yam*—which; *upāsate*—follow; *tu*—certainly; *āryāḥ*—those who are advanced in civilization.

TRANSLATION

My dear Lord, one's occupational duty is instructed in Śrīmad-Bhāgavatam and Bhagavad-gītā according to Your point of view,

which never deviates from the highest goal of life. Those who follow their occupational duties under Your supervision, being equal to all living entities, moving and nonmoving, and not considering high and low, are called Āryans. Such Āryans worship You, the Supreme Personality of Godhead.

PURPORT

Bhāgavata-dharma and *kṛṣṇa-kathā* are identical. Śrī Caitanya Mahāprabhu wanted everyone to become a *guru* and preach the instructions of Kṛṣṇa everywhere from *Bhagavad-gītā*, *Śrīmad-Bhāgavatam*, the *Purāṇas*, *Vedānta-sūtra* and similar Vedic literatures. Āryans, who are advanced in civilization, follow *bhāgavata-dharma*. Prahlāda Mahārāja, although merely a child of five years, recommended:

kaumāra ācaret prājño
dharmān bhāgavatān iha
durlabhaṁ mānuṣaṁ janma
tad apy adhruvam arthadam
(*Bhāg.* 7.6.1)

Prahlāda Mahārāja preached *bhāgavata-dharma* among his classmates as soon as an opportunity was afforded by the absence of his teachers from the classroom. He said that from the very beginning of life, from the age of five, children should be instructed about *bhāgavata-dharma* because the human form of life, which is very rarely obtained, is meant for understanding this subject.

Bhāgavata-dharma means living according to the instructions of the Supreme Personality of Godhead. In *Bhagavad-gītā* we find that the Supreme Lord has arranged human society in four social divisions, namely *brāhmaṇa*, *kṣatriya*, *vaiśya* and *śūdra*. Again, the *Purāṇas* and other Vedic literatures set forth four *āśramas*, which are the divisions of spiritual life. Therefore *bhāgavata-dharma* means the *varṇāśrama-dharma* of the four social and four spiritual divisions.

The members of human society who strictly follow the principles of *bhāgavata-dharma* and live according to the instructions of the Supreme Personality of Godhead are called Āryans or *ārya*. A civilization of Āryans who strictly follow the instructions of the Lord and never deviate from those instructions is perfect. Such civilized men do not discriminate between trees, animals, human beings and other living entities. *Paṇḍitāḥ sama-darśinaḥ:* because they are completely educated in Kṛṣṇa consciousness, they see all living beings equally. Āryans do not kill even a small plant unnecessarily, not to speak of cutting trees for sense gratification. At the present moment, throughout the world, killing is prominent. Men are killing trees, they are killing animals, and they are killing other human beings also, all for sense gratification. This is not an Āryan civilization. As stated here, *sthira-cara-sattva-kadambeṣv apṛthag-dhiyaḥ.* The word *apṛthag-dhiyaḥ* indicates that Āryans do not distinguish between lower and higher grades of life. All life should be protected. All living beings have a right to live, even the trees and plants. This is the basic principle of an Āryan civilization. Apart from the lower living entities, those who have come to the platform of human civilization should be divided into a society of *brāhmaṇas, kṣatriyas, vaiśyas* and *śūdras.* The *brāhmaṇas* should follow the instructions of the Supreme Personality of Godhead as stated in *Bhagavad-gītā* and other Vedic literatures. The criterion must be *guṇa* and *karma.* In other words, one should acquire the qualities of a *brāhmaṇa, kṣatriya, vaiśya* or *śūdra* and act accordingly. This is the civilization accepted by the Āryans. Why do they accept it? They accept it because they are very much eager to satisfy Kṛṣṇa. This is perfect civilization.

Āryans do not deviate from the instructions of Kṛṣṇa, nor do they have doubts about Kṛṣṇa, but non-Āryans and other demoniac people fail to follow the instructions of *Bhagavad-gītā* and *Śrīmad-Bhāgavatam.* This is because they have been trained in sense gratification at the cost of all other living entities. *Nūnaṁ pramattaḥ kurute vikarma:* their only business is to indulge in all kinds of forbidden activities for sense gratification. *Yad indriya-prītaya āpṛṇoti:* they deviate in this way because they want to gratify their senses. They have no other occupation or ambition. Their method of civilization is condemned in the previous verse. *Kaḥ kṣemo nija-parayoḥ kiyān vārthaḥ sva-para-druhā dharmeṇa:* "What is the meaning of a civilization that kills oneself and others?"

This verse, therefore, advises that everyone become a member of the Āryan civilization and accept the instructions of the Supreme Personality of Godhead. One should conduct his social, political and religious affairs according to His instructions. We are spreading the Kṛṣṇa consciousness movement to try to establish a society the way that Kṛṣṇa wants it. This is the meaning of Kṛṣṇa consciousness. We are therefore presenting *Bhagavad-gītā* as it is and kicking out all kinds of mental concoction. Fools and rascals interpret *Bhagavad-gītā* in their own way. When Kṛṣṇa says, *man-manā bhava mad-bhakto mad-yājī māṁ namaskuru*—"Always think of Me, become My devotee, worship Me and offer your homage unto Me"—they comment that it is not Kṛṣṇa to whom we must surrender. Thus they derive imaginary meanings from *Bhagavad-gītā*. The Kṛṣṇa consciousness movement, however, strictly follows *bhāgavata-dharma*, the instructions of *Bhagavad-gītā* and *Śrīmad-Bhāgavatam* for the complete welfare of human society. One who misinterprets *Bhagavad-gītā*, twisting out some meaning for his sense gratification, is a non-Āryan. Therefore commentaries on *Bhagavad-gītā* by such persons should be immediately rejected. One should try to follow *Bhagavad-gītā* as it is. In *Bhagavad-gītā* (12.6–7) Lord Śrī Kṛṣṇa says:

ye tu sarvāṇi karmāṇi
mayi sannyasya mat-parāḥ
ananyenaiva yogena
māṁ dhyāyanta upāsate

teṣām ahaṁ samuddhartā
mṛtyu-saṁsāra-sāgarāt
bhavāmi na cirāt pārtha
mayy āveśita-cetasām

"For one who worships Me, giving up all his activities unto Me and being devoted to Me without deviation, engaged in devotional service and always meditating upon Me, who has fixed his mind upon Me, O son of Pṛthā, for him I am the swift deliverer from the ocean of birth and death."

TEXT 44

न हि भगवन्नघटितमिदं
त्वद्दर्शनान्नृणामखिलपापक्षयः ।
यन्नामसकृच्छ्रवणात्
पुक्कशोऽपि विमुच्यते संसारात् ॥४४॥

na hi bhagavann aghaṭitam idaṁ
tvad-darśanān nṛṇām akhila-pāpa-kṣayaḥ
yan-nāma sakṛc chravaṇāt
pukkaśo 'pi vimucyate saṁsārāt

na—not; *hi*—indeed; *bhagavan*—O my Lord; *aghaṭitam*—not occurred; *idam*—this; *tvat*—of You; *darśanāt*—by seeing; *nṛṇām*—of all human beings; *akhila*—all; *pāpa*—of sins; *kṣayaḥ*—annihilation; *yat-nāma*—whose name; *sakṛt*—only once; *śravaṇāt*—by hearing; *pukkaśaḥ*—the lowest class, the *caṇḍāla; api*—also; *vimucyate*—is delivered; *saṁsārāt*—from the entanglement of material existence.

TRANSLATION

My Lord, it is not impossible for one to be immediately freed from all material contamination by seeing You. Not to speak of seeing You personally, merely by hearing the holy name of Your Lordship only once, even caṇḍālas, men of the lowest class, are freed from all material contamination. Under the circumstances, who will not be freed from material contamination simply by seeing You?

PURPORT

As stated in the *Śrīmad-Bhāgavatam* (9.5.16), *yan-nāma-śruti-mātreṇa pumān bhavati nirmalaḥ:* simply by hearing the holy name of the Lord, one is immediately purified. Therefore, in this age of Kali, when all people are very contaminated, the chanting of the holy name of the Lord is recommended as the only means of improvement.

harer nāma harer nāma
harer nāmaiva kevalam
kalau nāsty eva nāsty eva
nāsty eva gatir anyathā

"In this age of quarrel and hypocrisy the only means of deliverance is the chanting of the holy name of the Lord. There is no other way. There is no other way. There is no other way." (*Bṛhan-nāradīya Purāṇa*) Śrī

Caitanya Mahāprabhu introduced this chanting of the holy name five hundred years ago, and now through the Kṛṣṇa consciousness movement, the Hare Kṛṣṇa movement, we are actually seeing that men who are considered to belong to the lowest class are being delivered from all sinful activities simply by hearing the holy name of the Lord. *Saṁsāra*, material existence, is a result of sinful actions. Everyone in this material world is condemned, yet as there are different grades of prisoners, there are different grades of men. All of them, in all statuses of life, are suffering. To stop the suffering of material existence, one must take to the Hare Kṛṣṇa movement of *saṅkīrtana* or Kṛṣṇa conscious life.

Herein it is said, *yan-nāma sakṛc chravaṇāt:* the holy name of the Supreme Personality of Godhead is so powerful that if once heard without offenses, it can purify the lowest of men (*kirāta-hūṇāndhra-pulinda-pulkaśāḥ*). Such men, who are called *caṇḍālas*, are less than *śūdras*, but they also can be purified simply by hearing the holy name of the Lord, not to speak of personally seeing the Lord. From our present position, the Supreme Personality of Godhead can be personally seen as the Deity in the temple. The Deity of the Lord is not different from the Supreme Lord. Because we cannot see the Supreme Lord with our present blunt eyes, the Lord has kindly consented to come before us in a form we can see. Therefore the Deity in the temple should not be considered material. By offering food to the Deity and by decorating and serving the Deity, one gets the same result that one derives from serving the Lord personally in Vaikuṇṭha.

TEXT 45

अथ भगवन् वयमधुना
त्वदवलोकपरिमृष्टाशयमलाः ।
सुरऋषिणा यत् कथितं
तावकेन कथमन्यथा भवति ॥४५॥

atha bhagavan vayam adhunā
tvad-avaloka-parimṛṣṭāśaya-malāḥ
sura-ṛṣiṇā yat kathitaṁ
tāvakena katham anyathā bhavati

atha—therefore; *bhagavan*—O Supreme Personality of Godhead; *vayam*—we; *adhunā*—at the present moment; *tvat-avaloka*—by seeing You; *parimṛṣṭa*—wiped away; *āśaya-malāḥ*—contaminated desires in the heart; *sura-ṛṣiṇā*—by the great sage of the demigods (Nārada); *yat*—which; *kathitam*—spoken; *tāvakena*—who is Your devotee; *katham*—how; *anyathā*—otherwise; *bhavati*—can it be.

TRANSLATION

Therefore, my dear Lord, simply seeing You has now wiped away all the contamination of sinful activities and their results of material attachment and lusty desires, which always filled my mind and the core of my heart. Whatever is predicted by the great sage Nārada Muni cannot be otherwise. In other words, I have obtained Your audience as a result of being trained by Nārada Muni.

PURPORT

This is the process of the perfect way. One must take lessons from authorities like Nārada, Vyāsa and Asita, and follow their principles. Then one will be able to see the Supreme Personality of Godhead even with one's own eyes. One only needs training. *Ataḥ śrī-kṛṣṇa-nāmādi na bhaved grāhyam indriyaiḥ.* With our blunt eyes and other senses we cannot perceive the Supreme Personality of Godhead, but if we engage our senses in the service of the Lord according to the instructions of the authorities, it will be possible to see Him. As soon as one sees the Supreme Personality of Godhead, all the sinful reactions in the core of one's heart are certainly vanquished.

TEXT 46

विदितमनन्त समस्तं
तव जगदात्मनो जनैरिहाचरितम् ।
विज्ञाप्यं परमगुरोः
कियदिव सवितुरिव खद्योतैः ॥४६॥

viditam ananta samastaṁ
tava jagad-ātmano janair ihācaritam

vijñāpyaṁ parama-guroḥ
kiyad iva savitur iva khadyotaiḥ

viditam—well known; *ananta*—O unlimited; *samastam*—everything; *tava*—to You; *jagat-ātmanaḥ*—who are the Supersoul of all living entities; *janaiḥ*—by the mass of people, or all living entities; *iha*—within this material world; *ācaritam*—performed; *vijñāpyam*—to be informed; *parama-guroḥ*—to the Supreme Personality of Godhead, the supreme master; *kiyat*—how much; *iva*—certainly; *savituḥ*—to the sun; *iva*—like; *khadyotaiḥ*—by the fireflies.

TRANSLATION

O unlimited Supreme Personality of Godhead, whatever a living entity does in this material world is well known to You because You are the Supersoul. In the presence of the sun there is nothing to be revealed by the light of a glowworm. Similarly, because You know everything, in Your presence there is nothing for me to make known.

TEXT 47

नमस्तुभ्यं भगवते
सकलजगत्स्थितिलयोदयेशाय ।
दुरवसितात्मगतये
कुयोगिनां भिदा परमहंसाय ॥४७॥

namas tubhyaṁ bhagavate
sakala-jagat-sthiti-layodayeśāya
duravasitātma-gataye
kuyogināṁ bhidā paramahaṁsāya

namaḥ—all obeisances; *tubhyam*—unto You; *bhagavate*—Your Lordship; *sakala*—all; *jagat*—of the cosmic manifestation; *sthiti*—of the maintenance; *laya*—dissolution; *udaya*—and creation; *īśāya*—unto the Supreme Lord; *duravasita*—impossible to understand; *ātma-gataye*—whose own position; *ku-yoginām*—of those who are attached to the objects of the senses; *bhidā*—by the false understanding of separateness; *parama-haṁsāya*—unto the supreme pure.

TRANSLATION

My dear Lord, You are the creator, maintainer and annihilator of this cosmic manifestation, but persons who are too materialistic and who always see separateness do not have eyes with which to see You. They cannot understand Your real position, and therefore they conclude that the cosmic manifestation is independent of Your opulence. My Lord, You are the supreme pure, and You are full in all six opulences. Therefore I offer my respectful obeisances unto You.

PURPORT

Atheistic men think that the cosmic manifestation has come about by chance, by a combination of matter, without reference to God. Materialistic so-called chemists and atheistic philosophers always try to avoid even the name of God in relation to the cosmic manifestation. For them God's creation is impossible to understand because they are too materialistic. The Supreme Personality of Godhead is *paramahaṁsa*, or the supreme pure, whereas those who are sinful, being very much attached to material sense enjoyment and therefore engaging in material activities like asses, are the lowest of men. All their so-called scientific knowledge is null and void because of their atheistic temperament. Thus they cannot understand the Supreme Personality of Godhead.

TEXT 48

यं वै श्वसन्तमनु विश्वसृजः श्वसन्ति
यं चेकितानमनु चित्तय उच्चकन्ति ।
भूमण्डलं सर्षपायति यस्य मूर्ध्नि
तस्मै नमो भगवतेऽस्तु सहस्रमूर्ध्ने ॥४८॥

yaṁ vai śvasantam anu viśva-sṛjaḥ śvasanti
yaṁ cekitānam anu cittaya uccakanti
bhū-maṇḍalaṁ sarṣapāyati yasya mūrdhni
tasmai namo bhagavate 'stu sahasra-mūrdhne

yam—whom; *vai*—indeed; *śvasantam*—endeavoring; *anu*—after; *viśva-sṛjaḥ*—the directors of the cosmic creation; *śvasanti*—also endeavor; *yam*—whom; *cekitānam*—perceiving; *anu*—after; *cittayaḥ*—all the knowledge-gathering senses; *uccakanti*—perceive; *bhū-maṇḍalam*—the huge universe; *sarṣapāyati*—become like seeds of mustard; *yasya*—of whom; *mūrdhni*—on the head; *tasmai*—unto Him; *namaḥ*—obeisances; *bhagavate*—the Supreme Personality of Godhead, full with six opulences; *astu*—may there be; *sahasra-mūrdhne*—who has thousands of hoods.

TRANSLATION

My dear Lord, it is after You endeavor that Lord Brahmā, Indra and the other directors of the cosmic manifestation become occupied with their activities. It is after You perceive the material energy, My Lord, that the senses begin to perceive. The Supreme Personality of Godhead holds all the universes on His heads like seeds of mustard. I offer my respectful obeisances unto You, that Supreme Personality, who has thousands of hoods.

TEXT 49

श्रीशुक उवाच
संस्तुतो भगवानेवमनन्तस्तमभाषत ।
विद्याधरपतिं प्रीतश्चित्रकेतुं कुरूद्वह ॥४९॥

śrī-śuka uvāca
saṁstuto bhagavān evam
anantas tam abhāṣata
vidyādhara-patiṁ prītaś
citraketuṁ kurūdvaha

śrī-śukaḥ uvāca—Śrī Śukadeva Gosvāmī said; *saṁstutaḥ*—being worshiped; *bhagavān*—the Supreme Personality of Godhead; *evam*—in this way; *anantaḥ*—Lord Ananta; *tam*—unto him; *abhāṣata*—replied; *vidyādhara-patim*—the King of the Vidyādharas; *prītaḥ*—being very pleased; *citraketum*—King Citraketu; *kuru-udvaha*—O best of the Kuru dynasty, Mahārāja Parīkṣit.

TRANSLATION

Śukadeva Gosvāmī continued: The Lord, the Supreme Personality of Godhead, Anantadeva, being very much pleased with the prayers offered by Citraketu, the King of the Vidyādharas, replied to him as follows, O best of the Kuru dynasty, Mahārāja Parīkṣit.

TEXT 50

श्रीभगवानुवाच
यन्नारदाङ्गिरोभ्यां ते व्याहृतं मेऽनुशासनम् ।
संसिद्धोऽसि तया राजन् विद्यया दर्शनाच्च मे ॥५०॥

śrī-bhagavān uvāca
yan nāradāṅgirobhyāṁ te
vyāhṛtaṁ me 'nuśāsanam
saṁsiddho 'si tayā rājan
vidyayā darśanāc ca me

śrī-bhagavān uvāca—the Supreme Personality of Godhead, Saṅkarṣaṇa, replied; *yat*—which; *nārada-aṅgirobhyām*—by the great sages Nārada and Aṅgirā; *te*—unto you; *vyāhṛtam*—spoken; *me*—of Me; *anuśāsanam*—the worship; *saṁsiddhaḥ*—completely perfected; *asi*—you are; *tayā*—by that; *rājan*—O King; *vidyayā*—*mantra; darśanāt*—from the direct sight; *ca*—as well as; *me*—of Me.

TRANSLATION

The Supreme Personality of Godhead, Anantadeva, replied as follows: O King, as a result of your having accepted the instructions spoken about Me by the great sages Nārada and Aṅgirā, you have become completely aware of transcendental knowledge. Because you are now educated in the spiritual science, you have seen Me face to face. Therefore you are now completely perfect.

PURPORT

The perfection of life is to be spiritually educated and to understand the existence of the Lord and how He creates, maintains and annihilates the cosmic manifestation. When one is perfect in knowledge, he can develop his love of Godhead through the association of such perfect persons as Nārada and Aṅgirā and the members of their disciplic succession. Then one is able to see the unlimited Supreme Personality of Godhead face to face. Although the Lord is unlimited, by His causeless mercy He becomes visible to the devotee, who is then able to see Him. In our present position of conditioned life we cannot see or understand the Supreme Personality of Godhead.

ataḥ śrī-kṛṣṇa-nāmādi
na bhaved grāhyam indriyaiḥ
sevonmukhe hi jihvādau
svayam eva sphuraty adaḥ

"No one can understand the transcendental nature of the name, form, quality and pastimes of Śrī Kṛṣṇa through his materially contaminated senses. Only when one becomes spiritually saturated by transcendental service to the Lord are the transcendental name, form, quality and pastimes of the Lord revealed to him." (*Bhakti-rasāmṛta-sindhu* 1.2.234) If one takes to spiritual life under the direction of Nārada Muni or his representative and thus engages himself in the service of the Lord, he qualifies himself to see the Lord face to face. The *Brahma-saṁhitā* (5.38) states:

premāñjana-cchurita-bhakti-vilocanena
santaḥ sadaiva hṛdayeṣu vilokayanti
yaṁ śyāmasundaram acintya-guṇa-svarūpaṁ
govindam ādi-puruṣaṁ tam ahaṁ bhajāmi

"I worship the primeval Lord, Govinda, who is always seen by the devotee whose eyes are anointed with the pulp of love. He is seen in His eternal form of Śyāmasundara situated within the heart of the devotee." One must follow the instructions of the spiritual master. Thus one becomes qualified and later sees the Supreme Personality of Godhead, as evinced by Mahārāja Citraketu.

TEXT 51

अहं वै सर्वभूतानि भूतात्मा भूतभावनः ।
शब्दब्रह्म परं ब्रह्म ममोभे शाश्वती तनू ॥५१॥

ahaṁ vai sarva-bhūtāni
bhūtātmā bhūta-bhāvanaḥ
śabda-brahma paraṁ brahma
mamobhe śāśvatī tanū

aham—I; *vai*—indeed; *sarva-bhūtāni*—expanded in different forms of living entities; *bhūta-ātmā*—the Supersoul of all living entities (the supreme director and enjoyer of them); *bhūta-bhāvanaḥ*—the cause for the manifestation of all living entities; *śabda-brahma*—the transcendental sound vibration (the Hare Kṛṣṇa *mantra*); *param brahma*—the Supreme Absolute Truth; *mama*—My; *ubhe*—both (namely, the form of sound and the form of spiritual identity); *śāśvatī*—eternal; *tanū*—two bodies.

TRANSLATION

All living entities, moving and nonmoving, are My expansions and are separate from Me. I am the Supersoul of all living beings, who exist because I manifest them. I am the form of the transcendental vibrations like oṁkāra and Hare Kṛṣṇa Hare Rāma, and I am the Supreme Absolute Truth. These two forms of Mine—namely, the transcendental sound and the eternally blissful spiritual form of the Deity, are My eternal forms; they are not material.

PURPORT

The science of devotional service has been instructed by Nārada and Aṅgirā to Citraketu. Now, because of Citraketu's devotional service, he has seen the Supreme Personality of Godhead. By performing devotional service, one advances step by step, and when one is on the platform of love of Godhead (*premā pumartho mahān*) he sees the Supreme Lord at every moment. As stated in *Bhagavad-gītā*, when one engages in devotional service twenty-four hours a day (*teṣāṁ satata-yuktānāṁ bhajatāṁ prīti-pūrvakam*) in accordance with the instructions of the spiritual master, his devotional service becomes more and more pleasing. Then the Supreme Personality of Godhead, who is within the core of everyone's heart, speaks to the devotee (*dadāmi buddhi-yogaṁ taṁ yena mām upayānti te*). Citraketu Mahārāja was first instructed by his *gurus*, Aṅgirā and Nārada, and now, having followed their instructions, he has come to the stage of seeing the Supreme Lord face to face. Therefore the Lord is now instructing him in the essence of knowledge.

The essence of knowledge is that there are two kinds of *vastu*, or substances, One is real, and the other, being illusory or temporary, is sometimes called nonfactual. One must consider these two kinds of existence. The real *tattva*, or truth, consists of Brahman, Paramātmā, and Bhagavān. As stated in *Śrīmad-Bhāgavatam* (1.2.11):

vadanti tat tattva-vidas
tattvaṁ yaj jñānam advayam
brahmeti paramātmeti
bhagavān iti śabdyate

"Learned transcendentalists who know the Absolute Truth call this nondual substance Brahman, Paramātmā or Bhagavān." The Absolute Truth exists eternally in three features. Therefore, Brahman, Paramātmā and Bhagavān combined are the substance.

The categories of emanations from the nonsubstance are two—activities and forbidden activities (*karma* and *vikarma*). *Karma* refers to the pious life or material activities performed during the day and the mental activities of dreams at night. These are more or less desired activities. *Vikarma*, however, refers to illusory activities, which are something like the will-o'-the-wisp. These are activities that have no meaning. For example, modern scientists imagine that life can be produced from chemical combinations, and they are very busy trying to prove this in laboratories throughout the world, although no one in history has been able to produce the substance of life from material combinations. Such activities are called *vikarma*.

All material activities are actually illusory, and progress in illusion is simply a waste of time. These illusory activities are called *akārya*, and one must learn of them from the instructions of the Supreme Personality of Godhead. As stated in *Bhagavad-gītā* (4.17):

karmaṇo hy api boddhavyaṁ
boddhavyaṁ ca vikarmaṇaḥ
akarmaṇaś ca boddhavyaṁ
gahanā karmaṇo gatiḥ

"The intricacies of action are very hard to understand. Therefore one should know properly what action is, what forbidden action is, and what inaction is." One must learn of these directly from the Supreme Personality of Godhead, who, as Anantadeva, is instructing King Citraketu because of the advanced stage of devotional service he achieved by following the instructions of Nārada and Aṅgirā.

Herein it is said, *ahaṁ vai sarva-bhūtāni:* the Lord is everything (*sarva-bhūtāni*), including the living entities and the material or physical elements. As the Lord says in *Bhagavad-gītā* (7.4–5):

bhūmir āpo 'nalo vāyuḥ
khaṁ mano buddhir eva ca
ahaṅkāra itīyaṁ me
bhinnā prakṛtir aṣṭadhā

apareyam itas tv anyāṁ
prakṛtiṁ viddhi me parām
jīva-bhūtāṁ mahā-bāho
yayedaṁ dhāryate jagat

"Earth, water, fire, air, ether, mind, intelligence and false ego—all together these eight comprise My separated material energies. Besides this inferior nature, O mighty-armed Arjuna, there is a superior energy of Mine, which consists of the living entities, who are struggling with material nature and are sustaining the universe." The living entity tries to lord it over the material or physical elements, but both the physical elements and the spiritual spark are energies emanating from the Supreme Personality of Godhead. Therefore the Lord says, *ahaṁ vai sarva-bhūtāni:* "I am everything." Just as heat and light emanate from fire, these two energies—the physical elements and the living entities—

emanate from the Supreme Lord. Therefore the Lord says, *ahaṁ vai sarva-bhūtāni:* "I expand the physical and spiritual categories."

Again, the Lord, as the Supersoul, guides the living entities who are conditioned by the physical atmosphere. Therefore he is called *bhūtātmā bhūta-bhāvanaḥ.* He gives the living entity the intelligence with which to improve his position so that he may return home, back to Godhead, or if he does not want to go back to Godhead, the Lord gives him the intelligence with which to improve his material position. This is confirmed by the Lord Himself in *Bhagavad-gītā* (15.15). *Sarvasya cāhaṁ hṛdi sanniviṣṭo mattaḥ smṛtir jñānam apohanaṁ ca:* "I am seated in everyone's heart, and from Me come remembrance, knowledge and forgetfulness." From within, the Lord gives the living being the intelligence with which to work. Therefore the previous verse said that after the Supreme Personality of Godhead endeavors, our endeavors begin. We cannot independently endeavor or act upon anything. Therefore the Lord is *bhūta-bhāvanaḥ.*

Another specific feature of the knowledge given in this verse is that *śabda-brahma* is also a form of the Supreme Lord. In His eternal, blissful form, Lord Kṛṣṇa is accepted by Arjuna as *paraṁ brahma.* A living entity in the conditioned stage accepts something illusory as substantial. This is called *māyā* or *avidyā*—ignorance. Therefore according to the Vedic knowledge, one must become a devotee, and one must then distinguish between *avidyā* and *vidyā,* which are elaborately explained in the *Īśopaniṣad.* When one is actually on the platform of *vidyā,* he can personally understand the Personality of Godhead in His forms like those of Lord Rāma, Lord Kṛṣṇa and Saṅkarṣaṇa. The Vedic knowledge is described as the breathing of the Supreme Lord, and activities begin on the basis of Vedic knowledge. Therefore the Lord says that when He endeavors or breathes, the material universes come into existence, and various activities gradually develop. The Lord says in *Bhagavad-gītā, praṇavaḥ sarva-vedeṣu:* "I am the syllable *oṁ* in all the Vedic *mantras.*" Vedic knowledge begins with the vibration of the transcendental sound *praṇava, oṁkāra.* The same transcendental sound is Hare Kṛṣṇa, Hare Kṛṣṇa, Kṛṣṇa Kṛṣṇa, Hare Hare/ Hare Rāma, Hare Rāma, Rāma Rāma, Hare Hare. *Abhinnatvān nāma-nāminoḥ:* there is no difference between the holy name of the Lord and the Lord Himself.

TEXT 52

लोके विततमात्मानं लोकं चात्मनि सन्ततम् ।
उभयं च मया व्याप्तं मयि चैवोभयं कृतम् ॥५२॥

loke vitatam ātmānaṁ
lokaṁ cātmani santatam
ubhayaṁ ca mayā vyāptaṁ
mayi caivobhayaṁ kṛtam

loke—in this material world; *vitatam*—expanded (in the spirit of material enjoyment); *ātmānam*—the living entity; *lokam*—the material world; *ca*—also; *ātmani*—in the living entity; *santatam*—spread; *ubhayam*—both (the material world of material elements and the living entity); *ca*—and; *mayā*—by Me; *vyāptam*—pervaded; *mayi*—in Me; *ca*—also; *eva*—indeed; *ubhayam*—both of them; *kṛtam*—created.

TRANSLATION

In this world of matter, which the conditioned soul accepts as consisting of enjoyable resources, the conditioned soul expands, thinking that he is the enjoyer of the material world. Similarly, the material world expands in the living entity as a source of enjoyment. In this way they both expand, but because they are My energies, they are both pervaded by Me. As the Supreme Lord, I am the cause of these effects, and one should know that both of them rest in Me.

PURPORT

The Māyāvāda philosophy sees everything as being equal in quality with the Supreme Personality of Godhead, or the Supreme Brahman, and therefore sees everything as worshipable. This dangerous theory of the Māyāvāda school has turned people in general toward atheism. On the strength of this theory, one thinks that he is God, but this is not a fact. As stated in *Bhagavad-gītā* (*mayā tatam idaṁ sarvaṁ jagad avyakta-mūrtinā*), the fact is that the entire cosmic manifestation is an expansion of the Supreme Lord's energies, which are manifested in the physical elements and the living entities. The living entities wrongly consider the physical elements to be resources meant for their enjoyment, and they think themselves to be the enjoyers. However, neither of them is independent; they are both energies of the Lord. The original cause for the material energy and spiritual energy is the Supreme Personality of Godhead. However, although the expansion of the Lord's energies is the original cause, one should not think that the Lord Himself has expanded in different ways. To condemn the theories of the Māyāvādīs, the Lord clearly says in *Bhagavad-gītā, mat-sthāni sarva-bhūtāni na cāhaṁ teṣv avasthitaḥ:* "All beings are in Me, but I am not in them." Everything rests upon Him, and everything is but an expansion of His energies, but this does not mean that everything is as worshipable as the Lord Himself. The material expansion is temporary, but the Lord is not temporary. The living entities are parts of the Lord, but they are not the Lord Himself. The living entities in this material world are not inconceivable, but the Lord is. The theory that the Lord's energies, being expansions of the Lord, are as good as the Lord is mistaken.

TEXTS 53–54

यथा सुषुप्तः पुरुषो विश्वं पश्यति चात्मनि ।
आत्मानमेकदेशस्थं मन्यते स्वप्न उत्थितः ॥५३॥
एवं जागरणादीनि जीवस्थानानि चात्मनः ।
मायामात्राणि विज्ञाय तद्द्रष्टारं परं स्मरेत् ॥५४॥

yathā suṣuptaḥ puruṣo
viśvaṁ paśyati cātmani
ātmānam eka-deśa-sthaṁ
manyate svapna utthitaḥ

evaṁ jāgaraṇādīni
jīva-sthānāni cātmanaḥ
māyā-mātrāṇi vijñāya
tad-draṣṭāraṁ paraṁ smaret

yathā—just as; *suṣuptaḥ*—sleeping; *puruṣaḥ*—a person; *viśvam*—the whole universe; *paśyati*—perceives; *ca*—also; *ātmani*—in himself;

ātmānam—himself; *eka-deśa-stham*—lying down in one place; *manyate*—he considers; *svapne*—in the dreaming condition; *utthitaḥ*—waking up; *evam*—in this way; *jāgaraṇa-ādīni*—the states of wakefulness and so on; *jīva-sthānāni*—the living entity's different conditions of existence; *ca*—also; *ātmanaḥ*—of the Supreme Personality of Godhead; *māyā-mātrāṇi*—the exhibitions of the illusory potency; *vijñāya*—knowing; *tat*—of them; *draṣṭāram*—the creator or seer of all such conditions; *param*—the Supreme; *smaret*—one should always remember.

TRANSLATION

When a person is in deep sleep, he dreams and sees in himself many other objects, such as great mountains and rivers or perhaps even the entire universe, although they are far away. Sometimes when one awakens from a dream he sees that he is in a human form, lying in his bed in one place. Then he sees himself, in terms of various conditions, as belonging to a particular nationality, family and so on. All the conditions of deep sleep, dreaming and wakefulness are but energies of the Supreme Personality of Godhead. One should always remember the original creator of these conditions, the Supreme Lord, who is unaffected by them.

PURPORT

None of these conditions of the living entities—namely, deep sleep, dreaming and wakefulness—is substantial. They are simply displays of various phases of conditional life. There may be many mountains, rivers, trees, bees, tigers and snakes that are situated far away, but in a dream one may imagine them to be nearby. Similarly, as one has subtle dreams at night, when the living entity is awake he lives in gross dreams of nation, community, society, possessions, skyscrapers, bank balance, position and honor. Under the circumstances, one should know that his position is due to his contact with the material world. One is situated in different positions in various forms of life that are all but creations of the illusory energy, which works under the direction of the Supreme Personality of Godhead. Therefore the Supreme Lord is the ultimate actor, and the conditioned living entity should simply remember this original actor, Śrī Kṛṣṇa. As living entities, we are being carried away by the waves of *prakṛti*, or nature, which works under the Lord's direction (*mayādhyakṣeṇa prakṛtiḥ sūyate sa-carācaram*). Bhaktivinoda Ṭhākura sings, (*miche*) *māyāra vaśe, yāccha bhese', khāccha hābuḍubu, bhāi:* "Why are you being carried away by the waves of the illusory energy in various phases of dreaming and wakefulness? These are all creations of *māyā*." Our only duty is to remember the supreme director of this illusory energy—Kṛṣṇa. For us to do this, the *śāstra* advises us, *harer nāma harer nāma harer nāmaiva kevalam:* one should constantly chant the holy name of the Lord—Hare Kṛṣṇa, Hare Kṛṣṇa, Kṛṣṇa Kṛṣṇa, Hare Hare/ Hare Rāma, Hare Rāma, Rāma Rāma, Hare Hare. The Supreme Lord is realized in three different phases, as Brahman, Paramātmā and Bhagavān, but Bhagavān is the ultimate realization. One who realizes Bhagavān—the Supreme Personality of Godhead, Kṛṣṇa—is the most perfect *mahātmā* (*vāsudevaḥ sarvam iti sa mahātmā sudurlabhaḥ*). In the human form of life, one should understand the Supreme Personality of Godhead, for then one will understand everything else. *Yasmin vijñāte sarvam evaṁ vijñātaṁ bhavati.* According to this Vedic injunction, simply by understanding Kṛṣṇa one understands Brahman, Paramātmā, *prakṛti*, the illusory energy, the spiritual energy and everything else. Everything will be revealed. *Prakṛti*, the material nature, is working under the direction of the Supreme Lord, and we living entities are being carried away by various phases of *prakṛti*. For self-realization, one should always remember Kṛṣṇa. As stated in *Padma Purāṇa*, *smartavyaḥ satataṁ viṣṇuḥ:* we should always remember Lord Viṣṇu. *Vismartavyo na jātucit:* we should never forget the Lord. This is the perfection of life.

TEXT 55

येन प्रसुप्तः पुरुषः स्वापं वेदात्मनस्तदा ।
सुखं च निर्गुणं ब्रह्म तमात्मानमवेहि माम् ॥५५॥

yena prasuptaḥ puruṣaḥ
svāpaṁ vedātmanas tadā
sukhaṁ ca nirguṇaṁ brahma
tam ātmānam avehi mām

yena—by whom (the Supreme Brahman); *prasuptaḥ*—sleeping; *puruṣaḥ*—a man; *svāpam*—the subject of a dream; *veda*—knows; *āt-*

manaḥ—of himself; *tadā*—at that time; *sukham*—happiness; *ca*—also; *nirguṇam*—without contact with the material environment; *brahma*—the supreme spirit; *tam*—Him; *ātmānam*—the pervader; *avehi*—just know; *mām*—Me.

TRANSLATION

Know Me to be the Supreme Brahman, the all-pervading Supersoul through whom the sleeping living entity can understand his dreaming condition and his happiness beyond the activities of the material senses. That is to say, I am the cause of the activities of the sleeping living being.

PURPORT

When the living entity becomes free from false ego, he understands his superior position as a spirit soul, part and parcel of the pleasure potency of the Lord. Thus, due to Brahman, even while sleeping the living entity can enjoy. The Lord says, "That Brahman, that Paramātmā and that Bhagavān are I Myself." This is noted by Śrīla Jīva Gosvāmī in his *Krama-sandarbha.*

TEXT 56

उभयं स्मरतः पुंसः प्रस्वापप्रतिबोधयोः ।
अन्वेति व्यतिरिच्येत तज्ज्ञानं ब्रह्म तत् परम् ॥५६॥

ubhayaṁ smarataḥ puṁsaḥ
prasvāpa-pratibodhayoḥ
anveti vyatiricyeta
taj jñānaṁ brahma tat param

ubhayam—both types of consciousness (sleep and wakefulness); *smarataḥ*—remembering; *puṁsaḥ*—of the person; *prasvāpa*—of consciousness during sleep; *pratibodhayoḥ*—and of consciousness while awake; *anveti*—extends through; *vyatiricyeta*—may reach beyond; *tat*—that; *jñānam*—knowledge; *brahma*—the Supreme Brahman; *tat*—that; *param*—transcendental.

TRANSLATION

If one's dreams during sleep are merely subject matters witnessed by the Supersoul, how can the living entity, who is different from the Supersoul, remember the activities of dreams? The experiences of one person cannot be understood by another. Therefore the knower of the facts, the living entity who inquires into the incidents manifested in dreams and wakefulness, is different from the circumstantial activities. That knowing factor is Brahman. In other words, the quality of knowing belongs to the living entities and to the Supreme Soul. Thus the living entity can also experience the activities of dreams and wakefulness. In both stages the knower is unchanged, but is qualitatively one with the Supreme Brahman.

PURPORT

In knowledge the living entity is qualitatively one with the Supreme Brahman, but the quantity of the Supreme Brahman is not the same as that of the living entity, who is part of Brahman. Because the living entity is Brahman in quality, he can remember the past activities of dreams and also know the present activities of wakefulness.

TEXT 57

यदेतद्विस्मृतं पुंसो मद्भावं भिन्नमात्मनः ।
ततः संसार एतस्य देहाद्देहो मृतेर्मृतिः ॥५७॥

yad etad vismṛtaṁ puṁso
mad-bhāvaṁ bhinnam ātmanaḥ
tataḥ saṁsāra etasya
dehād deho mṛter mṛtiḥ

yat—which; *etat*—this; *vismṛtam*—forgotten; *puṁsaḥ*—of the living entity; *mat-bhāvam*—My spiritual position; *bhinnam*—separation; *ātmanaḥ*—from the Supreme Soul; *tataḥ*—from that; *saṁsāraḥ*—material, conditional life; *etasya*—of the living entity; *dehāt*—from one body; *dehaḥ*—another body; *mṛteḥ*—from one death; *mṛtiḥ*—another death.

TRANSLATION

When a living entity, thinking himself different from Me, forgets his spiritual identity of qualitative oneness with Me in eternity, knowledge and bliss, his material, conditional life begins. In other words, instead of identifying his interest with Mine, he becomes interested in his bodily expansions like his wife, children and material possessions. In this way, by the influence of his actions, one body comes from another, and after one death, another death takes place.

PURPORT

Generally the Māyāvādī philosophers or persons influenced by Māyāvādī philosophers think themselves as good as the Supreme Personality of Godhead. This is the cause of their conditional life. As stated by the Vaiṣṇava poet Jagadānanda Paṇḍita in his *Prema-vivarta:*

kṛṣṇa-bahirmukha hañā bhoga vāñchā kare
nikaṭa-stha māyā tāre jāpaṭiyā dhare

As soon as a living entity forgets his constitutional position and endeavors to become one with the Supreme, his conditional life begins. The conception that the Supreme Brahman and the living entity are equal not only in quality but also in quantity is the cause of conditional life. If one forgets the difference between the Supreme Lord and the living entity, his conditional life begins. Conditional life means giving up one body to accept another and undergoing death to accept death again. The Māyāvādī philosopher teaches the philosophy of *tat tvam asi,* saying, "You are the same as God." He forgets that *tat tvam asi* applies in terms of the marginal position of the living entity, who is like sunshine. There is heat and light in the sun, and there is heat and light in the sunshine, and thus they are qualitatively one. But one should not forget that the sunshine rests on the sun. As the Lord says in *Bhagavad-gītā, brahmaṇo hi pratiṣṭhāham:* "I am the original source of Brahman." The sunshine is important because of the presence of the sun globe. It is not that the sun globe is important because of the all-pervasiveness of the sunshine. Forgetfulness and misunderstanding of this fact is called *māyā.* Because of forgetfulness of one's constitutional position and that of the Supreme Lord, one comes into *māyā*, or *saṁsāra*—conditional life. In this regard, Madhvācārya says:

sarva-bhinnaṁ parātmānaṁ
vismaran saṁsared iha
abhinnaṁ saṁsmaran yāti
tamo nāsty atra saṁśayaḥ

When one thinks that the living entity is nondifferent in all respects from the Supreme Lord, there is no doubt that he is in ignorance (*tamaḥ*).

TEXT 58

लब्ध्वेह मानुषीं योनिं ज्ञानविज्ञानसम्भवाम् ।
आत्मानं यो न बुद्ध्येत न क्वचित् क्षेममाप्नुयात् ॥५८॥

labdhveha mānuṣīṁ yoniṁ
jñāna-vijñāna-sambhavām
ātmānaṁ yo na buddhyeta
na kvacit kṣemam āpnuyāt

labdhvā—achieving; *iha*—in this material world (especially in this pious land of Bhārata-varṣa, India); *mānuṣīm*—the human; *yonim*—species; *jñāna*—of knowledge through Vedic scriptures; *vijñāna*—and practical application of that knowledge in life; *sambhavām*—wherein there is a possibility; *ātmānam*—one's real identity; *yaḥ*—anyone who; *na*—not; *buddhyeta*—understands; *na*—never; *kvacit*—at any time; *kṣemam*—success in life; *āpnuyāt*—can obtain.

TRANSLATION

A human being can attain perfection in life by self-realization through the Vedic literature and its practical application. This is possible especially for a human being born in India, the land of piety. A man who obtains birth in such a convenient position but does not understand his self is unable to achieve the highest perfection, even if he is exalted to life in the higher planetary systems.

PURPORT

This statement is confirmed in *Caitanya-caritāmṛta* (*Ādi* 9.41). Lord Caitanya said:

bhārata-bhūmite haila manuṣya-janma yāra
janma sārthaka kari' kara para-upakāra

Everyone born in India, especially as a human being, can achieve the supreme success through the Vedic literature and its practical application in life. When one is perfect, he can render a service for the self-realization of the entire human society. This is the best way to perform humanitarian work.

TEXT 59

स्मृत्वेहायां परिक्लेशं ततः फलविपर्ययम् ।
अभयं चाप्यनीहायां सङ्कल्पाद्विरमेत्कविः ॥५९॥

smṛtvehāyāṁ parikleśaṁ
tataḥ phala-viparyayam
abhayaṁ cāpy anīhāyāṁ
saṅkalpād viramet kaviḥ

smṛtvā—remembering; *īhāyām*—in the field of activities with fruitive results; *parikleśam*—the waste of energy and the miserable conditions; *tataḥ*—from that; *phala-viparyayam*—the opposite of the desired result; *abhayam*—fearlessness; *ca*—also; *api*—indeed; *anīhāyām*—when there is no desire for fruitive results; *saṅkalpāt*—from material desire; *viramet*—should cease; *kaviḥ*—one who is advanced in knowledge.

TRANSLATION

Remembering the great trouble found in the field of activities performed for fruitive results, and remembering how one receives the reverse of the results one desires—whether from material actions or from the fruitive activities recommended in the Vedic literatures—an intelligent man should cease from the desire for

fruitive actions, for by such endeavors one cannot achieve the ultimate goal of life. On the other hand, if one acts without desires for fruitive results—in other words, if one engages in devotional activities—he can achieve the highest goal of life with freedom from miserable conditions. Considering this, one should cease from material desires.

TEXT 60

सुखाय दुःखमोक्षाय कुर्वाते दम्पती क्रियाः ।
ततोऽनिवृत्तिरप्राप्तिर्दुःखस्य च सुखस्य च ॥६०॥

sukhāya duḥkha-mokṣāya
kurvāte dampatī kriyāḥ
tato 'nivṛttir aprāptir
duḥkhasya ca sukhasya ca

sukhāya—for happiness; *duḥkha-mokṣāya*—for release from the unhappy state; *kurvāte*—perform; *dam-patī*—the wife and husband; *kriyāḥ*—activities; *tataḥ*—from that; *anivṛttiḥ*—no cessation; *aprāptiḥ*—no achievement; *duḥkhasya*—of distress; *ca*—also; *sukhasya*—of happiness; *ca*—also.

TRANSLATION

As husband and wife, a man and woman plan together to attain happiness and decrease unhappiness, working jointly in many ways, but because their activities are full of desires, these activities are never a source of happiness, and they never diminish distress. On the contrary, they are a cause of great unhappiness.

TEXTS 61–62

एवं विपर्ययं बुद्ध्वा नृणां विज्ञाभिमानिनाम् ।
आत्मनश्च गतिं सूक्ष्मां स्थानत्रयविलक्षणाम् ॥६१॥
दृष्टश्रुताभिर्मात्राभिर्निर्मुक्तः स्वेन तेजसा ।
ज्ञानविज्ञानसन्तृप्तो मद्भक्तः पुरुषो भवेत् ॥६२॥

evaṁ viparyayaṁ buddhvā
nṛṇāṁ vijñābhimāninām
ātmanaś ca gatiṁ sūkṣmāṁ
sthāna-traya-vilakṣaṇām

dṛṣṭa-śrutābhir mātrābhir
nirmuktaḥ svena tejasā
jñāna-vijñāna-santṛpto
mad-bhaktaḥ puruṣo bhavet

evam—in this way; *viparyayam*—reversal; *buddhvā*—realizing; *nṛṇām*—of men; *vijña-abhimāninām*—who think of themselves as full of scientific knowledge; *ātmanaḥ*—of the self; *ca*—also; *gatim*—the progress; *sūkṣmām*—extremely difficult to understand; *sthāna-traya*—the three conditions of life (deep sleep, dreaming and wakefulness); *vilakṣaṇām*—apart from; *dṛṣṭa*—directly perceived; *śrutābhiḥ*—or understood by information from authorities; *mātrābhiḥ*—from objects; *nirmuktaḥ*—being freed; *svena*—by one's own; *tejasā*—strength of consideration; *jñāna-vijñāna*—with knowledge and practical application of the knowledge; *santṛptaḥ*—being fully satisfied; *mat-bhaktaḥ*—My devotee; *puruṣaḥ*—a person; *bhavet*—should become.

TRANSLATION

One should understand that the activities of persons who are proud of their material experience bring only results contradictory to those such persons conceive while awake, sleeping and deeply sleeping. One should further understand that the spirit soul, although very difficult for the materialist to perceive, is above all these conditions, and by the strength of one's discrimination, one should give up the desire for fruitive results in the present life and in the next. Thus becoming experienced in transcendental knowledge, one should become My devotee.

TEXT 63

एतावानेव मनुजैर्योगनैपुण्यबुद्धिभिः ।
स्वार्थः सर्वात्मना ज्ञेयो यत्परात्मैकदर्शनम् ॥६३॥

etāvān eva manujair
yoga-naipuṇya-buddhibhiḥ
svārthaḥ sarvātmanā jñeyo
yat parātmaika-darśanam

etāvān—this much; *eva*—indeed; *manujaiḥ*—by human beings; *yoga*—by the process of linking with the Supreme by *bhakti-yoga;* *naipuṇya*—endowed with expertise; *buddhibhiḥ*—who have intelligence; *sva-arthaḥ*—the ultimate goal of life; *sarva-ātmanā*—by all means; *jñeyaḥ*—to be known; *yat*—which; *para*—of the transcendental Lord; *ātma*—and of the soul; *eka*—of the oneness; *darśanam*—understanding.

TRANSLATION

Persons who try to reach the ultimate goal of life must expertly observe the Supreme Absolute Person and the living entity, who are one in quality in their relationship as part and whole. This is the ultimate understanding of life. There is no better truth than this.

TEXT 64

त्वमेतच्छ्रद्धया राजन्नप्रमत्तो वचो मम ।
ज्ञानविज्ञानसम्पन्नो धारयन्नाशु सिध्यसि ॥६४॥

tvam etac chraddhayā rājann
apramatto vaco mama
jñāna-vijñāna-sampanno
dhārayann āśu sidhyasi

tvam—you; *etat*—this; *śraddhayā*—with great faith and allegiance; *rājan*—O King; *apramattaḥ*—without being mad or deviated to any other conclusion; *vacaḥ*—instruction; *mama*—of Me; *jñāna-vijñāna-sampannaḥ*—being fully aware of knowledge and its practical application in life; *dhārayan*—accepting; *āśu*—very soon; *sidhyasi*—you will become the most perfect.

TRANSLATION

O King, if you accept this conclusion of Mine, being unattached to material enjoyment, adhering to Me with great faith and thus

becoming proficient and fully aware of knowledge and its practical application in life, you will achieve the highest perfection by attaining Me.

TEXT 65

श्रीशुक उवाच
आश्वास्य भगवानित्थं चित्रकेतुं जगद्गुरुः ।
पश्यतस्तस्य विश्वात्मा ततश्चान्तर्दधे हरिः ॥६५॥

śrī-śuka uvāca
āśvāsya bhagavān itthaṁ
citraketuṁ jagad-guruḥ
paśyatas tasya viśvātmā
tataś cāntardadhe hariḥ

śrī-śukaḥ uvāca—Śrī Śukadeva Gosvāmī said; *āśvāsya*—assuring; *bhagavān*—the Supreme Personality of Godhead; *ittham*—thus; *citraketum*—King Citraketu; *jagat-guruḥ*—the supreme spiritual master; *paśyataḥ*—while looking on; *tasya*—he; *viśva-ātmā*—the Supersoul of the whole universe; *tataḥ*—from there; *ca*—also; *antar-dadhe*—disappeared; *hariḥ*—Lord Hari.

TRANSLATION

Śrī Śukadeva Gosvāmī continued: After thus instructing Citraketu and assuring him of perfection in this way, the Supreme Personality of Godhead, who is the supreme spiritual master, the supreme soul, Saṅkarṣaṇa, disappeared from that place as Citraketu looked on.

Thus end the Bhaktivedanta purports of the Sixth Canto, Sixteenth Chapter, of the Śrīmad-Bhāgavatam, *entitled "King Citraketu Meets the Supreme Lord."*

CHAPTER SEVENTEEN

Mother Pārvatī Curses Citraketu

The Seventeenth Chapter is summarized as follows. This chapter describes Citraketu's receiving the body of an *asura*, or demon, because of joking with Lord Śiva.

After personally talking with the Supreme Personality of Godhead, King Citraketu enjoyed life in his airplane with the women of the Vidyādhara planet. Engaging in the congregational chanting of the glories of the Lord, he began flying his plane and traveling in outer space. One day while traveling like this, he wandered into the bowers of Sumeru Mountain, where he came upon Lord Śiva embracing Pārvatī, surrounded by an assembly of Siddhas, Cāraṇas and great sages. Seeing Lord Śiva in that situation, Citraketu laughed very loudly, but Pārvatī became very angry at him and cursed him. Because of this curse, Citraketu later appeared as the demon Vṛtrāsura.

Citraketu, however, was not at all afraid of Pārvatī's curse, and thus he spoke as follows: "Everyone in human society enjoys happiness and distress according to his past deeds and in this way travels in the material world. Therefore no one is responsible for his happiness and distress. One is controlled by the influence of material nature in the material world, yet one thinks himself the doer of everything. In this material world, which is made of the external energy of the Supreme Lord, one is sometimes cursed and sometimes favored, and thus he sometimes enjoys in the upper planetary systems and sometimes suffers in the lower planets, but all these situations are the same because they are within this material world. None of these positions has any factual existence, for all of them are temporary. The Supreme Personality of Godhead is the ultimate controller because the material world is created, maintained and annihilated under His control while He nonetheless remains neutral to these different transformations of the material world in time and space. The material, external energy of the Supreme Personality of Godhead is in charge of this material world. The Lord helps the world by creating situations for the living entities within it."

When Citraketu spoke in this way, all the members in the great assembly in which Lord Śiva and Pārvatī were present were astonished. Then Lord Śiva began speaking about the devotees of the Lord. A devotee is neutral in all conditions of life, whether in the heavenly planets or hellish planets, whether liberated from the material world or conditioned by it, and whether blessed with happiness or subjected to distress. These are all merely dualities created by the external energy. Being influenced by the external energy, the living entity accepts a gross and subtle material body, and in this illusory position he apparently suffers miseries, although everyone is part and parcel of the Supreme Lord. The so-called demigods consider themselves independent lords, and in this way they are misled from understanding that all living entities are part of the Supreme. This chapter concludes by glorifying the devotee and the Supreme Personality of Godhead.

TEXT 1

श्रीशुक उवाच

यतश्चान्तर्हितोऽनन्तस्तस्यै कृत्वा दिशे नमः।
विद्याधरश्चित्रकेतुश्चचार गगनेचरः ॥ १ ॥

śrī-śuka uvāca
yataś cāntarhito 'nantas
tasyai kṛtvā diśe namaḥ
vidyādharaś citraketuś
cacāra gagane caraḥ

śrī-śukaḥ uvāca—Śrī Śukadeva Gosvāmī said; *yataḥ*—in which (direction); *ca*—and; *antarhitaḥ*—disappeared; *anantaḥ*—the unlimited Supreme Personality of Godhead; *tasyai*—unto that; *kṛtvā*—after offering; *diśe*—direction; *namaḥ*—obeisances; *vidyādharaḥ*—the King of the Vidyādhara planet; *citraketuḥ*—Citraketu; *cacāra*—traveled; *gagane*—in outer space; *caraḥ*—moving.

TRANSLATION

Śrīla Śukadeva Gosvāmī said: After offering obeisances to the direction from which Ananta, the Supreme Personality of God-

head, had disappeared, Citraketu began traveling in outer space as the head of the Vidyādharas.

TEXTS 2–3

स लक्षं वर्षलक्षाणामव्याहतबलेन्द्रियः ।
स्तूयमानो महायोगी मुनिभिः सिद्धचारणैः ॥ २ ॥
कुलाचलेन्द्रद्रोणीषु नानासङ्कल्पसिद्धिषु ।
रेमे विद्याधरस्त्रीभिर्गापयन् हरिमीश्वरम् ॥ ३ ॥

sa lakṣaṁ varṣa-lakṣāṇām
avyāhata-balendriyaḥ
stūyamāno mahā-yogī
munibhiḥ siddha-cāraṇaiḥ

kulācalendra-droṇīṣu
nānā-saṅkalpa-siddhiṣu
reme vidyādhara-strībhir
gāpayan harim īśvaram

saḥ—he (Citraketu); *lakṣam*—one hundred thousand; *varṣa*—of years; *lakṣāṇām*—one hundred thousand; *avyāhata*—without hindrance; *bala-indriyaḥ*—whose strength and power of the senses; *stūyamānaḥ*—being praised; *mahā-yogī*—the great mystic *yogī; munibhiḥ*—by saintly persons; *siddha-cāraṇaiḥ*—by the Siddhas and Cāraṇas; *kulācalendra-droṇīṣu*—within the valleys of the great mountain known as Kulācalendra, or Sumeru; *nānā-saṅkalpa-siddhiṣu*—where one becomes perfect in all kinds of mystic power; *reme*—enjoyed; *vidyādhara-strībhiḥ*—with the women of the Vidyādhara planet; *gāpayan*—causing to praise; *harim*—the Supreme Personality of Godhead, Hari; *īśvaram*—the controller.

TRANSLATION

Being praised by great sages and saints and by the inhabitants of Siddhaloka and Cāraṇaloka, Citraketu, the most powerful mystic yogī, wandered about enjoying life for millions of years. With bodily strength and senses free from deterioration, he traveled

within the valleys of Sumeru Mountain, which is the place of perfection for various kinds of mystic power. In those valleys he enjoyed life with the women of Vidyādhara-loka by chanting the glories of the Supreme Lord, Hari.

PURPORT

It is to be understood that Mahārāja Citraketu, although surrounded by beautiful women from Vidyādhara-loka, did not forget to glorify the Lord by chanting the holy name of the Lord. It has been proved in many places that one who is not contaminated by any material condition, who is a pure devotee engaged in chanting the glories of the Lord, should be understood to be perfect.

TEXTS 4–5

एकदा स विमानेन विष्णुदत्तेन भास्वता ।
गिरिशं ददृशे गच्छन् परीतं सिद्धचारणैः ॥ ४ ॥
आलिङ्गयाङ्कीकृतां देवीं बाहुना मुनिसंसदि ।
उवाच देव्याः शृण्वन्त्या जहासोच्चैस्तदन्तिके ॥ ५ ॥

ekadā sa vimānena
viṣṇu-dattena bhāsvatā
giriśaṁ dadṛśe gacchan
parītaṁ siddha-cāraṇaiḥ

āliṅgyāṅkīkṛtāṁ devīṁ
bāhunā muni-saṁsadi
uvāca devyāḥ śṛṇvantyā
jahāsoccais tad-antike

ekadā—one time; *saḥ*—he (King Citraketu); *vimānena*—with his airplane; *viṣṇu-dattena*—given to him by Lord Viṣṇu; *bhāsvatā*—shining brilliantly; *giriśam*—Lord Śiva; *dadṛśe*—he saw; *gacchan*—going; *parītam*—surrounded; *siddha*—by the inhabitants of Siddhaloka; *cāraṇaiḥ*—and the inhabitants of Cāraṇaloka; *āliṅgya*—embracing; *aṅkīkṛtām*—sitting on his lap; *devīm*—his wife, Pārvatī; *bāhunā*—with his arm; *muni-saṁsadi*—in the presence of great saintly persons;

uvāca—he said; *devyāḥ*—while the goddess Pārvatī; *śṛṇvantyāḥ*—was hearing; *jahāsa*—he laughed; *uccaiḥ*—very loudly; *tad-antike*—in the vicinity.

TRANSLATION

One time while King Citraketu was traveling in outer space on a brilliantly effulgent airplane given to him by Lord Viṣṇu, he saw Lord Śiva, surrounded by Siddhas and Cāraṇas. Lord Śiva was sitting in an assembly of great saintly persons and embracing Pārvatī on his lap with his arm. Citraketu laughed loudly and spoke, within the hearing of Pārvatī.

PURPORT

Śrīla Viśvanātha Cakravartī Ṭhākura says in this connection,

bhaktiṁ bhūtiṁ harir dattvā
sva-vicchedānubhūtaye
devyāḥ śāpena vṛtratvaṁ
nītvā taṁ svāntike 'nayat

The purport is that the Supreme Personality of Godhead wanted to bring Citraketu to Vaikuṇṭhaloka as soon as possible. The Lord's plan was that Citraketu be cursed by Pārvatī to become Vṛtrāsura so that in his next life he could quickly return home, back to Godhead. There have been many instances in which a devotee acting as a demon has been brought to the kingdom of God by the mercy of the Lord. For Pārvatī to be embraced by Lord Śiva was natural in a relationship between husband and wife; this was nothing extraordinary for Citraketu to see. Nonetheless, Citraketu laughed loudly to see Lord Śiva in that situation, even though he should not have done so. Thus he was eventually cursed, and this curse was the cause of his returning home, back to Godhead.

TEXT 6

चित्रकेतुरुवाच
एष लोकगुरुः साक्षाद्धर्मं वक्ता शरीरिणाम् ।
आस्ते मुख्यः सभायां वै मिथुनीभूय भार्यया ॥ ६ ॥

citraketur uvāca
eṣa loka-guruḥ sākṣād
dharmaṁ vaktā śarīriṇām
āste mukhyaḥ sabhāyāṁ vai
mithunī-bhūya bhāryayā

citraketuḥ uvāca—King Citraketu said; *eṣaḥ*—this; *loka-guruḥ*—the spiritual master of the people who follow Vedic instructions; *sākṣāt*—directly; *dharmam*—of religion; *vaktā*—the speaker; *śarīriṇām*—for all living entities who have accepted material bodies; *āste*—sits; *mukhyaḥ*—the chief; *sabhāyām*—in an assembly; *vai*—indeed; *mithunī-bhūya*—embracing; *bhāryayā*—with his wife.

TRANSLATION

Citraketu said: Lord Śiva, the spiritual master of the general populace, is the best of all living entities who have accepted material bodies. He enunciates the system of religion. Yet how wonderful it is that he is embracing his wife, Pārvatī, in the midst of an assembly of great saintly persons.

TEXT 7

जटाधरस्तीव्रतपा ब्रह्मवादिसभापतिः ।
अङ्गीकृत्य स्त्रियं चास्ते गतह्रीः प्राकृतो यथा ॥ ७ ॥

jaṭā-dharas tīvra-tapā
brahmavādi-sabhā-patiḥ
aṅkīkṛtya striyaṁ cāste
gata-hrīḥ prākṛto yathā

jaṭā-dharaḥ—keeping matted locks of hair; *tīvra-tapāḥ*—highly elevated due to undergoing fierce austerities and penances; *brahma-vādi*—of strict followers of the Vedic principles; *sabhā-patiḥ*—the president of an assembly; *aṅkīkṛtya*—embracing; *striyam*—a woman; *ca*—and; *āste*—sits; *gata-hrīḥ*—without shame; *prākṛtaḥ*—a person conditioned by material nature; *yathā*—just as.

TRANSLATION

Lord Śiva, whose hair is matted on his head, has certainly undergone great austerities and penances. Indeed, he is the president in the assembly of strict followers of Vedic principles. Nonetheless, he is seated with his wife on his lap in the midst of saintly persons and is embracing her as if he were a shameless, ordinary human being.

PURPORT

Citraketu appreciated the exalted position of Lord Śiva, and therefore he remarked at how wonderful it was that Lord Śiva was acting like an ordinary human being. He appreciated Lord Śiva's position, but when he saw Lord Śiva sitting in the midst of saintly persons and acting like a shameless, ordinary man, he was astonished. Śrīla Viśvanātha Cakravartī Ṭhākura remarks that although Citraketu criticized Lord Śiva, he did not offend Lord Śiva like Dakṣa. Dakṣa considered Lord Śiva insignificant, but Citraketu expressed his wonder at Lord Śiva's being situated in that way.

TEXT 8

प्रायशः प्राकृताश्चापि स्त्रियं रहसि बिभ्रति ।
अयं महाव्रतधरो बिभर्ति सदसि स्त्रियम् ॥ ८ ॥

prāyaśaḥ prākṛtāś cāpi
striyaṁ rahasi bibhrati
ayaṁ mahā-vrata-dharo
bibharti sadasi striyam

prāyaśaḥ—generally; *prākṛtāḥ*—conditioned souls; *ca*—also; *api*—although; *striyam*—a woman; *rahasi*—in a solitary place; *bibhrati*—embrace; *ayam*—this (Lord Śiva); *mahā-vrata-dharaḥ*—the master of great vows and austerities; *bibharti*—enjoys; *sadasi*—in an assembly of great saintly persons; *striyam*—his wife.

TRANSLATION

Ordinary conditioned persons generally embrace their wives and enjoy their company in solitary places. How wonderful it is

that Lord Mahādeva, although a great master of austerity, is embracing his wife openly in the midst of an assembly of great saints.

PURPORT

The word *mahā-vrata-dharaḥ* indicates a *brahmacārī* who has never fallen down. Lord Śiva is counted among the best of *yogīs*, yet he embraced his wife in the midst of great saintly persons. Citraketu appreciated how great Lord Śiva was to be unaffected even in that situation. Therefore Citraketu was not an offender; he merely expressed his wonder.

TEXT 9

श्रीशुक उवाच
भगवानपि तच्छ्रुत्वा प्रहस्यागाधधीर्नृप ।
तूष्णीं बभूव सदसि सभ्याश्च तदनुव्रताः ॥ ९ ॥

śrī-śuka uvāca
bhagavān api tac chrutvā
prahasyāgādha-dhīr nṛpa
tūṣṇīṁ babhūva sadasi
sabhyāś ca tad-anuvratāḥ

śrī-śukaḥ uvāca—Śrī Śukadeva Gosvāmī said; *bhagavān*—Lord Śiva; *api*—also; *tat*—that; *śrutvā*—hearing; *prahasya*—smiling; *agādha-dhīḥ*—whose intelligence is unfathomed; *nṛpa*—O King; *tūṣṇīm*—silent; *babhūva*—remained; *sadasi*—in the assembly; *sabhyāḥ*—everyone assembled there; *ca*—and; *tat-anuvratāḥ*—followed Lord Śiva (remained silent).

TRANSLATION

Śrīla Śukadeva Gosvāmī continued: My dear King, after hearing Citraketu's statement, Lord Śiva, the most powerful personality, whose knowledge is fathomless, simply smiled and remained silent, and all the members of the assembly followed the lord by not saying anything.

PURPORT

Citraketu's purpose in criticizing Lord Śiva is somewhat mysterious and cannot be understood by a common man. Śrīla Viśvanātha

Cakravartī Ṭhākura, however, has made the following observations. Lord Śiva, being the most exalted Vaiṣṇava and one of the most powerful demigods, is able to do anything he desires. Although he was externally exhibiting the behavior of a common man and not following etiquette, such actions cannot diminish his exalted position. The difficulty is that a common man, seeing Lord Śiva's behavior, might follow his example. As stated in *Bhagavad-gītā* (3.21):

yad yad ācarati śreṣṭhas
tat tad evetaro janaḥ
sa yat pramāṇaṁ kurute
lokas tad anuvartate

"Whatever action a great man performs, common men follow. And whatever standards he sets by exemplary acts, all the world pursues." A common man might also criticize Lord Śiva, like Dakṣa, who suffered the consequences for his criticism. King Citraketu desired that Lord Śiva cease this external behavior so that others might be saved from criticizing him and thus becoming offenders. If one thinks that Viṣṇu, the Supreme Personality of Godhead, is the only perfect personality whereas the demigods, even such demigods as Lord Śiva, are inclined to improper social affairs, he is an offender. Considering all this, King Citraketu was somewhat harsh in his behavior with Lord Śiva.

Lord Śiva, who is always deep in knowledge, could understand Citraketu's purpose, and therefore he was not at all angry; rather, he simply smiled and remained silent. The members of the assembly surrounding Lord Śiva could also understand Citraketu's purpose. Consequently, following the behavior of Lord Śiva, they did not protest; instead, following their master, they remained silent. If the members of the assembly thought that Citraketu had blasphemed Lord Śiva, they would certainly have left at once, blocking their ears with their hands.

TEXT 10

इत्यतद्वीर्यविदुषि ब्रुवाणे बह्वशोभनम् ।
रुषाह देवी धृष्टाय निर्जितात्माभिमानिने ॥१०॥

ity atad-vīrya-viduṣi
bruvāṇe bahv-aśobhanam
ruṣāha devī dhṛṣṭāya
nirjitātmābhimānine

iti—thus; *a-tat-vīrya-viduṣi*—when Citraketu, who did not know the prowess of Lord Śiva; *bruvāṇe*—spoke; *bahu-aśobhanam*—that which is not up to the standard of etiquette (the criticism of the exalted Lord Śiva); *ruṣā*—with anger; *āha*—said; *devī*—the goddess Pārvatī; *dhṛṣṭāya*—unto Citraketu, who was quite shameless; *nirjita-ātma*—as one who has controlled his senses; *abhimānine*—thinking of himself.

TRANSLATION

Not knowing the prowess of Lord Śiva and Pārvatī, Citraketu strongly criticized them. His statements were not at all pleasing, and therefore the goddess Pārvatī, being very angry, spoke as follows to Citraketu, who thought himself better than Lord Śiva in controlling the senses.

PURPORT

Although Citraketu never meant to insult Lord Śiva, he should not have criticized the lord, even though the lord was transgressing social customs. It is said, *tejīyasāṁ na doṣāya:* one who is very powerful should be understood to be faultless. For example, one should not find faults with the sun, although it evaporates urine from the street. The most powerful cannot be criticized by an ordinary man, or even by a great personality. Citraketu should have known that Lord Śiva, although sitting in that way, was not to be criticized. The difficulty was that Citraketu, having become a great devotee of Lord Viṣṇu, Saṅkarṣaṇa, was somewhat proud at having achieved Lord Saṅkarṣaṇa's favor and therefore thought that he could now criticize anyone, even Lord Śiva. This kind of pride in a devotee is never tolerated. A Vaiṣṇava should always remain very humble and meek and offer respect to others.

tṛṇād api sunīcena
taror api sahiṣṇunā

amāninā mānadena
kīrtanīyaḥ sadā hariḥ

"One should chant the holy name of the Lord in a humble state of mind, thinking oneself lower than the straw in the street; one should be more tolerant than a tree, devoid of all sense of false prestige and ready to offer all respect to others. In such a state of mind one can chant the holy name of the Lord constantly." A Vaiṣṇava should not try to minimize anyone else's position. It is better to remain humble and meek and chant the Hare Kṛṣṇa *mantra.* The word *nirjitātmābhimānine* indicates that Citraketu thought himself a better controller of the senses than Lord Śiva, although actually he was not. Because of all these considerations, mother Pārvatī was somewhat angry at Citraketu.

TEXT 11

श्रीपार्वत्युवाच
अयं किमधुना लोके शास्ता दण्डधरः प्रभुः ।
अस्मद्विधानां दुष्टानां निर्लज्जानां च विप्रकृत् ॥११॥

śrī-pārvaty uvāca
ayaṁ kim adhunā loke
śāstā daṇḍa-dharaḥ prabhuḥ
asmad-vidhānāṁ duṣṭānāṁ
nirlajjānāṁ ca viprakṛt

śrī-pārvatī uvāca—the goddess Pārvatī said; *ayam*—this; *kim*—whether; *adhunā*—now; *loke*—in the world; *śāstā*—the supreme controller; *daṇḍa-dharaḥ*—the carrier of the rod of punishment; *prabhuḥ*—the master; *asmat-vidhānām*—of persons like us; *duṣṭānām*—criminals; *nirlajjānām*—who have no shame; *ca*—and; *viprakṛt*—the restrainer.

TRANSLATION

The goddess Pārvatī said: Alas, has this upstart now received a post from which to punish shameless persons like us? Has he been

appointed ruler, carrier of the rod of punishment? Is he now the only master of everything?

TEXT 12

न वेद धर्मं किल पद्मयोनि-
र्न ब्रह्मपुत्रा भृगुनारदाद्याः ।
न वै कुमारः कपिलो मनुश्च
ये नो निषेधन्त्यतिवर्तिनं हरम् ॥१२॥

na veda dharmaṁ kila padmayonir
na brahma-putrā bhṛgu-nāradādyāḥ
na vai kumāraḥ kapilo manuś ca
ye no niṣedhanty ati-vartinaṁ haram

na—not; *veda*—knows; *dharmam*—the religious principles; *kila*—indeed; *padma-yoniḥ*—Lord Brahmā; *na*—nor; *brahma-putrāḥ*—the sons of Lord Brahmā; *bhṛgu*—Bhṛgu; *nārada*—Nārada; *ādyāḥ*—and so on; *na*—nor; *vai*—indeed; *kumāraḥ*—the four Kumāras (Sanaka, Sanat-kumāra, Sananda and Sanātana); *kapilaḥ*—Lord Kapila; *manuḥ*—Manu himself; *ca*—and; *ye*—who; *no*—not; *niṣedhanti*—order to stop; *ati-vartinam*—who is beyond laws and orders; *haram*—Lord Śiva.

TRANSLATION

Alas, Lord Brahmā, who has taken his birth from the lotus flower, does not know the principles of religion, nor do the great saints like Bhṛgu and Nārada, nor the four Kumāras, headed by Sanat-kumāra. Manu and Kapila have also forgotten the religious principles. I suppose it to be because of this that they have not tried to stop Lord Śiva from behaving improperly.

TEXT 13

एषामनुध्येयपदाब्जयुग्मं
जगद्गुरुं मङ्गलमङ्गलं स्वयम् ।

यः क्षत्रबन्धुः परिभूय सूरीन्
प्रशास्ति धृष्टस्तदयं हि दण्ड्यः ॥१३॥

eṣām anudhyeya-padābja-yugmaṁ
jagad-guruṁ maṅgala-maṅgalaṁ svayam
yaḥ kṣatra-bandhuḥ paribhūya sūrīn
praśāsti dhṛṣṭas tad ayaṁ hi daṇḍyaḥ

eṣām—of all these (exalted personalities); *anudhyeya*—to be constantly meditated upon; *pada-abja-yugmam*—whose two lotus feet; *jagat-gurum*—the spiritual master of the whole world; *maṅgala-maṅgalam*—personification of the topmost religious principle; *svayam*—himself; *yaḥ*—he who; *kṣatra-bandhuḥ*—the lowest of the *kṣatriyas; paribhūya*—overriding; *sūrīn*—the demigods (like Brahmā and the others); *praśāsti*—chastises; *dhṛṣṭaḥ*—impudent; *tat*—therefore; *ayam*—this person; *hi*—indeed; *daṇḍyaḥ*—to be punished.

TRANSLATION

This Citraketu is the lowest of kṣatriyas, for he has impudently overridden Brahmā and the other demigods by insulting Lord Śiva, upon whose lotus feet they always meditate. Lord Śiva is personified religion and the spiritual master of the entire world, and therefore Citraketu must be punished.

PURPORT

All the members of the assembly were exalted *brāhmaṇas* and self-realized souls, but they did not say anything about the conduct of Lord Śiva, who was embracing the goddess Pārvatī on his lap. Citraketu nonetheless criticized Lord Śiva, and therefore the opinion of Pārvatī was that he should be punished.

TEXT 14

नायमर्हति वैकुण्ठपादमूलोपसर्पणम् ।
सम्भावितमतिः स्तब्धः साधुभिः पर्युपासितम् ॥१४॥

nāyam arhati vaikuṇṭha-
pāda-mūlopasarpaṇam
sambhāvita-matiḥ stabdhaḥ
sādhubhiḥ paryupāsitam

na—not; *ayam*—this person; *arhati*—deserves; *vaikuṇṭha-pāda-mūla-upasarpaṇam*—the approaching of the shelter of Lord Viṣṇu's lotus feet; *sambhāvita-matiḥ*—considering himself highly esteemed; *stabdhaḥ*—impudent; *sādhubhiḥ*—by great saintly persons; *paryupāsitam*—worshiped.

TRANSLATION

This person is puffed up because of his achievements, thinking, "I am the best." He does not deserve to approach the shelter of Lord Viṣṇu's lotus feet, which are worshiped by all saintly persons, for he is impudent, thinking himself greatly important.

PURPORT

If a devotee thinks that he is very much advanced in devotional service, he is considered puffed up and unfit to sit beneath the shelter of the Lord's lotus feet. Again, this instruction by Lord Caitanya is applicable:

tṛṇād api sunīcena
taror api sahiṣṇunā
amāninā mānadena
kīrtanīyaḥ sadā hariḥ

"One should chant the holy name of the Lord in a humble state of mind, thinking oneself lower than the straw in the street; one should be more tolerant than a tree, devoid of all sense of false prestige and ready to offer all respect to others. In such a state of mind one can chant the holy name of the Lord constantly." Unless one is humble and meek, one cannot qualify to sit at the lotus feet of the Lord.

TEXT 15

अतः पापीयसीं योनिमासुरीं याहि दुर्मते ।
यथेह भूयो महतां न कर्ता पुत्र किल्बिषम् ॥१५॥

ataḥ pāpīyasīṁ yonim
āsurīṁ yāhi durmate
yatheha bhūyo mahatāṁ
na kartā putra kilbiṣam

ataḥ—therefore; *pāpīyasīm*—most sinful; *yonim*—to the species of life; *āsurīm*—demoniac; *yāhi*—go; *durmate*—O impudent one; *yathā*—so that; *iha*—in this world; *bhūyaḥ*—again; *mahatām*—to great personalities; *na*—not; *kartā*—will commit; *putra*—my dear son; *kilbiṣam*—any offense.

TRANSLATION

O impudent one, my dear son, now take birth in a low, sinful family of demons so that you will not commit such an offense again toward exalted, saintly persons in this world.

PURPORT

One should be very careful not to commit offenses at the lotus feet of Vaiṣṇavas, of whom Lord Śiva is the best. While instructing Śrīla Rūpa Gosvāmī, Śrī Caitanya Mahāprabhu described an offense at the lotus feet of a Vaiṣṇava as *hātī mātā,* a mad elephant. When a mad elephant enters a nice garden, it spoils the entire garden. Similarly, if one becomes like a mad elephant and commits offenses at the lotus feet of a Vaiṣṇava, his entire spiritual career is halted. One should therefore be very careful not to commit offenses at the lotus feet of a Vaiṣṇava.

Mother Pārvatī was justified in punishing Citraketu, for Citraketu impudently criticized the supreme father, Mahādeva, who is the father of the living entities conditioned within this material world. The goddess Durgā is called mother, and Lord Śiva is called father. A pure Vaiṣṇava should be very careful to engage in his specific duty without criticizing others. This is the safest position. Otherwise, if one tends to criticize others, he may commit the great offense of criticizing a Vaiṣṇava.

Because Citraketu was undoubtedly a Vaiṣṇava, he might have been surprised that Pārvatī had cursed him. Therefore the goddess Pārvatī addressed him as *putra,* or son. Everyone is the son of mother Durgā, but she is not an ordinary mother. As soon as there is a small discrepancy in a demon's behavior, mother Durgā immediately punishes the demon so that he may come to his senses. This is explained by Lord Kṛṣṇa in *Bhagavad-gītā* (7.14):

daivī hy eṣā guṇamayī
mama māyā duratyayā
mām eva ye prapadyante
māyām etāṁ taranti te

"This divine energy of Mine, consisting of the three modes of material nature, is difficult to overcome. But those who have surrendered unto Me can easily cross beyond it." To surrender to Kṛṣṇa means to surrender to His devotees also, for no one can be a proper servant of Kṛṣṇa unless he is a proper servant of a devotee. *Chāḍiyā vaiṣṇava-sevā nistāra pāyeche kebā:* without serving a servant of Kṛṣṇa, one cannot be elevated to being a servant of Kṛṣṇa Himself. Therefore mother Pārvatī spoke to Citraketu exactly like a mother who says to her naughty child, "My dear child, I am punishing you so that you won't do anything like this again." This tendency of a mother to punish her child is found even in mother Yaśodā, who became the mother of the Supreme Personality of Godhead. Mother Yaśodā punished Kṛṣṇa by binding Him and showing Him a stick. Thus it is the duty of a mother to chastise her beloved son, even in the case of the Supreme Lord. It is to be understood that mother Durgā was justified in punishing Citraketu. This punishment was a boon to Citraketu because after taking birth as the demon Vṛtrāsura, he was promoted directly to Vaikuṇṭha.

TEXT 16

श्रीशुक उवाच
एवं शप्तश्चित्रकेतुर्विमानादवरुह्य सः ।
प्रसादयामास सतीं मूर्ध्ना नम्रेण भारत ॥१६॥

śrī-śuka uvāca
evaṁ śaptaś citraketur
vimānād avaruhya saḥ
prasādayām āsa satīṁ
mūrdhnā namreṇa bhārata

śrī-śukaḥ uvāca—Śrī Śukadeva Gosvāmī said; *evam*—thus; *śaptaḥ*—cursed; *citraketuḥ*—King Citraketu; *vimānāt*—from his airplane; *avaruhya*—coming down; *saḥ*—he; *prasādayām āsa*—completely pleased; *satīm*—Pārvatī; *mūrdhnā*—by his head; *namreṇa*—bent low; *bhārata*—O King Parīkṣit.

TRANSLATION

Śrī Śukadeva Gosvāmī continued: My dear King Parīkṣit, when Citraketu was cursed by Pārvatī, he descended from his airplane, bowed before her with great humility and pleased her completely.

TEXT 17

चित्रकेतुरुवाच
प्रतिगृह्णामि ते शापमात्मनोऽञ्जलिनाम्बिके ।
देवैर्मर्त्याय यत्प्रोक्तं पूर्वदिष्टं हि तस्य तत् ॥१७॥

citraketur uvāca
pratigṛhṇāmi te śāpam
ātmano 'ñjalināmbike
devair martyāya yat proktaṁ
pūrva-diṣṭaṁ hi tasya tat

citraketuḥ uvāca—King Citraketu said; *pratigṛhṇāmi*—I accept; *te*—your; *śāpam*—curse; *ātmanaḥ*—my own; *añjalinā*—with folded hands; *ambike*—O mother; *devaiḥ*—by the demigods; *martyāya*—unto a mortal; *yat*—which; *proktam*—prescribed; *pūrva-diṣṭam*—fixed previously according to one's past deeds; *hi*—indeed; *tasya*—of him; *tat*—that.

TRANSLATION

Citraketu said: My dear mother, with my own hands folded together I accept the curse upon me. I do not mind the curse, for happiness and distress are given by the demigods as a result of one's past deeds.

PURPORT

Since Citraketu was a devotee of the Lord, he was not at all disturbed by the curse of mother Pārvatī. He knew very well that one suffers or enjoys the results of one's past deeds as ordained by *daiva-netra*—superior authority, or the agents of the Supreme Personality of Godhead. He knew that he had not committed any offense at the lotus feet of Lord Śiva or the goddess Pārvatī, yet he had been punished, and this means that the punishment had been ordained. Thus the King did not mind it. A devotee is naturally so humble and meek that he accepts any condition of life as a blessing from the Lord. *Tat te 'nukampāṁ susamīkṣamāṇaḥ* (*Bhāg.* 10.14.8). A devotee always accepts punishment from anyone as the mercy of the Lord. If one lives in this conception of life, he sees whatever reverses occur to be due to his past misdeeds, and therefore he never accuses anyone. On the contrary, he becomes increasingly attached to the Supreme Personality of Godhead because of his being purified by his suffering. Suffering, therefore, is also a process of purification.

Śrīla Viśvanātha Cakravartī Ṭhākura says in this connection that one who has developed Kṛṣṇa consciousness and who exists in love with Kṛṣṇa is no longer subject to suffering and happiness under the laws of *karma*. Indeed, he is beyond *karma*. The *Brahma-saṁhitā* says, *karmāṇi nirdahati kintu ca bhakti-bhājām:* a devotee is free from the reactions of his *karma* because he has taken to devotional service. This same principle is confirmed in *Bhagavad-gītā* (14.26). *Sa guṇān samatītyaitān brahma-bhūyāya kalpate:* one who is engaged in devotional service has already been freed from the reactions of his material *karma*, and thus he immediately becomes *brahma-bhūta*, or transcendental. This is also expressed in *Śrīmad-Bhāgavatam* (1.2.21). *Kṣīyante cāsya karmāṇi:* before attaining the stage of love, one becomes free from all the results of *karma*.

The Lord is very kind and affectionate toward His devotees, and therefore a devotee, in any condition, is not subjected to the results of *karma*. A devotee never aspires for the heavenly planets. The heavenly planets, liberation and hell are nondifferent for a devotee, for he does not discriminate between different positions in the material world. A devotee is always eager to return home, back to Godhead, and remain there as the Lord's associate. This ambition becomes increasingly fervent in his heart, and therefore he does not care about material changes in his life. Śrīla Viśvanātha Cakravartī Ṭhākura comments that Mahārāja Citraketu's being cursed by Pārvatī should be considered the mercy of the Lord. The Lord wanted Citraketu to return to Godhead as soon as possible, and therefore he terminated all the reactions of his past deeds. Acting through the heart of Pārvatī, the Lord, who is situated in everyone's heart, cursed Citraketu in order to end all his material reactions. Thus Citraketu became Vṛtrāsura in his next life and returned home, back to Godhead.

TEXT 18

संसारचक्र एतस्मिञ्जन्तुरज्ञानमोहितः ।
भ्राम्यन् सुखं च दुःखं च भुङ्क्ते सर्वत्र सर्वदा ॥१८॥

saṁsāra-cakra etasmiñ
jantur ajñāna-mohitaḥ
bhrāmyan sukhaṁ ca duḥkhaṁ ca
bhuṅkte sarvatra sarvadā

saṁsāra-cakre—in the wheel of material existence; *etasmin*—this; *jantuḥ*—the living entity; *ajñāna-mohitaḥ*—being bewildered by ignorance; *bhrāmyan*—wandering; *sukham*—happiness; *ca*—and; *duḥkham*—distress; *ca*—also; *bhuṅkte*—he undergoes; *sarvatra*—everywhere; *sarvadā*—always.

TRANSLATION

Deluded by ignorance, the living entity wanders in the forest of this material world, enjoying the happiness and distress resulting from his past deeds, everywhere and at all times. [Therefore, my dear mother, neither you nor I am to be blamed for this incident.]

PURPORT

As confirmed in *Bhagavad-gītā* (3.27):

prakṛteḥ kriyamāṇāni
guṇaiḥ karmāṇi sarvaśaḥ
ahaṅkāra-vimūḍhātmā
kartāham iti manyate

"The bewildered soul, under the influence of the three modes of material nature, thinks himself the doer of activities that are in actuality carried out by nature." Actually a conditioned soul is completely under the control of material nature. Wandering here and there—always and everywhere—he is subjected to the results of his past deeds. This is carried out by the laws of nature, but one foolishly thinks himself the doer, which in fact he is not. To get free from the *karma-cakra*, the wheel of the results of one's *karma*, one should take to *bhakti-mārga*—devotional service, or Kṛṣṇa consciousness. That is the only remedy. *Sarva-dharmān parityajya mām ekaṁ śaraṇaṁ vraja.*

TEXT 19

नैवात्मा न परश्चापि कर्ता स्यात् सुखदुःखयोः ।
कर्तारं मन्यतेऽत्राज्ञ आत्मानं परमेव च ॥१९॥

naivātmā na paraś cāpi
kartā syāt sukha-duḥkhayoḥ
kartāraṁ manyate 'trājña
ātmānaṁ param eva ca

na—not; *eva*—indeed; *ātmā*—the spirit soul; *na*—nor; *paraḥ*—another (friend or enemy); *ca*—also; *api*—indeed; *kartā*—the doer; *syāt*—can be; *sukha-duḥkhayoḥ*—of happiness and distress; *kartāram*—the doer; *manyate*—considers; *atra*—in this connection; *ajñaḥ*—a person not aware of the real fact; *ātmānam*—himself; *param*—another; *eva*—indeed; *ca*—also.

TRANSLATION

In this material world, neither the living entity himself nor others [friends and enemies] are the cause of material happiness and distress. But because of gross ignorance, the living entity thinks that he and others are the cause.

PURPORT

In this verse the word *ajña* is very significant. In the material world, all living entities are *ajña*, ignorant, in different degrees. This ignorance continues very strongly in the mode of ignorance presented by material nature. One must therefore promote himself to the stage of goodness through his character and behavior and then gradually come to the transcendental platform, or *adhokṣaja* platform, in which he realizes both his position and the position of others. Everything is done under the superintendence of the Supreme Personality of Godhead. The process by which the results of action are ordained is called *niyatam*, always working.

TEXT 20

गुणप्रवाह एतस्मिन् कः शापः को न्वनुग्रहः ।
कः स्वर्गो नरकः को वा किं सुखं दुःखमेव वा ॥२०॥

guṇa-pravāha etasmin
kaḥ śāpaḥ ko nv anugrahaḥ
kaḥ svargo narakaḥ ko vā
kiṁ sukhaṁ duḥkham eva vā

guṇa-pravāhe—in the current of the modes of material nature; *etasmin*—this; *kaḥ*—what; *śāpaḥ*—a curse; *kaḥ*—what; *nu*—indeed; *anugrahaḥ*—a favor; *kaḥ*—what; *svargaḥ*—elevation to heavenly planets; *narakaḥ*—hell; *kaḥ*—what; *vā*—or; *kim*—what; *sukham*—happiness; *duḥkham*—distress; *eva*—indeed; *vā*—or.

TRANSLATION

This material world resembles the waves of a constantly flowing river. Therefore, what is a curse and what is a favor? What are the heavenly planets, and what are the hellish planets? What is actually happiness, and what is actually distress? Because the waves flow constantly, none of them has an eternal effect.

PURPORT

Śrīla Bhaktivinoda Ṭhākura sings, (*miche*) *māyāra vaśe, yāccha bhese', khāccha hābuḍubu, bhāi:* "My dear living entities within this material world, why are you being carried away by the waves of the modes of material nature?" (*Jīva*) *kṛṣṇa-dāsa, ei viśvāsa, karle ta' āra duḥkha nāi:* "If the living entity tries to understand that he is an eternal servant of Kṛṣṇa, there will no longer be misery for him." Kṛṣṇa wants us to give up all other engagements and surrender unto Him. If we do so, where will the cause and effect of this material world be? There is nothing like cause and effect for the surrendered soul. Śrīla Viśvanātha Cakravartī Ṭhākura says in this regard that being put into this material world is like being thrown into a mine of salt. If one falls into a mine of salt, he tastes only salt wherever he goes. Similarly, this material world is full of miseries. The so-called temporary happiness of the world is also misery, but in ignorance we cannot understand this. That is the actual position. When one comes to his senses—when he becomes Kṛṣṇa conscious—he is no longer concerned with the various conditions of this material world. He is not concerned with happiness or distress, curses or favors, or heavenly or hellish planets. He sees no distinction between them.

TEXT 21

एकः सृजति भूतानि भगवानात्ममायया ।
एषां बन्धं च मोक्षं च सुखं दुःखं च निष्कलः ॥२१॥

ekaḥ sṛjati bhūtāni
bhagavān ātma-māyayā
eṣāṁ bandhaṁ ca mokṣaṁ ca
sukhaṁ duḥkhaṁ ca niṣkalaḥ

ekaḥ—one; *sṛjati*—creates; *bhūtāni*—different varieties of living entities; *bhagavān*—the Supreme Personality of Godhead; *ātma-māyayā*—by His personal potencies; *eṣām*—of all the conditioned souls; *bandham*—the conditional life; *ca*—and; *mokṣam*—the liberated life; *ca*—also; *sukham*—happiness; *duḥkham*—distresses; *ca*—and; *niṣkalaḥ*—not affected by the material qualities.

TRANSLATION

The Supreme Personality of Godhead is one. Unaffected by the conditions of the material world, He creates all the conditioned souls by His own personal potency. Because of being contaminated by the material energy, the living entity is put into ignorance and

thus into different conditions of bondage. Sometimes, by knowledge, the living entity is given liberation. In sattva-guṇa and rajo-guṇa, he is subjected to happiness and distress.

PURPORT

The question may be raised why the living entities are situated in different conditions and who has arranged this. The answer is that it has been done by the Supreme Personality of Godhead, without anyone's help. The Lord has His own energies (*parāsya śaktir vividhaiva śrūyate*), and one of them, namely the external energy, creates the material world and the varieties of happiness and distress for the conditioned souls under the supervision of the Lord. The material world consists of three modes of material nature—*sattva-guṇa, rajo-guṇa* and *tamo-guṇa.* By *sattva-guṇa* the Lord maintains the material world, by *rajo-guṇa* He creates it, and by *tamo-guṇa* He annihilates it. After the varieties of living entities are created, they are subject to happiness and distress according to their association. When they are in *sattva-guṇa*, the mode of goodness, they feel happiness, when in *rajo-guṇa* they are distressed, and when in *tamo-guṇa* they have no sense of what to do or what is right and wrong.

TEXT 22

न तस्य कश्चिद्दयितः प्रतीपो
न ज्ञातिबन्धुर्न परो न च स्वः ।
समस्य सर्वत्र निरञ्जनस्य
सुखे न रागः कुत एव रोषः ॥२२॥

na tasya kaścid dayitaḥ pratīpo
na jñāti-bandhur na paro na ca svaḥ
samasya sarvatra nirañjanasya
sukhe na rāgaḥ kuta eva roṣaḥ

na—not; *tasya*—of Him (the Supreme Lord); *kaścit*—anyone; *dayitaḥ*—dear; *pratīpaḥ*—not dear; *na*—nor; *jñāti*—kinsman; *bandhuḥ*—friend; *na*—nor; *paraḥ*—other; *na*—nor; *ca*—also; *svaḥ*—own; *samasya*—who is equal; *sarvatra*—everywhere; *nirañjanasya*—

without being affected by material nature; *sukhe*—in happiness; *na*—not; *rāgaḥ*—attachment; *kutaḥ*—from where; *eva*—indeed; *roṣaḥ*—anger.

TRANSLATION

The Supreme Personality of Godhead is equally disposed toward all living entities. Therefore no one is very dear to Him, and no one is a great enemy for Him; no one is His friend, and no one is His relative. Being unattached to the material world, He has no affection for so-called happiness or hatred for so-called distress. The two terms happiness and distress are relative. Since the Lord is always happy, for Him there is no question of distress.

TEXT 23

तथापि तच्छक्तिविसर्ग एषां
सुखाय दुःखाय हिताहिताय ।
बन्धाय मोक्षाय च मृत्युजन्मनोः
शरीरिणां संसृतयेऽवकल्पते ॥२३॥

tathāpi tac-chakti-visarga eṣāṁ
sukhāya duḥkhāya hitāhitāya
bandhāya mokṣāya ca mṛtyu-janmanoḥ
śarīriṇāṁ saṁsṛtaye 'vakalpate

tathāpi—still; *tat-śakti*—of the Lord's energy; *visargaḥ*—the creation; *eṣām*—of these (conditioned souls); *sukhāya*—for the happiness; *duḥkhāya*—for the distress; *hita-ahitāya*—for the profit and loss; *bandhāya*—for the bondage; *mokṣāya*—for the liberation; *ca*—also; *mṛtyu*—of death; *janmanoḥ*—and birth; *śarīriṇām*—of all those who accept material bodies; *saṁsṛtaye*—for the repetition; *avakalpate*—acts.

TRANSLATION

Although the Supreme Lord is unattached to our happiness and distress according to karma, and although no one is His enemy or favorite, He creates pious and impious activities through the

agency of His material potency. Thus for the continuation of the materialistic way of life He creates happiness and distress, good fortune and bad, bondage and liberation, birth and death.

PURPORT

Although the Supreme Personality of Godhead is the ultimate doer of everything, in His original transcendental existence He is not responsible for the happiness and distress, or bondage and liberation, of the conditioned souls. These are due to the results of the fruitive activities of the living entities within this material world. By the order of a judge, one person is released from jail, and another is imprisoned, but the judge is not responsible, for the distress and happiness of these different people is due to their own activities. Although the government is ultimately the supreme authority, the justice is administered by the departments of the government, and the government is not responsible for the individual judgments. Therefore the government is equal to all the citizens. Similarly, the Supreme Lord is neutral to everyone, but for the maintenance of law and order His supreme government has various departments, which control the activities of the living entities. Another example given in this regard is that lilies open or close because of the sunshine, and thus the bumblebees enjoy or suffer, but the sunshine and the sun globe are not responsible for the happiness and distress of the bumblebees.

TEXT 24

अथ प्रसादये न त्वां शापमोक्षाय भामिनि ।
यन्मन्यसे ह्यसाधूक्तं मम तत्क्षम्यतां सति ॥२४॥

atha prasādaye na tvāṁ
śāpa-mokṣāya bhāmini
yan manyase hy asādhūktaṁ
mama tat kṣamyatāṁ sati

atha—therefore; *prasādaye*—I am trying to please; *na*—not; *tvām*—you; *śāpa-mokṣāya*—for being released from your curse; *bhāmini*—O most angry one; *yat*—which; *manyase*—you consider; *hi*—indeed;

asādhu-uktam—improper speech; *mama*—my; *tat*—that; *kṣamyatām*—let it be excused; *sati*—O most chaste one.

TRANSLATION

O mother, you are now unnecessarily angry, but since all my happiness and distress are destined by my past activities, I do not plead to be excused or relieved from your curse. Although what I have said is not wrong, please let whatever you think is wrong be pardoned.

PURPORT

Being fully aware of how the results of one's *karma* accrue by the laws of nature, Citraketu did not want to be released from Pārvatī's curse. Nonetheless, he wanted to satisfy her because although his verdict was natural, she was displeased with him. As a matter of course, Mahārāja Citraketu begged pardon from Pārvatī.

TEXT 25

श्रीशुक उवाच
इति प्रसाद्य गिरिशौ चित्रकेतुररिन्दम ।
जगाम स्वविमानेन पश्यतोः स्मयतोस्तयोः ॥२५॥

śrī-śuka uvāca
iti prasādya giriśau
citraketur arindama
jagāma sva-vimānena
paśyatoḥ smayatos tayoḥ

śrī-śukaḥ uvāca—Śrī Śukadeva Gosvāmī said; *iti*—thus; *prasādya*—after satisfying; *giriśau*—Lord Śiva and his wife, Pārvatī; *citraketuḥ*—King Citraketu; *arim-dama*—O King Parīkṣit, who are always able to subdue the enemy; *jagāma*—went away; *sva-vimānena*—by his own airplane; *paśyatoḥ*—were watching; *smayatoḥ*—were smiling; *tayoḥ*—while Lord Śiva and Pārvatī.

TRANSLATION

Śrī Śukadeva Gosvāmī continued: O King Parīkṣit, subduer of the enemy, after Citraketu satisfied Lord Śiva and his wife, Pārvatī, he boarded his airplane and left as they looked on. When Lord Śiva and Pārvatī saw that Citraketu, although informed of the curse, was unafraid, they smiled, being fully astonished by his behavior.

TEXT 26

ततस्तु भगवान् रुद्रो रुद्राणीमिदमब्रवीत् ।
देवर्षिदैत्यसिद्धानां पार्षदानां च शृण्वताम् ॥२६॥

tatas tu bhagavān rudro
rudrāṇīm idam abravīt
devarṣi-daitya-siddhānāṁ
pārṣadānāṁ ca śṛṇvatām

tataḥ—thereafter; *tu*—then; *bhagavān*—the most powerful; *rudraḥ*—Lord Śiva; *rudrāṇīm*—unto his wife, Pārvatī; *idam*—this; *abravīt*—said; *devarṣi*—while the great sage Nārada; *daitya*—the demons; *siddhānām*—and the inhabitants of Siddhaloka, who are expert in yogic power; *pārṣadānām*—his personal associates; *ca*—also; *śṛṇvatām*—were listening.

TRANSLATION

Thereafter, in the presence of the great sage Nārada, the demons, the inhabitants of Siddhaloka, and his personal associates, Lord Śiva, who is most powerful, spoke to his wife, Pārvatī, while they all listened.

TEXT 27

श्रीरुद्र उवाच
दृष्टवत्यसि सुश्रोणि हरेरद्भुतकर्मणः ।
माहात्म्यं भृत्यभृत्यानां निःस्पृहाणां महात्मनाम् ॥२७॥

śrī-rudra uvāca
dṛṣṭavaty asi suśroṇi
harer adbhuta-karmaṇaḥ
māhātmyaṁ bhṛtya-bhṛtyānāṁ
niḥspṛhāṇāṁ mahātmanām

śrī-rudraḥ uvāca—Lord Śiva said; *dṛṣṭavatī asi*—have you seen; *suśroṇi*—O beautiful Pārvatī; *hareḥ*—of the Supreme Personality of Godhead; *adbhuta-karmaṇaḥ*—whose acts are wonderful; *māhātmyam*—the greatness; *bhṛtya-bhṛtyānām*—of the servants of the servants; *niḥspṛhāṇām*—who are without ambitions for sense gratification; *mahātmanām*—great souls.

TRANSLATION

Lord Śiva said: My dear beautiful Pārvatī, have you seen the greatness of the Vaiṣṇavas? Being servants of the servants of the Supreme Personality of Godhead, Hari, they are great souls and are not interested in any kind of material happiness.

PURPORT

Lord Śiva, the husband of Pārvatī, told his wife, "My dear Pārvatī, you are very beautiful in your bodily features. Certainly you are glorious. But I do not think that you can compete with the beauty and glory of devotees who have become servants of the servants of the Supreme Personality of Godhead." Of course, Lord Śiva smiled when he joked with his wife in that way, for others cannot speak like that. "The Supreme Lord," Śiva continued, "is always exalted in His activities, and here is another example of His wonderful influence upon King Citraketu, His devotee. Just see, although you cursed the King, he was not at all afraid or sorry. Rather, he offered respect to you, called you mother and accepted your curse, thinking himself faulty. He did not say anything in retaliation. This is the excellence of a devotee. By mildly tolerating your curse, he has certainly excelled the glory of your beauty and your power to curse him. I can impartially judge that this devotee, Citraketu, has defeated you and your excellence simply by becoming a pure devotee of the Lord." As stated by Śrī Caitanya Mahāprabhu, *taror api sahiṣṇunā.* Just like a tree, a devotee can tolerate all kinds of curses and reversals in life. This is the excellence of a devotee. Indirectly, Lord Śiva forbade Pārvatī to commit the mistake of cursing a devotee like Citraketu. He indicated that although she was powerful, the King, without showing any power, had excelled her power by his tolerance.

TEXT 28

नारायणपराः सर्वे न कुतश्चन बिभ्यति ।
स्वर्गापवर्गनरकेष्वपि तुल्यार्थदर्शिनः ॥२८॥

nārāyaṇa-parāḥ sarve
na kutaścana bibhyati
svargāpavarga-narakeṣv
api tulyārtha-darśinaḥ

nārāyaṇa-parāḥ—pure devotees, who are interested only in the service of Nārāyaṇa, the Supreme Personality of Godhead; *sarve*—all; *na*—not; *kutaścana*—anywhere; *bibhyati*—are afraid; *svarga*—in the higher planetary systems; *apavarga*—in liberation; *narakeṣu*—and in hell; *api*—even; *tulya*—equal; *artha*—value; *darśinaḥ*—who see.

TRANSLATION

Devotees solely engaged in the devotional service of the Supreme Personality of Godhead, Nārāyaṇa, never fear any condition of life. For them the heavenly planets, liberation and the hellish planets are all the same, for such devotees are interested only in the service of the Lord.

PURPORT

Pārvatī might naturally have inquired how devotees become so exalted. Therefore this verse explains that they are *nārāyaṇa-para,* simply dependent on Nārāyaṇa. They do not mind reverses in life because in the service of Nārāyaṇa they have learned to tolerate whatever hardships there may be. They do not care whether they are in heaven or in hell: they simply engage in the service of the Lord. This is their excellence. *Ānukūlyena kṛṣṇānuśīlanam:* they are liberally engaged in the service of the Lord, and therefore they are excellent. By using the word *bhṛtya-bhṛtyānām,* Lord Śiva pointed out that although Citraketu provided one example of tolerance and excellence, all the devotees who have taken shelter of the Lord as eternal servants are glorious. They have no eagerness to be happy by being placed in the heavenly planets, becoming liberated or becoming one with Brahman, the supreme effulgence. These benefits do not appeal to their minds. They are simply interested in giving direct service to the Lord.

TEXT 29

देहिनां देहसंयोगाद् द्वन्द्वानीश्वरलीलया ।
सुखं दुःखं मृतिर्जन्म शापोऽनुग्रह एव च ॥२९॥

dehināṁ deha-saṁyogād
dvandvānīśvara-līlayā
sukhaṁ duḥkhaṁ mṛtir janma
śāpo 'nugraha eva ca

dehinām—of all those who have accepted material bodies; *deha-saṁyogāt*—because of contact with the material body; *dvandvāni*—dualities; *īśvara-līlayā*—by the supreme will of the Lord; *sukham*—happiness; *duḥkham*—distress; *mṛtiḥ*—death; *janma*—birth; *śāpaḥ*—curse; *anugrahaḥ*—favor; *eva*—certainly; *ca*—and.

TRANSLATION

Because of the actions of the Supreme Lord's external energy, the living entities are conditioned in contact with material bodies. The dualities of happiness and distress, birth and death, curses and favors, are natural by-products of this contact in the material world.

PURPORT

In *Bhagavad-gītā* we find, *mayādhyakṣeṇa prakṛtiḥ sūyate sa-carācaram:* the material world works under the direction of the goddess Durgā, the material energy of the Lord, but she acts under the direction of the Supreme Personality of Godhead. This is also confirmed in the *Brahma-saṁhitā* (5.44):

sṛṣṭi-sthiti-pralaya-sādhana-śaktir ekā
chāyeva yasya bhuvanāni bibharti durgā

Durgā—the goddess Pārvatī, the wife of Lord Śiva—is extremely powerful. She can create, maintain and annihilate any number of universes by her sweet will, but she acts under the direction of the Supreme Personality of Godhead, Kṛṣṇa, not independently. Kṛṣṇa is impartial, but because this is the material world of duality, such relative terms as happiness and distress, curses and favors, are created by the will of the Supreme. Those who are not *nārāyaṇa-para,* pure devotees, must be disturbed by this duality of the material world, whereas devotees who are simply attached to the service of the Lord are not at all disturbed by it. For example, Haridāsa Ṭhākura was beaten with cane in twenty-two bazaars, but he was never disturbed; instead, he smilingly tolerated the beating. Despite the disturbing dualities of the material world, devotees are not disturbed at all. Because they fix their minds on the lotus feet of the Lord and concentrate on the holy name of the Lord, they do not feel the so-called pains and pleasures caused by the dualities of this material world.

TEXT 30

अविवेककृतः पुंसो ह्यर्थभेद इवात्मनि ।
गुणदोषविकल्पश्च भिदेव स्रजिवत्कृतः ॥३०॥

aviveka-kṛtaḥ puṁso
hy artha-bheda ivātmani
guṇa-doṣa-vikalpaś ca
bhid eva srajivat kṛtaḥ

aviveka-kṛtaḥ—done in ignorance, without mature consideration; *puṁsaḥ*—of the living entity; *hi*—indeed; *artha-bhedaḥ*—differentiation of value; *iva*—like; *ātmani*—in himself; *guṇa-doṣa*—of quality and fault; *vikalpaḥ*—imagination; *ca*—and; *bhit*—difference; *eva*—certainly; *sraji*—in a garland; *vat*—like; *kṛtaḥ*—made.

TRANSLATION

As one mistakenly considers a flower garland to be a snake or experiences happiness and distress in a dream, so, in the material

world, by a lack of careful consideration, we differentiate between happiness and distress, considering one good and the other bad.

PURPORT

The happiness and distress of the material world of duality are both mistaken ideas. In the *Caitanya-caritāmṛta* (*Antya* 4.176) it is said:

"dvaite" bhadrābhadra-jñāna, saba——"manodharma"
"ei bhāla, ei manda",——ei saba "bhrama"

The distinctions between happiness and distress in the material world of duality are simply mental concoctions, for the so-called happiness and distress are actually one and the same. They are like the happiness and distress in dreams. A sleeping man creates his happiness and distress by dreaming, although actually they have no existence.

The other example given in this verse is that a flower garland is originally very nice, but by mistake, for want of mature knowledge, one may consider it a snake. In this connection there is a statement by Prabodhānanda Sarasvatī: *viśvaṁ pūrṇa-sukhāyate.* Everyone in this material world is distressed by miserable conditions, but Śrīla Prabodhānanda Sarasvatī says that this world is full of happiness. How is this possible? He answers, *yat-kāruṇya-kaṭākṣa-vaibhavavatāṁ taṁ gauram eva stumaḥ.* A devotee accepts the distress of this material world as happiness only due to the causeless mercy of Śrī Caitanya Mahāprabhu. By His personal behavior, Śrī Caitanya Mahāprabhu showed that He was never distressed but always happy in chanting the Hare Kṛṣṇa *mahā-mantra.* One should follow in the footsteps of Śrī Caitanya Mahāprabhu and engage constantly in chanting the *mahā-mantra*—Hare Kṛṣṇa, Hare Kṛṣṇa, Kṛṣṇa Kṛṣṇa, Hare Hare/ Hare Rāma, Hare Rāma, Rāma Rāma, Hare Hare. Then he will never feel the distresses of the world of duality. In any condition of life one will be happy if he chants the holy name of the Lord.

In dreams we sometimes enjoy eating sweet rice and sometimes suffer as if one of our beloved family members had died. Because the same mind and body exist in the same material world of duality when we are awake, the so-called happiness and distress of this world are no better than the false, superficial happiness of dreams. The mind is the via medium in both dreams and wakefulness, and everything created by the mind in terms of *saṅkalpa* and *vikalpa*, acceptance and rejection, is called *manodharma*, or mental concoction.

TEXT 31

वासुदेवे भगवति भक्तिमुद्वहतां नृणाम् ।
ज्ञानवैराग्यवीर्याणां न हि कश्चिद् व्यपाश्रयः ॥३१॥

vāsudeve bhagavati
bhaktim udvahatāṁ nṛṇām
jñāna-vairāgya-vīryāṇāṁ
na hi kaścid vyapāśrayaḥ

vāsudeve—to Lord Vāsudeva, Kṛṣṇa; *bhagavati*—the Supreme Personality of Godhead; *bhaktim*—love and faith in devotional service; *udvahatām*—for those who are carrying; *nṛṇām*—men; *jñāna-vairāgya*—of real knowledge and detachment; *vīryāṇām*—possessing the powerful strength; *na*—not; *hi*—indeed; *kaścit*—anything; *vyapāśrayaḥ*—as interest or shelter.

TRANSLATION

Persons engaged in devotional service to Lord Vāsudeva, Kṛṣṇa, have naturally perfect knowledge and detachment from this material world. Therefore such devotees are not interested in the so-called happiness or so-called distress of this world.

PURPORT

Here is the distinction between a devotee and a philosopher who speculates on the subject matter of transcendence. A devotee does not need to cultivate knowledge to understand the falsity or temporary existence of this material world. Because of his unalloyed devotion to Vāsudeva, this knowledge and detachment are automatically manifested in his person. As confirmed elsewhere in *Śrīmad-Bhāgavatam* (1.2.7):

vāsudeve bhagavati
bhakti-yogaḥ prayojitaḥ

janayaty āśu vairāgyaṁ
jñānaṁ ca yad ahaitukam

One who engages in unalloyed devotional service to Vāsudeva, Kṛṣṇa, automatically becomes aware of this material world, and therefore he is naturally detached. This detachment is possible because of his high standard of knowledge. The speculative philosopher tries to understand that this material world is false by cultivating knowledge, but this understanding is automatically manifested in the person of a devotee, without separate endeavor. The Māyāvādī philosophers may be very proud of their so-called knowledge, but because they do not understand Vāsudeva (*vāsudevaḥ sarvam iti*), they do not understand the world of duality, which is a manifestation of Vāsudeva's external energy. Therefore, unless the so-called *jñānīs* take shelter of Vāsudeva, their speculative knowledge is imperfect. *Ye 'nye 'ravindākṣa vimukta-māninaḥ.* They simply think of becoming free from the contamination of the material world, but because they do not take shelter at the lotus feet of Vāsudeva, their knowledge is impure. When they actually become pure, they surrender to the lotus feet of Vāsudeva. Therefore, the Absolute Truth is easier to understand for a devotee than for *jñānīs* who simply speculate to understand Vāsudeva. Lord Śiva confirms this statement in the following verse.

TEXT 32

नाहं विरिञ्चो न कुमारनारदौ
न ब्रह्मपुत्रा मुनयः सुरेशाः ।
विदाम यस्येहितमंशकांशका
न तत्स्वरूपं पृथगीशमानिनः ॥३२॥

nāhaṁ viriñco na kumāra-nāradau
na brahma-putrā munayaḥ sureśāḥ
vidāma yasyehitam aṁśakāṁśakā
na tat-svarūpaṁ pṛthag-īśa-māninaḥ

na—not; *aham*—I (Lord Śiva); *viriñcaḥ*—Lord Brahmā; *na*—nor; *kumāra*—the Aśvinī-kumāras; *nāradau*—the great saint Nārada; *na*—

nor; *brahma-putrāḥ*—the sons of Lord Brahmā; *munayaḥ*—great saintly persons; *sura-īśāḥ*—all the great demigods; *vidāma*—know; *yasya*—of whom; *īhitam*—activity; *aṁśaka-aṁśakāḥ*—those who are parts of the parts; *na*—not; *tat*—His; *sva-rūpam*—real personality; *pṛthak*—separate; *īśa*—rulers; *māninaḥ*—who consider ourselves to be.

TRANSLATION

Neither I [Lord Śiva], nor Brahmā, nor the Aśvinī-kumāras, nor Nārada or the other great sages who are Brahmā's sons, nor even the demigods can understand the pastimes and personality of the Supreme Lord. Although we are part of the Supreme Lord, we consider ourselves independent, separate controllers, and thus we cannot understand His identity.

PURPORT

Brahma-saṁhitā (5.33) states:

advaitam acyutam anādim ananta-rūpam
ādyaṁ purāṇa-puruṣaṁ nava-yauvanaṁ ca
vedeṣu durlabham adurlabham ātma-bhaktau
govindam ādi-puruṣaṁ tam ahaṁ bhajāmi

"I worship the Supreme Personality of Godhead, Govinda, who is the original person. He is absolute, infallible and beginningless, and although expanded into unlimited forms, He is still the same original person, the oldest person, who always appears as a fresh youth. The eternal, blissful, all-knowing forms of the Lord can not be understood even by the best Vedic scholars, but they are always manifest to pure, unalloyed devotees." Lord Śiva places himself as one of the nondevotees, who cannot understand the identity of the Supreme Lord. The Lord, being *ananta,* has an unlimited number of forms. Therefore, how is it possible for an ordinary, common man to understand Him? Lord Śiva, of course, is above the ordinary human beings, yet he is unable to understand the Supreme Personality of Godhead. Lord Śiva is not among the ordinary living entities, nor is he in the category of Lord Viṣṇu. He is between Lord Viṣṇu and the common living entity.

TEXT 33

न ह्यस्यास्ति प्रियः कश्चिन्नाप्रियः स्वः परोऽपि वा ।
आत्मत्वात्सर्वभूतानां सर्वभूतप्रियो हरिः ॥३३॥

na hy asyāsti priyaḥ kaścin
nāpriyaḥ svaḥ paro 'pi vā
ātmatvāt sarva-bhūtānāṁ
sarva-bhūta-priyo hariḥ

na—not; *hi*—indeed; *asya*—of the Lord; *asti*—there is; *priyaḥ*—very dear; *kaścit*—anyone; *na*—nor; *apriyaḥ*—not dear; *svaḥ*—own; *paraḥ*—other; *api*—even; *vā*—or; *ātmatvāt*—due to being the soul of the soul; *sarva-bhūtānām*—of all living entities; *sarva-bhūta*—to all living entities; *priyaḥ*—very, very dear; *hariḥ*—Lord Hari.

TRANSLATION

He holds no one as very dear and no one as inimical. He has no one for His own relative, and no one is alien to Him. He is actually the soul of the soul of all living entities. Thus He is the auspicious friend of all living beings and is very near and dear to all of them.

PURPORT

The Supreme Personality of Godhead, in His second feature, is the Supersoul of all living entities. As one's self is extremely dear, the Superself of the self is still more dear. No one can be the enemy of the friendly Superself, who is equal to everyone. Relationships of dearness or enmity between the Supreme Lord and the living beings are due to the intervention of the illusory energy. Because the three modes of material nature intervene between the Lord and the living beings, these different relationships appear. Actually, the living entity in his pure condition is always very near and dear to the Lord, and the Lord is dear to him. There is no question of partiality or enmity.

TEXTS 34–35

तस्य चायं महाभागश्चित्रकेतुः प्रियोऽनुगः ।
सर्वत्र समदृक् शान्तो ह्यहं चैवाच्युतप्रियः ॥३४॥

तस्मान्न विस्मयः कार्यः पुरुषेषु महात्मसु ।
महापुरुषभक्तेषु शान्तेषु समदर्शिषु ॥३५॥

tasya cāyaṁ mahā-bhāgaś
citraketuḥ priyo 'nugaḥ
sarvatra sama-dṛk śānto
hy ahaṁ caivācyuta-priyaḥ

tasmān na vismayaḥ kāryaḥ
puruṣeṣu mahātmasu
mahāpuruṣa-bhakteṣu
śānteṣu sama-darśiṣu

tasya—of Him (the Lord); *ca*—and; *ayam*—this; *mahā-bhāgaḥ*—the most fortunate; *citraketuḥ*—King Citraketu; *priyaḥ*—beloved; *anugaḥ*—most obedient servant; *sarvatra*—everywhere; *sama-dṛk*—sees equally; *śāntaḥ*—very peaceful; *hi*—indeed; *aham*—I; *ca*—also; *eva*—certainly; *acyuta-priyaḥ*—very dear to Lord Kṛṣṇa, who never fails; *tasmāt*—therefore; *na*—no; *vismayaḥ*—wonder; *kāryaḥ*—to be done; *puruṣeṣu*—among persons; *mahā-ātmasu*—who are exalted souls; *mahā-puruṣa-bhakteṣu*—devotees of Lord Viṣṇu; *śānteṣu*—peaceful; *sama-darśiṣu*—equal to everyone.

TRANSLATION

This magnanimous Citraketu is a dear devotee of the Lord. He is equal to all living entities and is free from attachment and hatred. Similarly, I am also very dear to Lord Nārāyaṇa. Therefore, no one should be astonished to see the activities of the most exalted devotees of Nārāyaṇa, for they are free from attachment and envy. They are always peaceful, and they are equal to everyone.

PURPORT

It is said, *vaiṣṇavera kriyā, mudrā vijñeha nā bujhaya:* one should not be astonished to see the activities of exalted, liberated Vaiṣṇavas. As one should not be misled by the activities of the Supreme Personality of Godhead, one should also not be misled by the activities of His devotees. Both the Lord and His devotees are liberated. They are on the same platform, the only difference being that the Lord is the master and the devotees are servants. Qualitatively, they are one and the same. In *Bhagavad-gītā* (9.29) the Lord says:

samo 'haṁ sarva-bhūteṣu
na me dveṣyo 'sti na priyaḥ
ye bhajanti tu māṁ bhaktyā
mayi te teṣu cāpy aham

"I envy no one, nor am I partial to anyone. I am equal to all. But whoever renders service unto Me in devotion is a friend, is in Me, and I am also a friend to him." From this statement by the Supreme Personality of Godhead, it is clear that the devotees of the Lord are always extremely dear to Him. In effect, Lord Śiva told Pārvatī, "Both Citraketu and I are always very dear to the Supreme Lord. In other words, both he and I are on the same level as servants of the Lord. We are always friends, and sometimes we enjoy joking words between us. When Citraketu loudly laughed at my behavior, he did so on friendly terms, and therefore there was no reason to curse him." Thus Lord Śiva tried to convince his wife, Pārvatī, that her cursing of Citraketu was not very sensible.

Here is a difference between male and female that exists even in the higher statuses of life—in fact, even between Lord Śiva and his wife. Lord Śiva could understand Citraketu very nicely, but Pārvatī could not. Thus even in the higher statuses of life there is a difference between the understanding of a male and that of a female. It may be clearly said that the understanding of a woman is always inferior to the understanding of a man. In the Western countries there is now agitation to the effect that man and woman should be considered equal, but from this verse it appears that woman is always less intelligent than man.

It is clear that Citraketu wanted to criticize the behavior of his friend Lord Śiva because Lord Śiva was sitting with his wife on his lap. Then, too, Lord Śiva wanted to criticize Citraketu for externally posing as a great devotee but being interested in enjoying with the Vidyādharī women. These were all friendly jokes; there was nothing serious for which Citraketu should have been cursed by Pārvatī. Upon hearing the instructions of Lord Śiva, Pārvatī must have been very much ashamed for cursing Citraketu to become a demon. Mother Pārvatī could not appreciate Citraketu's position, and therefore she cursed him, but when she understood the instructions of Lord Śiva she was ashamed.

TEXT 36

श्रीशुक उवाच
इति श्रुत्वा भगवतः शिवस्योमाभिभाषितम् ।
बभूव शान्तधी राजन् देवी विगतविस्मया ॥३६॥

śrī-śuka uvāca
iti śrutvā bhagavataḥ
śivasyomābhibhāṣitam
babhūva śānta-dhī rājan
devī vigata-vismayā

śrī-śukaḥ uvāca—Śrī Śukadeva Gosvāmī said; *iti*—thus; *śrutvā*—hearing; *bhagavataḥ*—of the most powerful demigod; *śivasya*—of Lord Śiva; *umā*—Pārvatī; *abhibhāṣitam*—instruction; *babhūva*—became; *śānta-dhīḥ*—very peaceful; *rājan*—O King Parīkṣit; *devī*—the goddess; *vigata-vismayā*—released from astonishment.

TRANSLATION

Śrī Śukadeva Gosvāmī said: O King, after hearing this speech by her husband, the demigoddess [Umā, the wife of Lord Śiva] gave up her astonishment at the behavior of King Citraketu and became steady in intelligence.

PURPORT

Śrīla Viśvanātha Cakravartī Ṭhākura remarks that the word *śānta-dhīḥ* means *svīya-pūrva-svabhāva-smṛtyā.* When Pārvatī remembered her former behavior in cursing Citraketu, she became very much ashamed and covered her face with the skirt of her sari, admitting that she was wrong in cursing Citraketu.

TEXT 37

इति भागवतो देव्याः प्रतिशप्तुमलन्तमः ।
मूर्ध्ना स जगृहे शापमेतावत्साधुलक्षणम् ॥३७॥

iti bhāgavato devyāḥ
pratiśaptum alantamaḥ
mūrdhnā sa jagṛhe śāpam
etāvat sādhu-lakṣaṇam

iti—thus; *bhāgavataḥ*—the most exalted devotee; *devyāḥ*—of Pārvatī; *pratiśaptum*—to make a counter-curse; *alantamaḥ*—able in all respects; *mūrdhnā*—with his head; *saḥ*—he (Citraketu); *jagṛhe*—accepted; *śāpam*—the curse; *etāvat*—this much; *sādhu-lakṣaṇam*—the symptom of a devotee.

TRANSLATION

The great devotee Citraketu was so powerful that he was quite competent to curse mother Pārvatī in retaliation, but instead of doing so he very humbly accepted the curse and bowed his head before Lord Śiva and his wife. This is very much to be appreciated as the standard behavior of a Vaiṣṇava.

PURPORT

Upon being informed by Lord Śiva, mother Pārvatī could understand that she was wrong in cursing Citraketu. King Citraketu was so exalted in his character that in spite of being wrongly cursed by Pārvatī, he immediately descended from his airplane and bowed his head before the mother, accepting her curse. This has already been explained: *nārāyaṇa-parāḥ sarve na kutaścana bibhyati.* Citraketu very sportingly felt that since the mother wanted to curse him, he could accept this curse just to please her. This is called *sādhu-lakṣaṇam,* the characteristic of a *sādhu,* or a devotee. As explained by Śrī Caitanya Mahāprabhu, *tṛṇād api sunīcena taror api sahiṣṇunā.* A devotee should always be very humble and meek and should offer all respect to others, especially to superiors. Being protected by the Supreme Personality of Godhead, a devotee is always powerful, but a devotee does not wish to show his power unnecessarily. However, when a less intelligent person has some power, he wants to use it for sense gratification. This is not the behavior of a devotee.

TEXT 38

जज्ञे त्वष्टुर्दक्षिणाग्नौ दानवीं योनिमाश्रितः ।
वृत्र इत्यभिविख्यातो ज्ञानविज्ञानसंयुतः ॥३८॥

jajñe tvaṣṭur dakṣiṇāgnau
dānavīṁ yonim āśritaḥ
vṛtra ity abhivikhyāto
jñāna-vijñāna-saṁyutaḥ

jajñe—was born; *tvaṣṭuḥ*—of the *brāhmaṇa* known as Tvaṣṭā; *dakṣiṇa-agnau*—in the fire sacrifice known as *dakṣiṇāgni; dānavīm*—demoniac; *yonim*—species of life; *āśritaḥ*—taking shelter of; *vṛtraḥ*—Vṛtra; *iti*—thus; *abhivikhyātaḥ*—celebrated; *jñāna-vijñāna-saṁyutaḥ*—fully equipped with transcendental knowledge and practical application of that knowledge in life.

TRANSLATION

Being cursed by mother Durgā [Bhavānī, the wife of Lord Śiva], that same Citraketu accepted birth in a demoniac species of life. Although still fully equipped with transcendental knowledge and practical application of that knowledge in life, he appeared as a demon at the fire sacrifice performed by Tvaṣṭā, and thus he became famous as Vṛtrāsura.

PURPORT

The word *yoni* is generally understood to mean *jāti*—family, group or species. Although Vṛtrāsura appeared in a family of demons, it is clearly said that his knowledge of spiritual life still existed. *Jñāna-vijñāna-saṁyutaḥ:* his spiritual knowledge and the practical application of that knowledge in life were not lost. Therefore it is said that even if a devotee falls down for some reason, he is still not lost.

yatra kva vābhadram abhūd amuṣya kiṁ
ko vārtha āpto 'bhajatāṁ sva-dharmataḥ
(*Bhāg.* 1.5.17)

Once one is advanced in devotional service, his spiritual assets are never lost under any circumstances. Whatever spiritual advancement he has achieved continues. This is confirmed in *Bhagavad-gītā.* Even if a *bhakti-yogī* falls, he takes birth in a rich family or family of *brāhmaṇas,* in which he again starts devotional activities from the point where he left off. Although Vṛtrāsura was known as an *asura,* or demon, he did not lose his consciousness of Kṛṣṇa or devotional service.

TEXT 39

एतत्ते सर्वमाख्यातं यन्मां त्वं परिपृच्छसि ।
वृत्रस्यासुरजातेश्च कारणं भगवन्मतेः ॥३९॥

etat te sarvam ākhyātaṁ
yan māṁ tvaṁ paripṛcchasi
vṛtrasyāsura-jāteś ca
kāraṇaṁ bhagavan-mateḥ

etat—this; *te*—unto you; *sarvam*—all; *ākhyātam*—explained; *yat*—which; *mām*—me; *tvam*—you; *paripṛcchasi*—asked; *vṛtrasya*—of Vṛtrāsura; *asura-jāteḥ*—whose birth was in a species of *asuras; ca*—and; *kāraṇam*—the cause; *bhagavat-mateḥ*—of exalted intelligence in Kṛṣṇa consciousness.

TRANSLATION

My dear King Parīkṣit, you inquired from me how Vṛtrāsura, a great devotee, took birth in a demoniac family. Thus I have tried to explain to you everything about this.

TEXT 40

इतिहासमिमं पुण्यं चित्रकेतोर्महात्मनः ।
माहात्म्यं विष्णुभक्तानां श्रुत्वा बन्धाद्विमुच्यते॥४०॥

itihāsam imaṁ puṇyaṁ
citraketor mahātmanaḥ
māhātmyaṁ viṣṇu-bhaktānāṁ
śrutvā bandhād vimucyate

itihāsam—history; *imam*—this; *puṇyam*—very pious; *citraketoḥ*—of Citraketu; *mahā-ātmanaḥ*—the exalted devotee; *māhātmyam*—containing glory; *viṣṇu-bhaktānām*—from the devotees of Viṣṇu; *śrutvā*—hearing; *bandhāt*—from bondage or conditional, material life; *vimucyate*—is freed.

TRANSLATION

Citraketu was a great devotee [mahātmā]. If one hears this history of Citraketu from a pure devotee, the listener also is freed from the conditional life of material existence.

PURPORT

The historical incidents in the *Purāṇas,* such as the history of Citraketu explained in the *Bhāgavata Purāṇa,* are sometimes misunderstood by outsiders, or nondevotees. Therefore Śukadeva Gosvāmī advised that the history of Citraketu be heard from a devotee. Anything about devotional service or the characteristics of the Lord and His devotees must be heard from a devotee, not from a professional reciter. This is advised herein. Śrī Caitanya Mahāprabhu's secretary also advised that one learn the history of *Śrīmad-Bhāgavatam* from a devotee: *yāha, bhāgavata paḍa vaiṣṇavera sthāne.* One should not hear the statements of *Śrīmad-Bhāgavatam* from professional reciters, or else they will not be effective. Quoting from *Padma Purāṇa,* Śrī Sanātana Gosvāmī has strictly forbidden us to hear about the activities of the Lord and His devotees from the mouths of nondevotees:

avaiṣṇava-mukhodgīrṇaṁ
pūtaṁ hari-kathāmṛtam
śravaṇaṁ naiva kartavyaṁ
sarpocchiṣṭaṁ yathā payaḥ

"One should not hear anything about Kṛṣṇa from a non-Vaiṣṇava. Milk touched by the lips of a serpent has poisonous effects; similarly, talks about Kṛṣṇa given by a non-Vaiṣṇava are also poisonous." One must be a bona fide devotee, and then he can preach and impress devotional service upon his listeners.

TEXT 41

य एतत्प्रातरुत्थाय श्रद्धया वाग्यतः पठेत् ।
इतिहासं हरिं स्मृत्वा स याति परमां गतिम् ॥४१॥

ya etat prātar utthāya
śraddhayā vāg-yataḥ paṭhet
itihāsaṁ hariṁ smṛtvā
sa yāti paramāṁ gatim

yaḥ—any person who; *etat*—this; *prātaḥ*—early in the morning; *utthāya*—rising; *śraddhayā*—with faith; *vāk-yataḥ*—controlling the mind and words; *paṭhet*—may read; *itihāsam*—history; *hariṁ*—the Supreme Lord; *smṛtvā*—remembering; *saḥ*—that person; *yāti*—goes; *paramām gatim*—back home, back to Godhead.

TRANSLATION

One who rises from bed early in the morning and recites this history of Citraketu, controlling his words and mind and remembering the Supreme Personality of Godhead, will return home, back to Godhead, without difficulty.

Thus end the Bhaktivedanta purports of the Sixth Canto, Seventeenth Chapter, of the Śrīmad-Bhāgavatam *entitled, "Mother Pārvatī Curses Citraketu."*

CHAPTER EIGHTEEN

Diti Vows to Kill King Indra

This chapter gives the history of Diti, the wife of Kaśyapa, and how she followed a vow to have a son who would kill Indra. It also describes how Indra attempted to foil her plan by cutting to pieces the son within her womb.

In relation to Tvaṣṭā and his descendants, there is a description of the dynasty of the Ādityas (sons of Aditi) and other demigods. Pṛśni, the wife of Aditi's fifth son named Savitā, had three daughters—Sāvitrī, Vyāhṛti and Trayī—and very exalted sons named Agnihotra, Paśu, Soma, Cāturmāsya and the five Mahāyajñas. Siddhi, the wife of Bhaga, had three sons, named Mahimā, Vibhu and Prabhu, and she also had one daughter, whose name was Āśī. Dhātā had four wives—Kuhū, Sinīvālī, Rākā and Anumati—who had four sons, named Sāyam, Darśa, Prātaḥ and Pūrṇamāsa respectively. Kriyā, the wife of Vidhātā, gave birth to the five Purīṣyas, who are representatives of five kinds of fire-gods. Bhṛgu, the mind-born son of Brahmā, took his birth again from Carṣaṇī, the wife of Varuṇa, and the great sage Vālmīki appeared from Varuṇa's semen. Agastya and Vasiṣṭha were two sons of Varuṇa and Mitra. Upon seeing the beauty of Urvaśī, Mitra and Varuṇa discharged semen, which they kept in an earthen pot. From that pot, Agastya and Vasiṣṭha appeared. Mitra had a wife named Revatī, who gave birth to three sons—Utsarga, Ariṣṭa and Pippala. Aditi had twelve sons, of whom Indra was the eleventh. Indra's wife was named Paulomī (Śacīdevī). She gave birth to three sons—Jayanta, Ṛṣabha and Mīḍhuṣa. By His own powers, the Supreme Personality of Godhead appeared as Vāmanadeva. From His wife, whose name was Kīrti, appeared a son named Bṛhatśloka. Bṛhatśloka's first son was known as Saubhaga. This is a description of the sons of Aditi. A description of Āditya Urukrama, who is an incarnation of the Supreme Personality of Godhead, will be offered in the Eighth Canto.

The demons born of Diti are also described in this chapter. In the dynasty of Diti appeared the great saintly devotee Prahlāda and also Bali,

Prahlāda's grandson. Hiraṇyakaśipu and Hiraṇyākṣa were the first sons of Diti. Hiraṇyakaśipu and his wife, whose name was Kayādhu, had four sons—Saṁhlāda, Anuhlāda, Hlāda and Prahlāda. They also had one daughter, whose name was Siṁhikā. In association with the demon Vipracit, Siṁhikā bore a son named Rāhu, whose head was severed by the Supreme Personality of Godhead. Kṛti, the wife of Saṁhlāda, bore a son named Pañcajana. Hlāda's wife, whose name was Dhamani, gave birth to two sons—Vātāpi and Ilvala. Ilvala put Vātāpi into the form of a ram and gave him to Agastya to eat. Anuhlāda, in the womb of his wife, Sūryā, begot two sons, named Bāṣkala and Mahiṣa. Prahlāda's son was known as Virocana, and his grandson was known as Bali Mahārāja. Bali Mahārāja had one hundred sons, of whom Bāṇa was the eldest.

After describing the dynasty of the Ādityas and the other demigods, Śukadeva Gosvāmī describes Diti's sons known as the Maruts and how they were elevated to the position of demigods. Just to help Indra, Lord Viṣṇu had killed Hiraṇyākṣa and Hiraṇyakaśipu. Because of this, Diti was very envious, and she was eager to have a son who could kill Indra. By her service, she enchanted Kaśyapa Muni in order to beg from him a greater son to do this. In corroboration of the Vedic injunction *vidvāṁsam api karṣati*, Kaśyapa Muni was attracted to his beautiful wife and promised to grant her any request. When, however, she requested a son who would kill Indra, he condemned himself, and he advised his wife Diti to follow the Vaiṣṇava ritualistic ceremonies to purify herself. When Diti, following the instructions of Kaśyapa, engaged in devotional service, Indra could understand her purpose, and he began observing all her activities. One day, Indra had the opportunity to see her deviating from devotional service. Thus he entered her womb and cut her son into forty-nine parts. In this way the forty-nine kinds of air known as the Maruts appeared, but because Diti had performed the Vaiṣṇava ritualistic ceremonies, all the sons became Vaiṣṇavas.

TEXT 1

श्रीशुक उवाच

पृश्निस्तु पत्नी सवितुः सावित्रीं व्याहृतिं त्रयीम् ।
अग्निहोत्रं पशुं सोमं चातुर्मास्यं महामखान् ॥ १ ॥

śrī-śuka uvāca
pṛśnis tu patnī savituḥ
sāvitrīṁ vyāhṛtiṁ trayīm
agnihotraṁ paśuṁ somaṁ
cāturmāsyaṁ mahā-makhān

śrī-śukaḥ uvāca—Śrī Śukadeva Gosvāmī said; *pṛśniḥ*—Pṛśni; *tu*—then; *patnī*—wife; *savituḥ*—of Savitā; *sāvitrīm*—Sāvitrī; *vyāhṛtim*—Vyāhṛti; *trayīm*—Trayī; *agnihotram*—Agnihotra; *paśum*—Paśu; *somam*—Soma; *cāturmāsyam*—Cāturmāsya; *mahā-makhān*—the five Mahāyajñas.

TRANSLATION

Śrī Śukadeva Gosvāmī said: Pṛśni, who was the wife of Savitā, the fifth of the twelve sons of Aditi, gave birth to three daughters—Sāvitrī, Vyāhṛti and Trayī—and the sons named Agnihotra, Paśu, Soma, Cāturmāsya and the five Mahāyajñas.

TEXT 2

सिद्धिर्भगस्य भार्याङ्ग महिमानं विभुं प्रभुम् ।
आशिषं च वरारोहां कन्यां प्रासूत सुव्रताम् ॥ २ ॥

siddhir bhagasya bhāryāṅga
mahimānaṁ vibhuṁ prabhum
āśiṣaṁ ca varārohāṁ
kanyāṁ prāsūta suvratām

siddhiḥ—Siddhi; *bhagasya*—of Bhaga; *bhāryā*—the wife; *aṅga*—my dear King; *mahimānam*—Mahimā; *vibhum*—Vibhu; *prabhum*—Prabhu; *āśiṣam*—Āśī; *ca*—and; *varārohām*—very beautiful; *kanyām*—daughter; *prāsūta*—bore; *su-vratām*—virtuous.

TRANSLATION

O King, Siddhi, who was the wife of Bhaga, the sixth son of Aditi, bore three sons, named Mahimā, Vibhu and Prabhu, and one extremely beautiful daughter, whose name was Āśī.

TEXTS 3–4

धातुः कुहूः सिनीवाली राका चानुमतिस्तथा ।
सायं दर्शमथ प्रातः पूर्णमासमनुक्रमात् ॥ ३ ॥
अग्नीन् पुरीष्यानाधत्त क्रियायां समनन्तरः ।
चर्षणी वरुणस्यासीद्यस्यां जातो भृगुः पुनः ॥ ४ ॥

dhātuḥ kuhūḥ sinīvālī
rākā cānumatis tathā
sāyaṁ darśam atha prātaḥ
pūrṇamāsam anukramāt

agnīn purīṣyān ādhatta
kriyāyāṁ samanantaraḥ
carṣaṇī varuṇasyāsīd
yasyāṁ jāto bhṛguḥ punaḥ

dhātuḥ—of Dhātā; *kuhūḥ*—Kuhū; *sinīvālī*—Sinīvālī; *rākā*—Rākā; *ca*—and; *anumatiḥ*—Anumati; *tathā*—also; *sāyam*—Sāyam; *darśam*—Darśa; *atha*—also; *prātaḥ*—Prātaḥ; *pūrṇamāsam*—Pūrṇamāsa; *anukramāt*—respectively; *agnīn*—fire-gods; *purīṣyān*—called the Purīṣyas; *ādhatta*—begot; *kriyāyām*—in Kriyā; *samanantaraḥ*—the next son, Vidhātā; *carṣaṇī*—Carṣaṇī; *varuṇasya*—of Varuṇa; *āsīt*—was; *yasyām*—in whom; *jātaḥ*—took birth; *bhṛguḥ*—Bhṛgu; *punaḥ*—again.

TRANSLATION

Dhātā, the seventh son of Aditi, had four wives, named Kuhū, Sinīvālī, Rākā and Anumati. These wives begot four sons, named Sāyam, Darśa, Prātaḥ and Pūrṇamāsa respectively. The wife of Vidhātā, the eighth son of Aditi, was named Kriyā. In her Vidhātā begot the five fire-gods named the Purīṣyas. The wife of Varuṇa, the ninth son of Aditi, was named Carṣaṇī. Bhṛgu, the son of Brahmā, took birth again in her womb.

TEXT 5

वाल्मीकिश्च महायोगी वल्मीकादभवत्किल ।
अगस्त्यश्च वसिष्ठश्च मित्रावरुणयोर्ऋषी ॥ ५ ॥

vālmīkiś ca mahā-yogī
valmīkād abhavat kila
agastyaś ca vasiṣṭhaś ca
mitrā-varuṇayor ṛṣī

vālmīkiḥ—Vālmīki; *ca*—and; *mahā-yogī*—the great mystic; *valmīkāt*—from an anthill; *abhavat*—took birth; *kila*—indeed; *agastyaḥ*—Agastya; *ca*—and; *vasiṣṭhaḥ*—Vasiṣṭha; *ca*—also; *mitrā-varuṇayoḥ*—of Mitra and Varuṇa; *ṛṣī*—the two sages.

TRANSLATION

By the semen of Varuṇa, the great mystic Vālmīki took birth from an anthill. Bhṛgu and Vālmīki were specific sons of Varuṇa, whereas Agastya and Vasiṣṭha Ṛṣis were the common sons of Varuṇa and Mitra, the tenth son of Aditi.

TEXT 6

रेतः सिषिचतुः कुम्भे उर्वश्याः सन्निधौ द्रुतम् ।
रेवत्यां मित्र उत्सर्गमरिष्टं पिप्पलं व्यधात् ॥ ६ ॥

retaḥ siṣicatuḥ kumbhe
urvaśyāḥ sannidhau drutam
revatyāṁ mitra utsargam
ariṣṭaṁ pippalaṁ vyadhāt

retaḥ—semen; *siṣicatuḥ*—discharged; *kumbhe*—in an earthen pot; *urvaśyāḥ*—of Urvaśī; *sannidhau*—in the presence; *drutam*—flown; *revatyām*—in Revatī; *mitraḥ*—Mitra; *utsargam*—Utsarga; *ariṣṭam*—Ariṣṭa; *pippalam*—Pippala; *vyadhāt*—begot.

TRANSLATION

Upon seeing Urvaśī, the celestial society girl, both Mitra and Varuṇa discharged semen, which they preserved in an earthen pot. The two sons Agastya and Vasiṣṭha later appeared from that pot, and they are therefore the common sons of Mitra and Varuṇa. Mitra begot three sons in the womb of his wife, whose name was Revatī. Their names were Utsarga, Ariṣṭa and Pippala.

PURPORT

Modern science is trying to generate living entities in test tubes by processing semen, but even long, long ago it was possible for semen kept in a pot to develop into a child.

TEXT 7

पौलोम्यामिन्द्र आधत्त त्रीन् पुत्रानिति नः श्रुतम् ।
जयन्तमृषभं तात तृतीयं मीढुषं प्रभुः ॥७॥

paulomyām indra ādhatta
trīn putrān iti naḥ śrutam
jayantam ṛṣabhaṁ tāta
tṛtīyaṁ mīḍhuṣaṁ prabhuḥ

paulomyām—in Paulomī (Śacīdevī); *indraḥ*—Indra; *ādhatta*—begot; *trīn*—three; *putrān*—sons; *iti*—thus; *naḥ*—by us; *śrutam*—heard; *jayantam*—Jayanta; *ṛṣabham*—Ṛṣabha; *tāta*—my dear King; *tṛtīyam*—third; *mīḍhuṣam*—Mīḍhuṣa; *prabhuḥ*—the lord.

TRANSLATION

O King Parīkṣit, Indra, the King of the heavenly planets and eleventh son of Aditi, begot three sons, named Jayanta, Ṛṣabha and Mīḍhuṣa, in the womb of his wife, Paulomī. Thus we have heard.

TEXT 8

उरुक्रमस्य देवस्य मायावामनरूपिणः ।
कीर्तौ पत्न्यां बृहच्छ्लोकस्तस्यासन् सौभगादयः ॥८॥

urukramasya devasya
māyā-vāmana-rūpiṇaḥ
kīrtau patnyāṁ bṛhacchlokas
tasyāsan saubhagādayaḥ

urukramasya—of Urukrama; *devasya*—the Lord; *māyā*—by His internal potency; *vāmana-rūpiṇaḥ*—having the form of a dwarf; *kīrtau*—in Kīrti; *patnyām*—His wife; *bṛhacchlokaḥ*—Bṛhatśloka; *tasya*—of him; *āsan*—were; *saubhaga-ādayaḥ*—sons beginning with Saubhaga.

TRANSLATION

By His own potency, the Supreme Personality of Godhead, who has multifarious potencies, appeared in the form of a dwarf as Urukrama, the twelfth son of Aditi. In the womb of His wife, whose name was Kīrti, He begot one son, named Bṛhatśloka, who had many sons, headed by Saubhaga.

PURPORT

As the Lord says in *Bhagavad-gītā* (4.6):

ajo 'pi sann avyayātmā
bhūtānām īśvaro 'pi san
prakṛtiṁ svām adhiṣṭhāya
sambhavāmy ātma-māyayā

"Although I am unborn and My transcendental body never deteriorates, and although I am the Lord of all sentient beings, I still appear in every millennium in My original transcendental form." When the Supreme Personality of Godhead incarnates, He does not need any help from the external energy, for He appears as He is by His own potency. The spiritual potency is also called *māyā*. It is said, *ato māyāmayaṁ viṣṇuṁ pravadanti manīṣiṇaḥ:* the body accepted by the Supreme Personality of Godhead is called *māyāmaya*. This does not mean that He is formed of the external energy; this *māyā* refers to His internal potency.

TEXT 9

तत्कर्मगुणवीर्याणि काश्यपस्य महात्मनः ।
पश्चाद्वक्ष्यामहेऽदित्यां यथैवावततार ह ॥ ९ ॥

tat-karma-guṇa-vīryāṇi
kāśyapasya mahātmanaḥ
paścād vakṣyāmahe 'dityāṁ
yathaivāvatatāra ha

tat—His; *karma*—activities; *guṇa*—qualities; *vīryāṇi*—and power; *kāśyapasya*—of the son of Kaśyapa; *mahā-ātmanaḥ*—the great soul; *paścāt*—later; *vakṣyāmahe*—I shall describe; *adityām*—in Aditi; *yathā*—how; *eva*—certainly; *avatatāra*—descended; *ha*—indeed.

TRANSLATION

Later [in the Eighth Canto of Śrīmad-Bhāgavatam] I shall describe how Urukrama, Lord Vāmanadeva, appeared as the son of the great sage Kaśyapa and how He covered the three worlds with three steps. I shall describe the uncommon activities He performed, His qualities, His power and how He took birth from the womb of Aditi.

TEXT 10

अथ कश्यपदायादान् दैतेयान् कीर्तयामि ते ।
यत्र भागवतः श्रीमान् प्रह्लादो बलिरेव च ॥१०॥

atha kaśyapa-dāyādān
daiteyān kīrtayāmi te
yatra bhāgavataḥ śrīmān
prahrādo balir eva ca

atha—now; *kaśyapa-dāyādān*—the sons of Kaśyapa; *daiteyān*—born of Diti; *kīrtayāmi*—I shall describe; *te*—to you; *yatra*—where; *bhāgavataḥ*—the great devotee; *śrī-mān*—glorious; *prahrādaḥ*—Prahlāda; *baliḥ*—Bali; *eva*—certainly; *ca*—also.

TRANSLATION

Now let me describe the sons of Diti, who were begotten by Kaśyapa but who became demons. In this demoniac family the great devotee Prahlāda Mahārāja appeared, and Bali Mahārāja also appeared in that family. The demons are technically known as Daityas because they proceeded from the womb of Diti.

TEXT 11

दितेर्द्वावेव दायादौ दैत्यदानववन्दितौ ।
हिरण्यकशिपुर्नाम हिरण्याक्षश्च कीर्तितौ ॥११॥

diter dvāv eva dāyādau
daitya-dānava-vanditau
hiraṇyakaśipur nāma
hiraṇyākṣaś ca kīrtitau

diteḥ—of Diti; *dvau*—two; *eva*—certainly; *dāyādau*—sons; *daitya-dānava*—by the Daityas and Dānavas; *vanditau*—worshiped; *hiraṇyakaśipuḥ*—Hiraṇyakaśipu; *nāma*—named; *hiraṇyākṣaḥ*—Hiraṇyākṣa; *ca*—also; *kīrtitau*—known.

TRANSLATION

First the two sons named Hiraṇyakaśipu and Hiraṇyākṣa took birth from Diti's womb. Both of them were very powerful and were worshiped by the Daityas and Dānavas.

TEXTS 12–13

हिरण्यकशिपोर्भार्या कयाधुर्नाम दानवी ।
जम्भस्य तनया सा तु सुषुवे चतुरः सुतान् ॥१२॥
संह्लादं प्रागनुह्लादं ह्लादं प्रह्लादमेव च ।
तत्स्वसा सिंहिका नाम राहुं विप्रचित्तोऽग्रहीत् ॥१३॥

hiraṇyakaśipor bhāryā
kayādhur nāma dānavī

jambhasya tanayā sā tu
suṣuve caturaḥ sutān

saṁhrādaṁ prāg anuhrādaṁ
hrādaṁ prahrādam eva ca
tat-svasā siṁhikā nāma
rāhuṁ vipracito 'grahīt

hiraṇyakaśipoḥ—of Hiraṇyakaśipu; *bhāryā*—the wife; *kayādhuḥ*—Kayādhu; *nāma*—named; *dānavī*—descendant of Danu; *jambhasya*—of Jambha; *tanayā*—daughter; *sā*—she; *tu*—indeed; *suṣuve*—gave birth to; *caturaḥ*—four; *sutān*—sons; *saṁhrādam*—Saṁhlāda; *prāk*—first; *anuhrādam*—Anuhlāda; *hrādam*—Hlāda; *prahrādam*—Prahlāda; *eva*—also; *ca*—and; *tat-svasā*—his sister; *siṁhikā*—Siṁhikā; *nāma*—named; *rāhum*—Rāhu; *vipracitaḥ*—from Vipracit; *agrahīt*—received.

TRANSLATION

The wife of Hiraṇyakaśipu was known as Kayādhu. She was the daughter of Jambha and a descendant of Danu. She gave birth to four consecutive sons, known as Saṁhlāda, Anuhlāda, Hlāda and Prahlāda. The sister of these four sons was known as Siṁhikā. She married the demon named Vipracit and gave birth to another demon, named Rāhu.

TEXT 14

शिरोऽहरद्यस्य हरिश्चक्रेण पिबतोऽमृतम् ।
संह्रादस्य कृतिर्भार्यासूत पञ्चजनं ततः ॥१४॥

śiro 'harad yasya hariś
cakreṇa pibato 'mṛtam
saṁhrādasya kṛtir bhāryā-
sūta pañcajanaṁ tataḥ

śiraḥ—the head; *aharat*—cut off; *yasya*—of whom; *hariḥ*—Hari; *cakreṇa*—with the disc; *pibataḥ*—drinking; *amṛtam*—nectar;

saṁhrādasya—of Saṁhlāda; *kṛtiḥ*—Kṛti; *bhāryā*—the wife; *asūta*—gave birth to; *pañcajanam*—Pañcajana; *tataḥ*—from him.

TRANSLATION

While Rāhu, in disguise, was drinking nectar among the demigods, the Supreme Personality of Godhead severed his head. The wife of Saṁhlāda was named Kṛti. By union with Saṁhlāda, Kṛti gave birth to a son named Pañcajana.

TEXT 15

ह्रादस्य धमनिर्भार्यासूत वातापिमिल्वलम् ।
योऽगस्त्याय त्वतिथये पेचे वातापिमिल्वलः ॥१५॥

hrādasya dhamanir bhāryā-
sūta vātāpim ilvalam
yo 'gastyāya tv atithaye
pece vātāpim ilvalaḥ

hrādasya—of Hlāda; *dhamaniḥ*—Dhamani; *bhāryā*—the wife; *asūta*—gave birth to; *vātāpim*—Vātāpi; *ilvalam*—Ilvala; *yaḥ*—he who; *agastyāya*—to Agastya; *tu*—but; *atithaye*—his guest; *pece*—cooked; *vātāpim*—Vātāpi; *ilvalaḥ*—Ilvala.

TRANSLATION

The wife of Hlāda was named Dhamani. She gave birth to two sons, named Vātāpi and Ilvala. When Agastya Muni became Ilvala's guest, Ilvala served him a feast by cooking Vātāpi, who was in the shape of a ram.

TEXT 16

अनुह्रादस्य सूर्यायां बाष्कलो महिषस्तथा ।
विरोचनस्तु प्राह्रादिर्देव्यां तस्याभवद्बलिः ॥१६॥

anuhrādasya sūryāyāṁ
bāṣkalo mahiṣas tathā

virocanas tu prāhrādir
devyāṁ tasyābhavad baliḥ

anuhrādasya—of Anuhlāda; *sūryāyām*—through Sūryā; *bāṣkalaḥ*—Bāṣkala; *mahiṣaḥ*—Mahiṣa; *tathā*—also; *virocanaḥ*—Virocana; *tu*—indeed; *prāhrādiḥ*—the son of Prahlāda; *devyām*—through his wife; *tasya*—of him; *abhavat*—was; *baliḥ*—Bali.

TRANSLATION

The wife of Anuhlāda was named Sūryā. She gave birth to two sons, named Bāṣkala and Mahiṣa. Prahlāda had one son, Virocana, whose wife gave birth to Bali Mahārāja.

TEXT 17

बाणज्येष्ठं पुत्रशतमशनायां ततोऽभवत् ।
तस्यानुभावं सुश्लोक्यं पश्चादेवाभिधास्यते ॥१७॥

bāṇa-jyeṣṭhaṁ putra-śatam
aśanāyāṁ tato 'bhavat
tasyānubhāvaṁ suślokyaṁ
paścād evābhidhāsyate

bāṇa-jyeṣṭham—having Bāṇa as the eldest; *putra-śatam*—one hundred sons; *aśanāyām*—through Aśanā; *tataḥ*—from him; *abhavat*—there were; *tasya*—his; *anubhāvam*—character; *su-ślokyam*—laudable; *paścāt*—later; *eva*—certainly; *abhidhāsyate*—will be described.

TRANSLATION

Thereafter, Bali Mahārāja begot one hundred sons in the womb of Aśanā. Of these one hundred sons, King Bāṇa was the eldest. The activities of Bali Mahārāja, which are very laudable, will be described later [in the Eighth Canto].

TEXT 18

बाण आराध्य गिरिशं लेभे तद्गणमुख्यताम् ।
यत्पार्श्वे भगवानास्ते ह्यद्यापि पुरपालकः ॥१८॥

bāṇa ārādhya giriśaṁ
lebhe tad-gaṇa-mukhyatām
yat-pārśve bhagavān āste
hy adyāpi pura-pālakaḥ

bāṇaḥ—Bāṇa; *ārādhya*—having worshiped; *giriśam*—Lord Śiva; *lebhe*—obtained; *tat*—of him (Lord Śiva); *gaṇa-mukhyatām*—the platform of being one of the chief associates; *yat-pārśve*—beside whom; *bhagavān*—Lord Śiva; *āste*—remains; *hi*—because of which; *adya*—now; *api*—even; *pura-pālakaḥ*—the protector of the capital.

TRANSLATION

Since King Bāṇa was a great worshiper of Lord Śiva, he became one of Lord Śiva's most celebrated associates. Even now, Lord Śiva protects King Bāṇa's capital and always stands beside him.

TEXT 19

मरुतश्च दितेः पुत्राश्चत्वारिंशन्नवाधिकाः ।
त आसन्नप्रजाः सर्वे नीता इन्द्रेण सात्मताम् ॥१९॥

marutaś ca diteḥ putrāś
catvāriṁśan navādhikāḥ
ta āsann aprajāḥ sarve
nītā indreṇa sātmatām

marutaḥ—the Maruts; *ca*—and; *diteḥ*—of Diti; *putrāḥ*—sons; *catvāriṁśat*—forty; *nava-adhikāḥ*—plus nine; *te*—they; *āsan*—were; *aprajāḥ*—without sons; *sarve*—all; *nītāḥ*—were brought; *indreṇa*—by Indra; *sa-ātmatām*—to the position of demigods.

TRANSLATION

The forty-nine Marut demigods were also born from the womb of Diti. None of them had sons. Although they were born of Diti, King Indra gave them a position as demigods.

PURPORT

Apparently even demons can be elevated to positions as demigods when their atheistic character is reformed. There are two kinds of men throughout the universe. Those who are devotees of Lord Viṣṇu are called demigods, and those who are just the opposite are called demons. Even the demons can be transformed into demigods, as the statement of this verse proves.

TEXT 20

श्रीराजोवाच

कथं त आसुरं भावमपोह्यौत्पत्तिकं गुरो ।
इन्द्रेण प्रापिताः सात्म्यं किं तत्साधु कृतं हि तैः ॥२०॥

śrī-rājovāca
kathaṁ ta āsuraṁ bhāvam
apohyautpattikaṁ guro
indreṇa prāpitāḥ sātmyaṁ
kiṁ tat sādhu kṛtaṁ hi taiḥ

śrī-rājā uvāca—King Parīkṣit said; *katham*—why; *te*—they; *āsuram*—demoniac; *bhāvam*—mentality; *apohya*—giving up; *autpattikam*—due to birth; *guro*—my dear lord; *indreṇa*—by Indra; *prāpitāḥ*—were converted; *sa-ātmyam*—to demigods; *kim*—whether; *tat*—therefore; *sādhu*—pious activities; *kṛtam*—performed; *hi*—indeed; *taiḥ*—by them.

TRANSLATION

King Parīkṣit inquired: My dear lord, due to their birth, the forty-nine Maruts must have been obsessed with a demoniac mentality. Why did Indra, the King of heaven, convert them into demigods? Did they perform any rituals or pious activities?

TEXT 21

इमे श्रद्दधते ब्रह्मन्नृषयो हि मया सह ।
परिज्ञानाय भगवंस्तन्नो व्याख्यातुमर्हसि ॥२१॥

ime śraddadhate brahmann
ṛṣayo hi mayā saha
parijñānāya bhagavaṁs
tan no vyākhyātum arhasi

ime—these; *śraddadhate*—are eager; *brahman*—O *brāhmaṇa; ṛṣayaḥ*—sages; *hi*—indeed; *mayā saha*—with me; *parijñānāya*—to know; *bhagavan*—O great soul; *tat*—therefore; *naḥ*—to us; *vyākhyātum arhasi*—please explain.

TRANSLATION

My dear brāhmaṇa, I and all the sages present with me are eager to know about this. Therefore, O great soul, kindly explain to us the reason.

TEXT 22

श्रीसूत उवाच
तद्विष्णुरातस्य स बादरायणि-
र्वचो निशम्याद्दतमल्पमर्थवत् ।
सभाजयन् संनिभृतेन चेतसा
जगाद सत्रायण सर्वदर्शनः ॥२२॥

śrī-sūta uvāca
tad viṣṇurātasya sa bādarāyaṇir
vaco niśamyādṛtam alpam arthavat
sabhājayan san nibhṛtena cetasā
jagāda satrāyaṇa sarva-darśanaḥ

śrī-sūtaḥ uvāca—Śrī Sūta Gosvāmī said; *tat*—those; *viṣṇurātasya*—of Mahārāja Parīkṣit; *saḥ*—he; *bādarāyaṇiḥ*—Śukadeva Gosvāmī; *vacaḥ*—words; *niśamya*—hearing; *ādṛtam*—respectful; *alpam*—brief;

artha-vat—meaningful; *sabhājayan san*—praising; *nibhṛtena cetasā*—with great pleasure; *jagāda*—replied; *satrāyaṇa*—O Śaunaka; *sarva-darśanaḥ*—who is aware of everything.

TRANSLATION

Śrī Sūta Gosvāmī said: O great sage Śaunaka, after hearing Mahārāja Parīkṣit speak respectfully and briefly on topics essential to hear, Śukadeva Gosvāmī, who was well aware of everything, praised his endeavor with great pleasure and replied.

PURPORT

Mahārāja Parīkṣit's question was very much appreciated by Śukadeva Gosvāmī because although it was composed of a small number of words, it contained meaningful inquiries about how the sons of Diti, although born as demons, became demigods. Śrīla Viśvanātha Cakravartī Ṭhākura stresses that even though Diti was very envious, her heart was purified because of a devotional attitude. Another significant topic is that although Kaśyapa Muni was a learned scholar and was advanced in spiritual consciousness, he nonetheless fell a victim to the inducement of his beautiful wife. All these questions were posed in a small number of words, and therefore Śukadeva Gosvāmī very much appreciated Mahārāja Parīkṣit's inquiry.

TEXT 23

श्रीशुक उवाच
हतपुत्रा दितिः शक्रपार्ष्णिग्राहेण विष्णुना ।
मन्युना शोकदीप्तेन ज्वलन्ती पर्यचिन्तयत् ॥२३॥

śrī-śuka uvāca
hata-putrā ditiḥ śakra-
pārṣṇi-grāheṇa viṣṇunā
manyunā śoka-dīptena
jvalantī paryacintayat

śrī-śukaḥ uvāca—Śrī Śukadeva Gosvāmī said; *hata-putrā*—whose sons were killed; *ditiḥ*—Diti; *śakra-pārṣṇi-grāheṇa*—who was helping

Lord Indra; *viṣṇunā*—by Lord Viṣṇu; *manyunā*—with anger; *śoka-dīptena*—kindled by lamentation; *jvalantī*—burning; *paryacintayat*—thought.

TRANSLATION

Śrī Śukadeva Gosvāmī said: Just to help Indra, Lord Viṣṇu killed the two brothers Hiraṇyākṣa and Hiraṇyakaśipu. Because of their being killed, their mother, Diti, overwhelmed with lamentation and anger, contemplated as follows.

TEXT 24

कदा नु भ्रातृहन्तारमिन्द्रियाराममुल्बणम् ।
अक्लिन्नहृदयं पापं घातयित्वा शये सुखम् ॥२४॥

kadā nu bhrātṛ-hantāram
indriyārāmam ulbaṇam
aklinna-hṛdayaṁ pāpaṁ
ghātayitvā śaye sukham

kadā—when; *nu*—indeed; *bhrātṛ-hantāram*—the killer of the brothers; *indriya-ārāmam*—very fond of sense gratification; *ulbaṇam*—cruel; *aklinna-hṛdayam*—hardhearted; *pāpam*—sinful; *ghātayitvā*—having caused to be killed; *śaye*—shall I rest; *sukham*—happily.

TRANSLATION

Lord Indra, who is very much fond of sense gratification, has killed the two brothers Hiraṇyākṣa and Hiraṇyakaśipu by means of Lord Viṣṇu. Therefore Indra is cruel, hardhearted and sinful. When will I, having killed him, rest with a pacified mind?

TEXT 25

कृमिविड्भस्मसंज्ञासीद्यस्येशाभिहितस्य च ।
भूतध्रुक् तत्कृते स्वार्थं किं वेद निरयो यतः ॥२५॥

kṛmi-viḍ-bhasma-saṁjñāsīd
yasyeśābhihitasya ca

bhūta-dhruk tat-kṛte svārthaṁ
kiṁ veda nirayo yataḥ

kṛmi—worms; *viṭ*—stool; *bhasma*—ashes; *saṁjñā*—name; *āsīt*—becomes; *yasya*—of which (body); *īśa-abhihitasya*—although designated as king; *ca*—also; *bhūta-dhruk*—he who harms others; *tat-kṛte*—for the sake of that; *sva-artham*—his self-interest; *kim veda*—does he know; *nirayaḥ*—punishment in hell; *yataḥ*—from which.

TRANSLATION

When dead, the bodies of all the rulers known as kings and great leaders will be transformed into worms, stool or ashes. If one enviously kills others for the protection of such a body, does he actually know the true interest of life? Certainly he does not, for if one is envious of other entities, he surely goes to hell.

PURPORT

The material body, even if possessed by a great king, is ultimately transformed into stool, worms or ashes. When one is too attached to the bodily conception of life, he is certainly not very intelligent.

TEXT 26

आशासानस्य तस्येदं ध्रुवमुन्नद्धचेतसः ।
मदशोषक इन्द्रस्य भूयाद्येन सुतो हि मे ॥२६॥

āśāsānasya tasyedaṁ
dhruvam unnaddha-cetasaḥ
mada-śoṣaka indrasya
bhūyād yena suto hi me

āśāsānasya—thinking; *tasya*—of him; *idam*—this (body); *dhruvam*—eternal; *unnaddha-cetasaḥ*—whose mind is unrestrained; *mada-śoṣakaḥ*—who can remove the madness; *indrasya*—of Indra; *bhūyāt*—may there be; *yena*—by which; *sutaḥ*—a son; *hi*—certainly; *me*—of me.

TRANSLATION

Diti thought: Indra considers his body eternal, and thus he has become unrestrained. I therefore wish to have a son who can remove Indra's madness. Let me adopt some means to help me in this.

PURPORT

One who is in the bodily conception of life is compared in the *śāstras* to animals like cows and asses. Diti wanted to punish Indra, who had become like a lower animal.

TEXTS 27–28

इति भावेन सा भर्तुराचचारासकृत्प्रियम् ।
शुश्रूषयानुरागेण प्रश्रयेण दमेन च ॥२७॥
भक्त्या परमया राजन् मनोज्ञैर्वल्गुभाषितैः ।
मनो जग्राह भावज्ञा सस्मितापाङ्गवीक्षणैः ॥२८॥

iti bhāvena sā bhartur
ācacārāsakṛt priyam
śuśrūṣayānurāgeṇa
praśrayeṇa damena ca

bhaktyā paramayā rājan
manojñair valgu-bhāṣitaiḥ
mano jagrāha bhāva-jñā
sasmitāpāṅga-vīkṣaṇaiḥ

iti—thus; *bhāvena*—with the intention; *sā*—she; *bhartuḥ*—of the husband; *ācacāra*—performed; *asakṛt*—constantly; *priyam*—pleasing activities; *śuśrūṣayā*—with service; *anurāgeṇa*—with love; *praśrayeṇa*—with humility; *damena*—with self-control; *ca*—also; *bhaktyā*—with devotion; *paramayā*—great; *rājan*—O King; *manojñaiḥ*—charming; *valgu-bhāṣitaiḥ*—with sweet words; *manaḥ*—his mind; *jagrāha*—brought under her control; *bhāva-jñā*—knowing his nature; *sa-smita*—with smiling; *apāṅga-vīkṣaṇaiḥ*—by glancing.

TRANSLATION

Thinking in this way [with a desire for a son to kill Indra], Diti began constantly acting to satisfy Kaśyapa by her pleasing behavior. O King, Diti always carried out Kaśyapa's orders very faithfully, as he desired. With service, love, humility and control, with words spoken very sweetly to satisfy her husband, and with smiles and glances at him, Diti attracted his mind and brought it under her control.

PURPORT

When a woman wants to endear herself to her husband and make him very faithful, she must try to please him in all respects. When the husband is pleased with his wife, the wife can receive all necessities, ornaments and full satisfaction for her senses. Herein this is indicated by the behavior of Diti.

TEXT 29

एवं स्त्रिया जडीभूतो विद्वानपि मनोज्ञया ।
बाढमित्याह विवशो न तच्चित्रं हि योषिति ॥२९॥

evaṁ striyā jaḍībhūto
vidvān api manojñayā
bāḍham ity āha vivaśo
na tac citraṁ hi yoṣiti

evam—thus; *striyā*—by the woman; *jaḍībhūtaḥ*—enchanted; *vidvān*—very learned; *api*—although; *manojñayā*—very expert; *bāḍham*—yes; *iti*—thus; *āha*—said; *vivaśaḥ*—under her control; *na*—not; *tat*—that; *citram*—astonishing; *hi*—indeed; *yoṣiti*—in the matter of women.

TRANSLATION

Although Kaśyapa Muni was a learned scholar, he was captivated by Diti's artificial behavior, which brought him under her control. Therefore he assured his wife that he would fulfill her desires. Such a promise by a husband is not at all astonishing.

TEXT 30

विलोक्यैकान्तभूतानि भूतान्यादौ प्रजापतिः ।
स्त्रियं चक्रे स्वदेहार्धं यया पुंसां मतिर्हृता ॥३०॥

vilokyaikānta-bhūtāni
bhūtāny ādau prajāpatiḥ
striyaṁ cakre sva-dehārdhaṁ
yayā puṁsāṁ matir hṛtā

vilokya—seeing; *ekānta-bhūtāni*—detached; *bhūtāni*—the living entities; *ādau*—in the beginning; *prajāpatiḥ*—Lord Brahmā; *striyam*—the woman; *cakre*—created; *sva-deha*—of his body; *ardham*—half; *yayā*—by whom; *puṁsām*—of men; *matiḥ*—the mind; *hṛtā*—carried away.

TRANSLATION

In the beginning of creation, Lord Brahmā, the father of the living entities of the universe, saw that all the living entities were unattached. To increase population, he then created woman from the better half of man's body, for woman's behavior carries away a man's mind.

PURPORT

This entire universe is going on under the spell of sexual attachment, which was created by Lord Brahmā to increase the population of the entire universe, not only in human society but also in other species. As stated by Ṛṣabhadeva in the Fifth Canto, *puṁsaḥ striyā mithunī-bhāvam etam:* the entire world is going on under the spell of sexual attraction and desire between man and woman. When man and woman unite, the hard knot of this attraction becomes increasingly tight, and thus a man is implicated in the materialistic way of life. This is the illusion of the material world. This illusion acted upon Kaśyapa Muni, although he was very learned and advanced in spiritual knowledge. As stated in the *Manu-saṁhitā* (2.215) and *Śrīmad-Bhāgavatam* (9.19.17):

mātrā svasrā duhitrā vā
nāviviktāsano bhavet

balavān indriya-grāmo
vidvāṁsam api karṣati

"A man should not associate with a woman in a solitary place, not even with his mother, sister or daughter, for the senses are so strong that they lead astray even a person advanced in knowledge." When a man remains in a solitary place with a woman, his sexual desires undoubtedly increase. Therefore the words *ekānta-bhūtāni,* which are used here, indicate that to avoid sexual desires one should avoid the company of women as far as possible. Sexual desire is so powerful that one is saturated with it if he stays in a solitary place with any woman, even his mother, sister or daughter.

TEXT 31

एवं शुश्रूषितस्तात भगवान् कश्यपः स्त्रिया ।
प्रहस्य परमप्रीतो दितिमाहाभिनन्द्य च ॥३१॥

evaṁ śuśrūṣitas tāta
bhagavān kaśyapaḥ striyā
prahasya parama-prīto
ditim āhābhinandya ca

evam—thus; *śuśrūṣitaḥ*—being served; *tāta*—O dear one; *bhagavān*—the powerful; *kaśyapaḥ*—Kaśyapa; *striyā*—by the woman; *prahasya*—smiling; *parama-prītaḥ*—being very pleased; *ditim*—to Diti; *āha*—said; *abhinandya*—approving; *ca*—also.

TRANSLATION

O my dear one, the most powerful sage Kaśyapa, being extremely pleased by the mild behavior of his wife Diti, smiled and spoke to her as follows.

TEXT 32

श्रीकश्यप उवाच

वरं वरय वामोरु प्रीतस्तेऽहमनिन्दिते ।
स्त्रिया भर्तरि सुप्रीते कः काम इह चागमः ॥३२॥

śrī-kaśyapa uvāca
varaṁ varaya vāmoru
prītas te 'ham anindite
striyā bhartari suprīte
kaḥ kāma iha cāgamaḥ

śrī-kaśyapaḥ uvāca—Kaśyapa Muni said; *varam*—benediction; *varaya*—ask; *vāmoru*—O beautiful woman; *prītaḥ*—pleased; *te*—with you; *aham*—I; *anindite*—O irreproachable lady; *striyāḥ*—for the woman; *bhartari*—when the husband; *su-prīte*—pleased; *kaḥ*—what; *kāmaḥ*—desire; *iha*—here; *ca*—and; *agamaḥ*—difficult to obtain.

TRANSLATION

Kaśyapa Muni said: O beautiful woman, O irreproachable lady, since I am very much pleased by your behavior, you may ask me for any benediction you want. If a husband is pleased, what desires are difficult for his wife to obtain, either in this world or in the next?

TEXTS 33–34

पतिरेव हि नारीणां दैवतं परमं स्मृतम् ।
मानसः सर्वभूतानां वासुदेवः श्रियः पतिः ॥३३॥
स एव देवतालिङ्गैर्नामरूपविकल्पितैः ।
इज्यते भगवान् पुम्भिः स्त्रीभिश्च पतिरूपधृक् ॥३४॥

patir eva hi nārīṇāṁ
daivataṁ paramaṁ smṛtam
mānasaḥ sarva-bhūtānāṁ
vāsudevaḥ śriyaḥ patiḥ

sa eva devatā-liṅgair
nāma-rūpa-vikalpitaiḥ
ijyate bhagavān pumbhiḥ
strībhiś ca pati-rūpa-dhṛk

patiḥ—the husband; *eva*—indeed; *hi*—certainly; *nārīṇām*—of women; *daivatam*—demigod; *paramam*—supreme; *smṛtam*—is considered; *mānasaḥ*—situated in the heart; *sarva-bhūtānām*—of all living entities; *vāsudevaḥ*—Vāsudeva; *śriyaḥ*—of the goddess of fortune; *patiḥ*—the husband; *saḥ*—He; *eva*—certainly; *devatā-liṅgaiḥ*—by the forms of the demigods; *nāma*—names; *rūpa*—forms; *vikalpitaiḥ*—conceived; *ijyate*—is worshiped; *bhagavān*—the Supreme Personality of Godhead; *pumbhiḥ*—by men; *strībhiḥ*—by women; *ca*—also; *pati-rūpa-dhṛk*—in the form of the husband.

TRANSLATION

A husband is the supreme demigod for a woman. The Supreme Personality of Godhead, Lord Vāsudeva, the husband of the goddess of fortune, is situated in everyone's heart and is worshiped through the various names and forms of the demigods by fruitive workers. Similarly, a husband represents the Lord as the object of worship for a woman.

PURPORT

The Lord says in *Bhagavad-gītā* (9.23):

ye 'py anya-devatā-bhaktā
yajante śraddhayānvitāḥ
te 'pi mām eva kaunteya
yajanty avidhi-pūrvakam

"Whatever a man may sacrifice to other gods, O son of Kuntī, is really meant for Me alone, but it is offered without true understanding." The demigods are various assistants who act like the hands and legs of the Supreme Personality of Godhead. One who is not in direct touch with the Supreme Lord and cannot conceive of the exalted position of the Lord is sometimes advised to worship the demigods as various parts of the Lord. If women, who are usually very much attached to their husbands, worship their husbands as representatives of Vāsudeva, the women benefit, just as Ajāmila benefited by calling for Nārāyaṇa, his son. Ajāmila was concerned with his son, but because of his attachment to the name of Nārāyaṇa, he attained salvation simply by chanting that name. In India a husband is still called *pati-guru*, the husband spiritual master. If husband and wife are attached to one another for advancement in Kṛṣṇa consciousness, their relationship of cooperation is very effective for such advancement. Although the names of Indra and Agni are sometimes uttered in the Vedic *mantras* (*indrāya svāhā, agnaye svāhā*), the Vedic sacrifices are actually performed for the satisfaction of Lord Viṣṇu. As long as one is very much attached to material sense gratification, the worship of the demigods or the worship of one's husband is recommended.

TEXT 35

तस्मात्पतिव्रता नार्यः श्रेयस्कामाः सुमध्यमे ।
यजन्तेऽनन्यभावेन पतिमात्मानमीश्वरम् ॥३५॥

tasmāt pati-vratā nāryaḥ
śreyas-kāmāḥ sumadhyame
yajante 'nanya-bhāvena
patim ātmānam īśvaram

tasmāt—therefore; *pati-vratāḥ*—devoted to the husband; *nāryaḥ*—women; *śreyaḥ-kāmāḥ*—conscientious; *su-madhyame*—O thin-waisted woman; *yajante*—worship; *ananya-bhāvena*—with devotion; *patim*—the husband; *ātmānam*—the Supersoul; *īśvaram*—representative of the Supreme Personality of Godhead.

TRANSLATION

My dear wife, whose body is so beautiful, your waist being thin, a conscientious wife should be chaste and should abide by the orders of her husband. She should very devoutly worship her husband as a representative of Vāsudeva.

TEXT 36

सोऽहं त्वयार्चितो भद्रे ईदृग्भावेन भक्तितः ।
तं ते सम्पादये काममसतीनां सुदुर्लभम् ॥३६॥

so 'haṁ tvayārcito bhadre
īdṛg-bhāvena bhaktitaḥ

taṁ te sampādaye kāmam
asatīnāṁ sudurlabham

saḥ—such a person; *aham*—I; *tvayā*—by you; *arcitaḥ*—worshiped; *bhadre*—O gentle woman; *īdṛk-bhāvena*—in such a way; *bhaktitaḥ*—with devotion; *tam*—that; *te*—your; *sampādaye*—shall fulfill; *kāmam*—desire; *asatīnām*—for unchaste women; *su-durlabham*—not obtainable.

TRANSLATION

My dear gentle wife, because you have worshiped me with great devotion, considering me a representative of the Supreme Personality of Godhead, I shall reward you by fulfilling your desires, which are unobtainable for an unchaste wife.

TEXT 37

दितिरुवाच
वरदो यदि मे ब्रह्मन् पुत्रमिन्द्रहणं वृणे ।
अमृत्युं मृतपुत्राहं येन मे घातितौ सुतौ ॥३७॥

ditir uvāca
varado yadi me brahman
putram indra-haṇaṁ vṛṇe
amṛtyuṁ mṛta-putrāhaṁ
yena me ghātitau sutau

ditiḥ uvāca—Diti said; *vara-daḥ*—the giver of benedictions; *yadi*—if; *me*—to me; *brahman*—O great soul; *putram*—a son; *indra-haṇam*—who can kill Indra; *vṛṇe*—I am asking for; *amṛtyum*—immortal; *mṛta-putrā*—whose sons are dead; *aham*—I; *yena*—by whom; *me*—my; *ghātitau*—were caused to be killed; *sutau*—two sons.

TRANSLATION

Diti replied: O my husband, O great soul, I have now lost my sons. If you want to give me a benediction, I ask you for an immor-

tal son who can kill Indra. I pray for this because Indra, with the help of Viṣṇu, has killed my two sons Hiraṇyākṣa and Hiraṇyakaśipu.

PURPORT

The word *indra-haṇam* means "one who can kill Indra," but it also means "one who follows Indra." The word *amṛtyum* refers to the demigods, who do not die like ordinary human beings because they have extremely long durations of life. For example, the duration of Lord Brahmā's life is stated in *Bhagavad-gītā: sahasra-yuga-paryantam ahar yad brahmaṇo viduḥ.* Even the duration of one day, or twelve hours, of Brahmā is 4,300,000 years multiplied by one thousand. Thus the duration of his life is inconceivable for an ordinary human being. The demigods are therefore sometimes called *amara*, which means "one who has no death." In this material world, however, everyone has to die. Therefore the word *amṛtyum* indicates that Diti wanted a son who would be equal in status to the demigods.

TEXT 38

निशम्य तद्वचो विप्रो विमनाः पर्यतप्यत ।
अहो अधर्मः सुमहानद्य मे समुपस्थितः ॥३८॥

niśamya tad-vaco vipro
vimanāḥ paryatapyata
aho adharmaḥ sumahān
adya me samupasthitaḥ

niśamya—hearing; *tat-vacaḥ*—her words; *vipraḥ*—the *brāhmaṇa; vimanāḥ*—aggrieved; *paryatapyata*—lamented; *aho*—alas; *adharmaḥ*—impiety; *su-mahān*—very great; *adya*—today; *me*—upon me; *samupasthitaḥ*—has come.

TRANSLATION

Upon hearing Diti's request, Kaśyapa Muni was very much aggrieved. "Alas," he lamented, "now I face the danger of the impious act of killing Indra."

PURPORT

Although Kaśyapa Muni was eager to fulfill the desire of his wife Diti, when he heard that she wanted a son to kill Indra his jubilation was immediately reduced to nothing because he was averse to the idea.

TEXT 39

अहो अर्थेन्द्रियारामो योषिन्मय्येह मायया ।
गृहीतचेताः कृपणः पतिष्ये नरके ध्रुवम् ॥३९॥

aho arthendriyārāmo
yoṣin-mayyeha māyayā
gṛhīta-cetāḥ kṛpaṇaḥ
patiṣye narake dhruvam

aho—alas; *artha-indriya-ārāmaḥ*—too attached to material enjoyment; *yoṣit-mayyā*—in the form of a woman; *iha*—here; *māyayā*—by the illusory energy; *gṛhīta-cetāḥ*—my mind being captivated; *kṛpaṇaḥ*—wretched; *patiṣye*—I shall fall; *narake*—to hell; *dhruvam*—surely.

TRANSLATION

Kaśyapa Muni thought: Alas, I have now become too attached to material enjoyment. Taking advantage of this, my mind has been attracted by the illusory energy of the Supreme Personality of Godhead in the form of a woman [my wife]. Therefore I am surely a wretched person who will glide down toward hell.

TEXT 40

कोऽतिक्रमोऽनुवर्तन्त्याः स्वभावमिह योषितः ।
धिङ् मां बताबुधं स्वार्थे यदहं त्वजितेन्द्रियः ॥४०॥

ko 'tikramo 'nuvartantyāḥ
svabhāvam iha yoṣitaḥ
dhiṅ māṁ batābudhaṁ svārthe
yad ahaṁ tv ajitendriyaḥ

kaḥ—what; *atikramaḥ*—offense; *anuvartantyāḥ*—following; *sva-bhāvam*—her nature; *iha*—here; *yoṣitaḥ*—of the woman; *dhik*—condemnation; *mām*—unto me; *bata*—alas; *abudham*—not conversant; *sva-arthe*—in what is good for me; *yat*—because; *aham*—I; *tu*—indeed; *ajita-indriyaḥ*—unable to control my senses.

TRANSLATION

This woman, my wife, has adopted a means that follows her nature, and therefore she is not to be blamed. But I am a man. Therefore, all condemnation upon me! I am not at all conversant with what is good for me, since I could not control my senses.

PURPORT

The natural instinct of a woman is to enjoy the material world. She induces her husband to enjoy this world by satisfying his tongue, belly and genitals, which are called *jihvā, udara* and *upastha.* A woman is expert in cooking palatable dishes so that she can easily satisfy her husband in eating. When one eats nicely, his belly is satisfied, and as soon as the belly is satisfied the genitals become strong. Especially when a man is accustomed to eating meat and drinking wine and similar passionate things, he certainly becomes sexually inclined. It should be understood that sexual inclinations are meant not for spiritual progress but for gliding down to hell. Thus Kaśyapa Muni considered his situation and lamented. In other words, to be a householder is very risky unless one is trained and the wife is a follower of her husband. A husband should be trained at the very beginning of his life. *Kaumāra ācaret prājño dharmān bhāgavatān iha* (*Bhāg.* 7.6.1). During the time of *brahmacarya,* or student life, a *brahmacārī* should be taught to be expert in *bhāgavata-dharma,* devotional service. Then when he marries, if his wife is faithful to her husband and follows him in such life, the relationship between husband and wife is very desirable. However, a relationship between husband and wife without spiritual consciousness but strictly for sense gratification is not at all good. It is said in *Śrīmad-Bhāgavatam* (12.2.3) that especially in this age, Kali-yuga, *dām-patye 'bhirucir hetuḥ:* the relationship between husband and wife will be based on sexual power. Therefore householder life in this Kali-yuga is extremely dangerous unless both the wife and husband take to Kṛṣṇa consciousness.

TEXT 41

शरत्पद्मोत्सवं वक्त्रं वचश्च श्रवणामृतम् ।
हृदयं क्षुरधाराभं स्त्रीणां को वेद चेष्टितम् ॥४१॥

śarat-padmotsavaṁ vaktraṁ
vacaś ca śravaṇāmṛtam
hṛdayaṁ kṣura-dhārābhaṁ
strīṇāṁ ko veda ceṣṭitam

śarat—in the autumn; *padma*—a lotus flower; *utsavam*—blossoming; *vaktram*—face; *vacaḥ*—words; *ca*—and; *śravaṇa*—to the ear; *amṛtam*—giving pleasure; *hṛdayam*—heart; *kṣura-dhārā*—the blade of a razor; *ābham*—like; *strīṇām*—of women; *kaḥ*—who; *veda*—knows; *ceṣṭitam*—the dealings.

TRANSLATION

A woman's face is as attractive and beautiful as a blossoming lotus flower during autumn. Her words are very sweet, and they give pleasure to the ear, but if we study a woman's heart, we can understand it to be extremely sharp, like the blade of a razor. In these circumstances, who could understand the dealings of a woman?

PURPORT

Woman is now depicted very well from the materialistic point of view by Kaśyapa Muni. Women are generally known as the fair sex, and especially in youth, at the age of sixteen or seventeen, women are very attractive to men. Therefore a woman's face is compared to a blooming lotus flower in autumn. Just as a lotus is extremely beautiful in autumn, a woman at the threshold of youthful beauty is extremely attractive. In Sanskrit a woman's voice is called *nārī-svara* because women generally sing and their singing is very attractive. At the present moment, cinema artists, especially female singers, are especially welcome. Some of them earn fabulous amounts of money simply by singing. Therefore, as taught by Śrī Caitanya Mahāprabhu, a woman's singing is dangerous because it can make a *sannyāsī* fall a victim to the woman. *Sannyāsa* means giving up the company of women, but if a *sannyāsī* hears the voice of a woman and sees her beautiful face, he certainly becomes attracted and is sure to fall down. There have been many examples. Even the great sage Viśvāmitra fell a victim to Menakā. Therefore a person desiring to advance in spiritual consciousness must be especially careful not to see a woman's face or hear a woman's voice. To see a woman's face and appreciate its beauty or to hear a woman's voice and appreciate her singing as very nice is a subtle falldown for a *brahmacārī* or *sannyāsī*. Thus the description of a woman's features by Kaśyapa Muni is very instructive.

When a woman's bodily features are attractive, when her face is beautiful and when her voice is sweet, she is naturally a trap for a man. The *śāstras* advise that when such a woman comes to serve a man, she should be considered to be like a dark well covered by grass. In the fields there are many such wells, and a man who does not know about them drops through the grass and falls down. Thus there are many such instructions. Since the attraction of the material world is based on attraction for women, Kaśyapa Muni thought, "Under the circumstances, who can understand the heart of a woman?" Cāṇakya Paṇḍita has also advised, *viśvāso naiva kartavyaḥ strīṣu rāja-kuleṣu ca:* "There are two persons one should not trust—a politician and a woman." These, of course, are authoritative śāstric injunctions, and we should therefore be very careful in our dealings with women.

Sometimes our Kṛṣṇa consciousness movement is criticized for mingling men and women, but Kṛṣṇa consciousness is meant for anyone. Whether one is a man or woman does not matter. Lord Kṛṣṇa personally says, *striyo vaiśyās tathā śūdrās te 'pi yānti parāṁ gatim:* whether one is a woman, *śūdra* or *vaiśya*, not to speak of being a *brāhmaṇa* or *kṣatriya*, everyone is fit to return home, back to Godhead, if he strictly follows the instructions of the spiritual master and *śāstra*. We therefore request all the members of the Kṛṣṇa consciousness movement—both men and women—not to be attracted by bodily features but only to be attracted by Kṛṣṇa. Then everything will be all right. Otherwise there will be danger.

TEXT 42

न हि कश्चित्प्रियः स्त्रीणामञ्जसा स्वाशिषात्मनाम् ।
पतिं पुत्रं भ्रातरं वा घ्नन्त्यर्थे घातयन्ति च ॥४२॥

na hi kaścit priyaḥ strīṇām
añjasā svāśiṣātmanām
patiṁ putraṁ bhrātaraṁ vā
ghnanty arthe ghātayanti ca

na—not; *hi*—certainly; *kaścit*—anyone; *priyaḥ*—dear; *strīṇām*—to women; *añjasā*—actually; *sva-āśiṣā*—for their own interests; *ātmanām*—most dear; *patim*—husband; *putram*—son; *bhrātaram*—brother; *vā*—or; *ghnanti*—they kill; *arthe*—for their own interests; *ghātayanti*—cause to be killed; *ca*—also.

TRANSLATION

To satisfy their own interests, women deal with men as if the men were most dear to them, but no one is actually dear to them. Women are supposed to be very saintly, but for their own interests they can kill even their husbands, sons or brothers, or cause them to be killed by others.

PURPORT

A woman's nature has been particularly well studied by Kaśyapa Muni. Women are self-interested by nature, and therefore they should be protected by all means so that their natural inclination to be too self-interested will not be manifested. Women need to be protected by men. A woman should be cared for by her father in her childhood, by her husband in her youth and by her grown sons in her old age. This is the injunction of Manu, who says that a woman should not be given independence at any stage. Women must be cared for so that they will not be free to manifest their natural tendency for gross selfishness. There have been many cases, even in the present day, in which women have killed their husbands to take advantage of their insurance policies. This is not a criticism of women but a practical study of their nature. Such natural instincts of a woman or a man are manifested only in the bodily conception of life. When either a man or a woman is advanced in spiritual consciousness, the bodily conception of life practically vanishes. We should see all women as spiritual units (*ahaṁ brahmāsmi*), whose only duty is to satisfy Kṛṣṇa. Then the influences of the different modes of material nature, which result from one's possessing a material body, will not act.

The Kṛṣṇa consciousness movement is so beneficial that it can very easily counteract the contamination of material nature, which results from one's possessing a material body. *Bhagavad-gītā* therefore teaches, in the very beginning, that whether one is a man or a woman, one must know that he or she is not the body but a spiritual soul. Everyone should be interested in the activities of the spirit soul, not the body. As long as one is activated by the bodily conception of life, there is always the danger of being misled, whether one is a man or a woman. The soul is sometimes described as *puruṣa* because whether one is dressed as a man or a woman, one is inclined to enjoy this material world. One who has this spirit of enjoyment is described as *puruṣa*. Whether one is a man or a woman, he is not interested in serving others; everyone is interested in satisfying his or her own senses. Kṛṣṇa consciousness, however, provides first-class training for a man or a woman. A man should be trained to be a first-class devotee of Lord Kṛṣṇa, and a woman should be trained to be a very chaste follower of her husband. That will make the lives of both of them happy.

TEXT 43

प्रतिश्रुतं ददामीति वचस्तन्न मृषा भवेत् ।
वधं नार्हति चेन्द्रोऽपि तत्रेदमुपकल्पते ॥४३॥

pratiśrutaṁ dadāmīti
vacas tan na mṛṣā bhavet
vadhaṁ nārhati cendro 'pi
tatredam upakalpate

pratiśrutam—promised; *dadāmi*—I shall give; *iti*—thus; *vacaḥ*—statement; *tat*—that; *na*—not; *mṛṣā*—false; *bhavet*—can be; *vadham*—killing; *na*—not; *arhati*—is suitable; *ca*—and; *indraḥ*—Indra; *api*—also; *tatra*—in that connection; *idam*—this; *upakalpate*—is suitable.

TRANSLATION

I promised to give her a benediction, and this promise cannot be violated, but Indra does not deserve to be killed. In these circumstances, the solution I have is quite suitable.

PURPORT

Kaśyapa Muni concluded, "Diti is eager to have a son who can kill Indra, since she is a woman, after all, and is not very intelligent. I shall train her in such a way that instead of always thinking of how to kill Indra, she will become a Vaiṣṇava, a devotee of Kṛṣṇa. If she agrees to follow the rules and regulations of the Vaiṣṇava principles, the unclean core of her heart will certainly be cleansed." *Ceto-darpaṇa-mārjanam.* This is the process of devotional service. Anyone can be purified by following the principles of devotional service in Kṛṣṇa consciousness, for Kṛṣṇa consciousness is so powerful that it can purify even the dirtiest class of men and transform them into the topmost Vaiṣṇavas. Śrī Caitanya Mahāprabhu's movement aims at this purpose. Narottama dāsa Ṭhākura says:

vrajendra-nandana yei, śacī-suta haila sei,
balarāma ha-ila nitāi
dīna-hīna yata chila, hari-nāme uddhārila,
ta'ra sākṣī jagāi-mādhāi

The appearance of Śrī Caitanya Mahāprabhu in this Kali-yuga is especially meant to deliver the fallen souls, who are always planning something for material enjoyment. He gave the people of this age the advantage of being able to chant the Hare Kṛṣṇa *mantra* and thus become fully pure, free from all material contamination. Once one becomes a pure Vaiṣṇava, he transcends all material conceptions of life. Thus Kaśyapa Muni tried to transform his wife into a Vaiṣṇavī so that she might give up the idea of killing Indra. He wanted both her and her sons to be purified so that they would be fit to become pure Vaiṣṇavas. Of course, sometimes a practitioner deviates from the Vaiṣṇava principles, and there is a chance that he may fall down, but Kaśyapa Muni thought that even if one falls while practicing the Vaiṣṇava principles, he is still not a loser. Even a fallen Vaiṣṇava is eligible for better results, as confirmed in *Bhagavad-gītā*. *Svalpam apy asya dharmasya trāyate mahato bhayāt:* even practicing the Vaiṣṇava principles to a small extent can save one from the greatest danger of material existence. Thus Kaśyapa Muni planned to instruct his wife Diti to become a Vaiṣṇava because he wanted to save the life of Indra.

TEXT 44

इति संचिन्त्य भगवान्मारीचः कुरुनन्दन ।
उवाच किञ्चित् कुपित आत्मानं च विगर्हयन् ॥४४॥

iti sañcintya bhagavān
mārīcaḥ kurunandana
uvāca kiñcit kupita
ātmānaṁ ca vigarhayan

iti—thus; *sañcintya*—thinking; *bhagavān*—the powerful; *mārīcaḥ*—Kaśyapa Muni; *kuru-nandana*—O descendant of Kuru; *uvāca*—spoke; *kiñcit*—somewhat; *kupitaḥ*—angry; *ātmānam*—himself; *ca*—and; *vigarhayan*—condemning.

TRANSLATION

Śrī Śukadeva Gosvāmī said: Kaśyapa Muni, thinking in this way, became somewhat angry. Condemning himself, O Mahārāja Parīkṣit, descendant of Kuru, he spoke to Diti as follows.

TEXT 45

श्रीकश्यप उवाच
पुत्रस्ते भविता भद्रे इन्द्रहादेवबान्धवः ।
संवत्सरं व्रतमिदं यद्यञ्जो धारयिष्यसि ॥४५॥

śrī-kaśyapa uvāca
putras te bhavitā bhadre
indra-hādeva-bāndhavaḥ
saṁvatsaraṁ vratam idaṁ
yady añjo dhārayiṣyasi

śrī-kaśyapaḥ uvāca—Kaśyapa Muni said; *putraḥ*—son; *te*—your; *bhavitā*—will be; *bhadre*—O gentle woman; *indra-hā*—killer of Indra, or follower of Indra; *adeva-bāndhavaḥ*—friend of the demons (or *deva-bāndhavaḥ*—friend of the demigods); *saṁvatsaram*—for a year; *vratam*—vow; *idam*—this; *yadi*—if; *añjaḥ*—properly; *dhārayiṣyasi*—you will execute.

TRANSLATION

Kaśyapa Muni said: My dear gentle wife, if you follow my instructions regarding this vow for at least one year, you will surely get a son who will be able to kill Indra. However, if you deviate from this vow of following the Vaiṣṇava principles, you will get a son who will be favorable to Indra.

PURPORT

The word *indra-hā* refers to an *asura* who is always eager to kill Indra. An enemy of Indra is naturally a friend to the *asuras*, but the word *indra-hā* also refers to one who follows Indra or who is obedient to him. When one becomes a devotee of Indra, he is certainly a friend to the demigods. Thus the words *indra-hādeva-bāndhavaḥ* are equivocal, for they say, "Your son will kill Indra, but he will be very friendly to the demigods." If a person actually became a friend of the demigods, he certainly would not be able to kill Indra.

TEXT 46

दितिरुवाच

धारयिष्ये व्रतं ब्रह्मन्ब्रूहि कार्याणि यानि मे ।
यानि चेह निषिद्धानि न व्रतं घ्नन्ति यान्युत ॥४६॥

ditir uvāca
dhārayiṣye vrataṁ brahman
brūhi kāryāṇi yāni me
yāni ceha niṣiddhāni
na vrataṁ ghnanti yāny uta

ditiḥ uvāca—Diti said; *dhārayiṣye*—I shall accept; *vratam*—vow; *brahman*—my dear *brāhmaṇa; brūhi*—please state; *kāryāṇi*—must be done; *yāni*—what; *me*—to me; *yāni*—what; *ca*—and; *iha*—here; *niṣiddhāni*—is forbidden; *na*—not; *vratam*—the vow; *ghnanti*—break; *yāni*—what; *uta*—also.

TRANSLATION

Diti replied: My dear brāhmaṇa, I must accept your advice and follow the vow. Now let me understand what I have to do, what is forbidden and what will not break the vow. Please clearly state all this to me.

PURPORT

As stated above, a woman is generally inclined to serve her own purposes. Kaśyapa Muni proposed to train Diti to fulfill her desires within one year, and since she was eager to kill Indra, she immediately agreed, saying, "Please let me know what the vow is and how I have to follow it. I promise that I shall do the needful and not break the vow." This is another side of a woman's psychology. Even though a woman is very fond of fulfilling her own plans, when someone instructs her, especially her husband, she innocently follows, and thus she can be trained for better purposes. By nature a woman wants to be a follower of a man; therefore if the man is good the woman can be trained for a good purpose.

TEXT 47

श्रीकश्यप उवाच
न हिंस्याद्भूतजातानि न शपेन्नानृतं वदेत् ।
नच्छिन्द्यान्नखरोमाणि न स्पृशेद्यदमङ्गलम् ॥४७॥

śrī-kaśyapa uvāca
na hiṁsyād bhūta-jātāni
na śapen nānṛtaṁ vadet
na chindyān nakha-romāṇi
na spṛśed yad amaṅgalam

śrī-kaśyapaḥ uvāca—Kaśyapa Muni said; *na hiṁsyāt*—must not harm; *bhūta-jātāni*—the living entities; *na śapet*—must not curse; *na*—not; *anṛtam*—a lie; *vadet*—must speak; *na chindyāt*—must not cut; *nakha-romāṇi*—the nails and hair; *na spṛśet*—must not touch; *yat*—that which; *amaṅgalam*—impure.

TRANSLATION

Kaśyapa Muni said: My dear wife, to follow this vow, do not be violent or cause harm to anyone. Do not curse anyone, and do not speak lies. Do not cut your nails and hair, and do not touch impure things like skulls and bones.

PURPORT

Kaśyapa Muni's first instruction to his wife was not to be envious. The general tendency of anyone within this material world is to be envious, and therefore, to become a Kṛṣṇa conscious person, one must curb this tendency, as stated in *Śrīmad-Bhāgavatam* (*paramo nirmatsarāṇām*). A Kṛṣṇa conscious person is always nonenvious, whereas others are always envious. Thus Kaśyapa Muni's instruction that his wife not be envious indicates that this is the first stage of advancement in Kṛṣṇa consciousness. Kaśyapa Muni desired to train his wife to be a Kṛṣṇa conscious person, for this would suffice to protect both her and Indra.

TEXT 48

नाप्सु स्नायान्न कुप्येत न सम्भाषेत दुर्जनैः ।
न वसीताधौतवासः स्रजं च विधृतां क्वचित् ॥४८॥

nāpsu snāyān na kupyeta
na sambhāṣeta durjanaiḥ
na vasītādhauta-vāsaḥ
srajaṁ ca vidhṛtāṁ kvacit

na—not; *apsu*—in water; *snāyāt*—must bathe; *na kupyeta*—must not become angry; *na sambhāṣeta*—must not speak; *durjanaiḥ*—with wicked persons; *na vasīta*—must not wear; *adhauta-vāsaḥ*—unwashed clothes; *srajam*—flower garland; *ca*—and; *vidhṛtām*—which was already worn; *kvacit*—ever.

TRANSLATION

Kaśyapa Muni continued: My dear gentle wife, never enter the water while bathing, never be angry, and do not even speak or associate with wicked people. Never wear clothes that have not been properly washed, and do not put on a garland that has already been worn.

TEXT 49

नोच्छिष्टं चण्डिकान्नं च सामिषं वृषलाहृतम् ।
भुञ्जीतोदक्यया दृष्टं पिबेन्नाञ्जलिना त्वपः ॥४९॥

nocchiṣṭaṁ caṇḍikānnaṁ ca
sāmiṣaṁ vṛṣalāhṛtam
bhuñjītodakyayā dṛṣṭaṁ
piben nāñjalinā tv apaḥ

na—not; *ucchiṣṭam*—leftover food; *caṇḍikā-annam*—food offered to the goddess Kālī; *ca*—and; *sa-āmiṣam*—mixed with flesh; *vṛṣala-āhṛtam*—brought by a *śūdra; bhuñjīta*—must eat; *udakyayā*—by a woman in her menstrual period; *dṛṣṭam*—seen; *pibet na*—must not drink; *añjalinā*—by joining and cupping the two palms; *tu*—also; *apaḥ*—water.

TRANSLATION

Never eat leftover food, never eat prasāda offered to the goddess Kālī [Durgā], and do not eat anything contaminated by flesh or fish. Do not eat anything brought or touched by a śūdra nor anything seen by a woman in her menstrual period. Do not drink water by joining your palms.

PURPORT

Generally the goddess Kālī is offered food containing meat and fish, and therefore Kaśyapa Muni strictly forbade his wife to take the remnants of such food. Actually a Vaiṣṇava is not allowed to take any food offered to the demigods. A Vaiṣṇava is always fixed in accepting *prasāda* offered to Lord Viṣṇu. Through all these instructions, Kaśyapa Muni, in a negative way, instructed his wife Diti how to become a Vaiṣṇavī.

TEXT 50

नोच्छिष्टास्पृष्टसलिला सन्ध्यायां मुक्तमूर्धजा ।
अनर्चितासंयतवाक् नासंवीता बहिश्चरेत् ॥५०॥

nocchiṣṭāspṛṣṭa-salilā
sandhyāyāṁ mukta-mūrdhajā
anarcitāsaṁyata-vāk
nāsaṁvītā bahiś caret

na—not; *ucchiṣṭā*—after eating; *aspṛṣṭa-salilā*—without washing; *sandhyāyām*—in the evening; *mukta-mūrdhajā*—with the hair loose; *anarcitā*—without ornaments; *asaṁyata-vāk*—without being grave; *na*—not; *asaṁvītā*—without being covered; *bahiḥ*—outside; *caret*—should go.

TRANSLATION

After eating, you should not go out to the street without having washed your mouth, hands and feet. You should not go out in the evening or with your hair loose, nor should you go out unless you are properly decorated with ornaments. You should not leave the house unless you are very grave and are sufficiently covered.

PURPORT

Kaśyapa Muni advised his wife not to go out onto the street unless she was well decorated and well dressed. He did not encourage the miniskirts that have now become fashionable. In Oriental civilization, when a woman goes out onto the street, she must be fully covered so that no man will recognize who she is. All these methods are to be accepted for purification. If one takes to Kṛṣṇa consciousness, one is fully purified, and thus one remains always transcendental to the contamination of the material world.

TEXT 51

नाधौतपादाप्रयता नार्द्रपादा उदक्शिराः ।
शयीत नापराङ्नान्यैर्न नग्ना न च सन्ध्ययोः ॥५१॥

nādhauta-pādāprayatā
nārdra-pādā udak-śirāḥ
śayīta nāparāṅ nānyair
na nagnā na ca sandhyayoḥ

na—not; *adhauta-pādā*—without washing the feet; *aprayatā*—without being purified; *na*—not; *ardra-pādā*—with wet feet; *udak-śirāḥ*—with the head toward the north; *śayīta*—should lie down; *na*—not; *aparāk*—with the head pointed west; *na*—not; *anyaiḥ*—with other women; *na*—not; *nagnā*—naked; *na*—not; *ca*—and; *sandhyayoḥ*—at sunrise and sunset.

TRANSLATION

You should not lie down without having washed both of your feet or without being purified, nor with wet feet or with your head pointed west or north. You should not lie naked, or with other women, or during the sunrise or sunset.

TEXT 52

धौतवासा शुचिर्नित्यं सर्वमङ्गलसंयुता ।
पूजयेत्प्रातराशात्प्राग्गोविप्राञ् श्रियमच्युतम् ।।५२।।

dhauta-vāsā śucir nityaṁ
sarva-maṅgala-saṁyutā
pūjayet prātarāśāt prāg
go-viprāñ śriyam acyutam

dhauta-vāsā—wearing washed cloth; *śuciḥ*—being purified; *nityam*—always; *sarva-maṅgala*—with all auspicious items; *saṁyutā*—adorned; *pūjayet*—one should worship; *prātaḥ-āśāt prāk*—before breakfast; *go-viprān*—the cows and *brāhmaṇas; śriyam*—the goddess of fortune; *acyutam*—the Supreme Personality of Godhead.

TRANSLATION

Putting on washed clothing, being always pure and being adorned with turmeric, sandalwood pulp and other auspicious

items, before breakfast one should worship the cows, the brāhmaṇas, the goddess of fortune and the Supreme Personality of Godhead.

PURPORT

If one is trained to honor and worship the cows and *brāhmaṇas,* he is actually civilized. The worship of the Supreme Lord is recommended, and the Lord is very fond of the cows and *brāhmaṇas* (*namo brahmaṇya-devāya go-brāhmaṇa-hitāya ca*). In other words, a civilization in which there is no respect for the cows and *brāhmaṇas* is condemned. One cannot become spiritually advanced without acquiring the brahminical qualifications and giving protection to cows. Cow protection insures sufficient food prepared with milk, which is needed for an advanced civilization. One should not pollute civilization by eating the flesh of cows. A civilization must do something progressive, and then it is an Āryan civilization. Instead of killing the cow to eat flesh, civilized men must prepare various milk products that will enhance the condition of society. If one follows the brahminical culture, he will become competent in Kṛṣṇa consciousness.

TEXT 53

स्त्रियो वीरवतीश्चार्चेत्स्रग्गन्धबलिमण्डनैः ।
पतिं चार्च्योपतिष्ठेत ध्यायेत्कोष्ठगतं च तम् ॥५३॥

striyo vīravatīś cārcet
srag-gandha-bali-maṇḍanaiḥ
patiṁ cārcyopatiṣṭheta
dhyāyet koṣṭha-gataṁ ca tam

striyaḥ—women; *vīra-vatīḥ*—possessing husbands and sons; *ca*—and; *arcet*—she should worship; *srak*—with garlands; *gandha*—sandalwood; *bali*—presentations; *maṇḍanaiḥ*—and with ornaments; *patim*—the husband; *ca*—and; *ārcya*—worshiping; *upatiṣṭheta*—should offer prayers; *dhyāyet*—should meditate; *koṣṭha-gatam*—situated in the womb; *ca*—also; *tam*—upon him.

TRANSLATION

With flower garlands, sandalwood pulp, ornaments and other paraphernalia, a woman following this vow should worship women who have sons and whose husbands are living. The pregnant wife should worship her husband and offer him prayers. She should meditate upon him, thinking that he is situated in her womb.

PURPORT

The child in the womb is a part of the husband's body. Therefore the husband, through his representative, indirectly remains within the womb of his pregnant wife.

TEXT 54

सांवत्सरं पुंसवनं व्रतमेतदविप्लुतम् ।
धारयिष्यसि चेत्तुभ्यं शक्रहा भविता सुतः ॥५४॥

sāṁvatsaraṁ puṁsavanaṁ
vratam etad aviplutam
dhārayiṣyasi cet tubhyaṁ
śakra-hā bhavitā sutaḥ

sāṁvatsaram—for one year; *puṁsavanam*—called *puṁsavana; vratam*—vow; *etat*—this; *aviplutam*—without violation; *dhārayiṣyasi*—you will perform; *cet*—if; *tubhyam*—for you; *śakra-hā*—the killer of Indra; *bhavitā*—will be; *sutaḥ*—a son.

TRANSLATION

Kaśyapa Muni continued: If you perform this ceremony called puṁsavana, adhering to the vow with faith for at least one year, you will give birth to a son destined to kill Indra. But if there is any discrepancy in the discharge of this vow, the son will be a friend to Indra.

TEXT 55

बाढमित्यभ्युपेत्याथ दिती राजन् महामनाः ।
काश्यपाद् गर्भमाधत्त व्रतं चाञ्जो दधार सा ॥५५॥

bāḍham ity abhyupetyātha
ditī rājan mahā-manāḥ
kaśyapād garbham ādhatta
vrataṁ cāñjo dadhāra sā

bāḍham—yes; *iti*—thus; *abhyupetya*—accepting; *atha*—then; *ditiḥ*—Diti; *rājan*—O King; *mahā-manāḥ*—jubilant; *kaśyapāt*—from Kaśyapa; *garbham*—semen; *ādhatta*—obtained; *vratam*—the vow; *ca*—and; *añjaḥ*—properly; *dadhāra*—discharged; *sā*—she.

TRANSLATION

O King Parīkṣit, Diti, the wife of Kaśyapa, agreed to undergo the purificatory process known as puṁsavana. "Yes," she said, "I shall do everything according to your instructions." With great jubilation she became pregnant, having taken semen from Kaśyapa, and faithfully began discharging the vow.

TEXT 56

मातृष्वसुरभिप्रायमिन्द्र आज्ञाय मानद ।
शुश्रूषणेनाश्रमस्थां दितिं पर्यचरत्कविः ॥५६॥

mātṛ-ṣvasur abhiprāyam
indra ājñāya mānada
śuśrūṣaṇenāśrama-sthāṁ
ditiṁ paryacarat kaviḥ

mātṛ-svasuḥ—of his mother's sister; *abhiprāyam*—the intention; *indraḥ*—Indra; *ājñāya*—understanding; *māna-da*—O King Parīkṣit, who give respect to everyone; *śuśrūṣaṇena*—with service; *āśrama-sthām*—residing in an *āśrama;* *ditim*—Diti; *paryacarat*—attended upon; *kaviḥ*—seeing his own interest.

TRANSLATION

O King, who are respectful to everyone, Indra understood Diti's purpose, and thus he contrived to fulfill his own interests. Following the logic that self-preservation is the first law of nature, he

wanted to break Diti's promise. Thus he engaged himself in the service of Diti, his aunt, who was residing in an āśrama.

TEXT 57

नित्यं वनात्सुमनसः फलमूलसमित्कुशान् ।
पत्राङ्कुरमृदोऽपश्च काले काल उपाहरत् ॥५७॥

nityaṁ vanāt sumanasaḥ
phala-mūla-samit-kuśān
patrāṅkura-mṛdo 'paś ca
kāle kāla upāharat

nityam—daily; *vanāt*—from the forest; *sumanasaḥ*—flowers; *phala*—fruits; *mūla*—roots; *samit*—wood for the sacrificial fire; *kuśān*—and *kuśa* grass; *patra*—leaves; *aṅkura*—sprouts; *mṛdaḥ*—and earth; *apaḥ*—water; *ca*—also; *kāle kāle*—at the proper time; *upāharat*—brought.

TRANSLATION

Indra served his aunt daily by bringing flowers, fruits, roots and wood for yajñas from the forest. He also brought kuśa grass, leaves, sprouts, earth and water exactly at the proper time.

TEXT 58

एवं तस्या व्रतस्थाया व्रतच्छिद्रं हरिर्नृप ।
प्रेप्सुः पर्यचरज्जिह्मो मृगहेव मृगाकृतिः ॥५८॥

evaṁ tasyā vrata-sthāyā
vrata-cchidraṁ harir nṛpa
prepsuḥ paryacaraj jihmo
mṛga-heva mṛgākṛtiḥ

evam—thus; *tasyāḥ*—of her; *vrata-sthāyāḥ*—who was faithfully discharging her vow; *vrata-chidram*—a fault in the execution of the vow; *hariḥ*—Indra; *nṛpa*—O King; *prepsuḥ*—desiring to find; *paryacarat*—

served; *jihmaḥ*—deceitful; *mṛga-hā*—a hunter; *iva*—like; *mṛga-ākṛtiḥ*—in the form of a deer.

TRANSLATION

O King Parīkṣit, as the hunter of a deer becomes like a deer by covering his body with deerskin and serving the deer, so Indra, although at heart the enemy of the sons of Diti, became outwardly friendly and served Diti in a faithful way. Indra's purpose was to cheat Diti as soon as he could find some fault in the way she discharged the vows of the ritualistic ceremony. However, he wanted to be undetected, and therefore he served her very carefully.

TEXT 59

नाध्यगच्छद्व्रतच्छिद्रं तत्परोऽथ महीपते ।
चिन्तां तीव्रां गतः शक्रः केन मे स्याच्छिवं त्विह ॥५९॥

nādhyagacchad vrata-cchidraṁ
tat-paro 'tha mahī-pate
cintāṁ tīvrāṁ gataḥ śakraḥ
kena me syāc chivaṁ tv iha

na—not; *adhyagacchat*—could find; *vrata-chidram*—a fault in the execution of the vow; *tat-paraḥ*—intent upon that; *atha*—thereupon; *mahī-pate*—O master of the world; *cintām*—anxiety; *tīvrām*—intense; *gataḥ*—obtained; *śakraḥ*—Indra; *kena*—how; *me*—my; *syāt*—can there be; *śivam*—well-being; *tu*—then; *iha*—here.

TRANSLATION

O master of the entire world, when Indra could find no faults, he thought, "How will there be good fortune for me?" Thus he was full of deep anxiety.

TEXT 60

एकदा सा तु सन्ध्यायामुच्छिष्टा व्रतकर्शिता ।
अस्पृष्टवार्यधौताङ्घ्रिः सुष्वाप विधिमोहिता ॥६०॥

ekadā sā tu sandhyāyām
ucchiṣṭā vrata-karśitā
aspṛṣṭa-vāry-adhautāṅghriḥ
suṣvāpa vidhi-mohitā

ekadā—once; *sā*—she; *tu*—but; *sandhyāyām*—during the evening twilight; *ucchiṣṭā*—just after eating; *vrata*—from the vow; *karśitā*—weak and thin; *aspṛṣṭa*—not touched; *vāri*—water; *adhauta*—not washed; *aṅghriḥ*—her feet; *suṣvāpa*—went to sleep; *vidhi*—by fate; *mohitā*—bewildered.

TRANSLATION

Having grown weak and thin because of strictly following the principles of the vow, Diti once unfortunately neglected to wash her mouth, hands and feet after eating and went to sleep during the evening twilight.

TEXT 61

लब्ध्वा तदन्तरं शक्रो निद्रापहृतचेतसः ।
दितेः प्रविष्ट उदरं योगेशो योगमायया ॥६१॥

labdhvā tad-antaraṁ śakro
nidrāpahṛta-cetasaḥ
diteḥ praviṣṭa udaraṁ
yogeśo yoga-māyayā

labdhvā—finding; *tat-antaram*—after that; *śakraḥ*—Indra; *nidrā*—by sleep; *apahṛta-cetasaḥ*—unconscious; *diteḥ*—of Diti; *praviṣṭaḥ*—entered; *udaram*—the womb; *yoga-īśaḥ*—the master of *yoga; yoga*—of yogic perfections; *māyayā*—by the power.

TRANSLATION

Finding this fault, Indra, who has all the mystic powers [the yoga-siddhis such as aṇimā and laghimā], entered Diti's womb while she was unconscious, being fast asleep.

PURPORT

A perfectly successful *yogī* is expert in eight kinds of perfection. By one of them, called *aṇimā-siddhi,* he can become smaller than an atom, and in that state he can enter anywhere. With this yogic power, Indra entered the womb of Diti while she was pregnant.

TEXT 62

चकर्त सप्तधा गर्भं वज्रेण कनकप्रभम् ।
रुदन्तं सप्तधैकैकं मा रोदीरिति तान् पुनः ॥६२॥

cakarta saptadhā garbhaṁ
vajreṇa kanaka-prabham
rudantaṁ saptadhaikaikaṁ
mā rodīr iti tān punaḥ

cakarta—he cut; *sapta-dhā*—into seven pieces; *garbham*—the embryo; *vajreṇa*—by his thunderbolt; *kanaka*—of gold; *prabham*—which had the appearance; *rudantam*—crying; *sapta-dhā*—into seven pieces; *eka-ekam*—each one; *mā rodīḥ*—do not cry; *iti*—thus; *tān*—them; *punaḥ*—again.

TRANSLATION

After entering Diti's womb, Indra, with the help of his thunderbolt, cut into seven pieces her embryo, which appeared like glowing gold. In seven places, seven different living beings began crying. Indra told them, "Do not cry," and then he cut each of them into seven pieces again.

PURPORT

Śrīla Viśvanātha Cakravartī Ṭhākura remarks that Indra, by his yogic power, first expanded the body of the one Marut into seven, and then when he cut each of the seven parts of the original body into pieces, there were forty-nine. When each body was cut into seven, other living entities entered the new bodies, and thus they were like plants, which become separate entities when cut into various parts and planted on a hill. The first body was one, and when it was cut into many pieces, many other living entities entered the new bodies.

TEXT 63

तमूचुः पाट्यमानास्ते सर्वे प्राञ्जलयो नृप ।
किं न इन्द्र जिघांससि भ्रातरो मरुतस्तव ॥६३॥

tam ūcuḥ pāṭyamānās te
sarve prāñjalayo nṛpa
kiṁ na indra jighāṁsasi
bhrātaro marutas tava

tam—to him; *ūcuḥ*—said; *pāṭyamānāḥ*—being aggrieved; *te*—they; *sarve*—all; *prāñjalayaḥ*—with folded hands; *nṛpa*—O King; *kim*—why; *naḥ*—us; *indra*—O Indra; *jighāṁsasi*—do you want to kill; *bhrātaraḥ*—brothers; *marutaḥ*—Maruts; *tava*—your.

TRANSLATION

O King, being very much aggrieved, they pleaded to Indra with folded hands, saying, "Dear Indra, we are the Maruts, your brothers. Why are you trying to kill us?"

TEXT 64

मा भैष्ट भ्रातरो मह्यं यूयमित्याह कौशिकः ।
अनन्यभावान् पार्षदानात्मनो मरुतां गणान् ॥६४॥

mā bhaiṣṭa bhrātaro mahyaṁ
yūyam ity āha kauśikaḥ
ananya-bhāvān pārṣadān
ātmano marutāṁ gaṇān

mā bhaiṣṭa—do not fear; *bhrātaraḥ*—brothers; *mahyam*—my; *yūyam*—you; *iti*—thus; *āha*—said; *kauśikaḥ*—Indra; *ananya-bhāvān*—devoted; *pārṣadān*—followers; *ātmanaḥ*—his; *marutām gaṇān*—the Maruts.

TRANSLATION

When Indra saw that actually they were his devoted followers, he said to them: If you are all my brothers, you have nothing more to fear from me.

TEXT 65

न ममार दितेर्गर्भः श्रीनिवासानुकम्पया ।
बहुधा कुलिशक्षुण्णो द्रौण्यस्त्रेण यथा भवान् ॥६५॥

na mamāra diter garbhaḥ
śrīnivāsānukampayā
bahudhā kuliśa-kṣuṇṇo
drauṇy-astreṇa yathā bhavān

na—not; *mamāra*—died; *diteḥ*—of Diti; *garbhaḥ*—the embryo; *śrī-nivāsa*—of Lord Viṣṇu, the resting place of the goddess of fortune; *anukampayā*—by the mercy; *bahu-dhā*—into many pieces; *kuliśa*—by the thunderbolt; *kṣuṇṇaḥ*—cut; *drauṇi*—of Aśvatthāmā; *astreṇa*—by the weapon; *yathā*—just as; *bhavān*—you.

TRANSLATION

Śukadeva Gosvāmī said: My dear King Parīkṣit, you were burned by the brahmāstra of Aśvatthāmā, but when Lord Kṛṣṇa entered the womb of your mother, you were saved. Similarly, although the one embryo was cut into forty-nine pieces by the thunderbolt of Indra, they were all saved by the mercy of the Supreme Personality of Godhead.

TEXTS 66–67

सकृदिष्ट्वादिपुरुषं पुरुषो याति साम्यताम् ।
संवत्सरं किञ्चिदूनं दित्या यद्धरिरर्चितः ॥६६॥
सजूरिन्द्रेण पञ्चाशद्देवास्ते मरुतोऽभवन् ।
व्यपोह्य मातृदोषं ते हरिणा सोमपाः कृताः ॥६७॥

sakṛd iṣṭvādi-puruṣaṁ
puruṣo yāti sāmyatām
saṁvatsaraṁ kiñcid ūnaṁ
dityā yad dharir arcitaḥ

sajūr indreṇa pañcāśad
devās te maruto 'bhavan
vyapohya mātṛ-doṣaṁ te
hariṇā soma-pāḥ kṛtāḥ

sakṛt—once; *iṣṭvā*—worshiping; *ādi-puruṣam*—the original person; *puruṣaḥ*—a person; *yāti*—goes to; *sāmyatām*—possessing the same bodily feature as the Lord; *saṁvatsaram*—a year; *kiñcit ūnam*—a little less than; *dityā*—by Diti; *yat*—because; *hariḥ*—Lord Hari; *arcitaḥ*—was worshiped; *sajūḥ*—with; *indreṇa*—Indra; *pañcāśat*—fifty; *devāḥ*—demigods; *te*—they; *marutaḥ*—the Maruts; *abhavan*—became; *vyapohya*—removing; *mātṛ-doṣam*—the fault of their mother; *te*—they; *hariṇā*—by Lord Hari; *soma-pāḥ*—drinkers of *soma-rasa;* *kṛtāḥ*—were made.

TRANSLATION

If one worships the Supreme Personality of Godhead, the original person, even once, he receives the benefit of being promoted to the spiritual world and possessing the same bodily features as Viṣṇu. Diti worshiped Lord Viṣṇu for almost one year, adhering to a great vow. Because of such strength in spiritual life, the forty-nine Maruts were born. How, then, is it wonderful that the Maruts, although born from the womb of Diti, became equal to the demigods by the mercy of the Supreme Lord?

TEXT 68

दितिरुत्थाय ददृशे कुमाराननलप्रभान् ।
इन्द्रेण सहितान् देवी पर्यतुष्यदनिन्दिता ॥६८॥

ditir utthāya dadṛśe
kumārān anala-prabhān

indreṇa sahitān devī
paryatuṣyad aninditā

ditiḥ—Diti; *utthāya*—getting up; *dadṛśe*—saw; *kumārān*—children; *anala-prabhān*—as brilliant as fire; *indreṇa sahitān*—with Indra; *devī*—the goddess; *paryatuṣyat*—was pleased; *aninditā*—being purified.

TRANSLATION

Because of worshiping the Supreme Personality of Godhead, Diti was completely purified. When she got up from bed, she saw her forty-nine sons along with Indra. These forty-nine sons were all as brilliant as fire and were in friendship with Indra, and therefore she was very pleased.

TEXT 69

अथेन्द्रमाह ताताहमादित्यानां भयावहम् ।
अपत्यमिच्छन्त्यचरं व्रतमेतत्सुदुष्करम् ॥६९॥

athendram āha tātāham
ādityānāṁ bhayāvaham
apatyam icchanty acaraṁ
vratam etat suduṣkaram

atha—thereafter; *indram*—to Indra; *āha*—spoke; *tāta*—dear one; *aham*—I; *ādityānām*—to the Ādityas; *bhaya-āvaham*—fearful; *apatyam*—a son; *icchantī*—desiring; *acaram*—executed; *vratam*—vow; *etat*—this; *su-duṣkaram*—very difficult to perform.

TRANSLATION

Thereafter, Diti said to Indra: My dear son, I adhered to this difficult vow just to get a son to kill you twelve Ādityas.

TEXT 70

एकः सङ्कल्पितः पुत्रः सप्त सप्ताभवन् कथम् ।
यदि ते विदितं पुत्र सत्यं कथय मा मृषा ॥७०॥

ekaḥ saṅkalpitaḥ putraḥ
sapta saptābhavan katham
yadi te viditaṁ putra
satyaṁ kathaya mā mṛṣā

ekaḥ—one; *saṅkalpitaḥ*—was prayed for; *putraḥ*—son; *sapta sapta*—forty-nine; *abhavan*—came to be; *katham*—how; *yadi*—if; *te*—by you; *viditam*—known; *putra*—my dear son; *satyam*—the truth; *kathaya*—speak; *mā*—do not (speak); *mṛṣā*—lies.

TRANSLATION

I prayed for only one son, but now I see that there are forty-nine. How has this happened? My dear son Indra, if you know, please tell me the truth. Do not try to speak lies.

TEXT 71

इन्द्र उवाच
अम्ब तेऽहं व्यवसितमुपधार्यागतोऽन्तिकम् ।
लब्धान्तरोऽच्छिदं गर्भमर्थबुद्धिर्न धर्मदृक् ॥७१॥

indra uvāca
amba te 'haṁ vyavasitam
upadhāryāgato 'ntikam
labdhāntaro 'cchidaṁ garbham
artha-buddhir na dharma-dṛk

indraḥ uvāca—Indra said; *amba*—O mother; *te*—your; *aham*—I; *vyavasitam*—vow; *upadhārya*—understanding; *āgataḥ*—came; *antikam*—nearby; *labdha*—having found; *antaraḥ*—a fault; *acchidam*—I cut; *garbham*—the embryo; *artha-buddhiḥ*—being self-interested; *na*—not; *dharma-dṛk*—possessing vision of religion.

TRANSLATION

Indra replied: My dear mother, because I was grossly blinded by selfish interests, I lost sight of religion. When I understood that you were observing a great vow in spiritual life, I wanted to find

some fault in you. When I found such a fault, I entered your womb and cut the embryo to pieces.

PURPORT

When Diti, Indra's aunt, explained to Indra without reservations what she had wanted to do, Indra explained his intentions to her. Thus both of them, instead of being enemies, freely spoke the truth. This is the qualification that results from contact with Viṣṇu. As stated in *Śrīmad-Bhāgavatam* (5.18.12):

yasyāsti bhaktir bhagavaty akiñcanā
sarvair guṇais tatra samāsate surāḥ

If one develops a devotional attitude and becomes purified by worshiping the Supreme Lord, all the good qualities are certainly manifested in his body. Because of being touched by worship of Viṣṇu, both Diti and Indra were purified.

TEXT 72

कृत्तो मे सप्तधा गर्भ आसन् सप्त कुमारकाः ।
तेऽपि चैकैकशो वृक्णाः सप्तधा नापि मम्रिरे ॥७२॥

kṛtto me saptadhā garbha
āsan sapta kumārakāḥ
te 'pi caikaikaśo vṛkṇāḥ
saptadhā nāpi mamrire

kṛttaḥ—cut; *me*—by me; *sapta-dhā*—into seven; *garbhaḥ*—the embryo; *āsan*—there came to be; *sapta*—seven; *kumārakāḥ*—babies; *te*—they; *api*—although; *ca*—also; *eka-ekaśaḥ*—each one; *vṛkṇāḥ*—cut; *sapta-dhā*—into seven; *na*—not; *api*—still; *mamrire*—died.

TRANSLATION

First I cut the child in the womb into seven pieces, which became seven children. Then I cut each of the children into seven

pieces again. By the grace of the Supreme Lord, however, none of them died.

TEXT 73

ततस्तत्परमाश्चर्यं वीक्ष्य व्यवसितं मया ।
महापुरुषपूजायाः सिद्धिः काप्यानुषङ्गिणी ॥७३॥

tatas tat paramāścaryaṁ
vīkṣya vyavasitaṁ mayā
mahāpuruṣa-pūjāyāḥ
siddhiḥ kāpy ānuṣaṅgiṇī

tataḥ—then; *tat*—that; *parama-āścaryam*—great wonder; *vīkṣya*—seeing; *vyavasitam*—it was decided; *mayā*—by me; *mahā-puruṣa*—of Lord Viṣṇu; *pūjāyāḥ*—of worship; *siddhiḥ*—result; *kāpi*—some; *ānuṣaṅgiṇī*—secondary.

TRANSLATION

My dear mother, when I saw that all forty-nine sons were alive, I was certainly struck with wonder. I decided that this was a secondary result of your having regularly executed devotional service in worship of Lord Viṣṇu.

PURPORT

For one who engages in worshiping Lord Viṣṇu, nothing is very wonderful. This is a fact. In *Bhagavad-gītā* (18.78) it is said:

yatra yogeśvaraḥ kṛṣṇo
yatra pārtho dhanur-dharaḥ
tatra śrīr vijayo bhūtir
dhruvā nītir matir mama

"Wherever there is Kṛṣṇa, the master of all mystics, and wherever there is Arjuna, the supreme archer, there will also certainly be opulence, victory, extraordinary power, and morality. That is my opinion." Yogeśvara is the Supreme Personality of Godhead, the master of all mystic *yoga*, who can do anything and everything He likes. This is the omnipotence of the Supreme Lord. For one who pleases the Supreme Lord, no achievement is wonderful. Everything is possible for him.

TEXT 74

आराधनं भगवत ईहमाना निराशिषः ।
ये तु नेच्छन्त्यपि परं ते स्वार्थकुशलाः स्मृताः ॥७४॥

ārādhanaṁ bhagavata
īhamānā nirāśiṣaḥ
ye tu necchanty api paraṁ
te svārtha-kuśalāḥ smṛtāḥ

ārādhanam—the worship; *bhagavataḥ*—of the Supreme Personality of Godhead; *īhamānāḥ*—being interested in; *nirāśiṣaḥ*—without material desires; *ye*—those who; *tu*—indeed; *na icchanti*—do not desire; *api*—even; *param*—liberation; *te*—they; *sva-artha*—in their own interest; *kuśalāḥ*—expert; *smṛtāḥ*—are considered.

TRANSLATION

Although those who are interested only in worshiping the Supreme Personality of Godhead do not desire anything material from the Lord and do not even want liberation, Lord Kṛṣṇa fulfills all their desires.

PURPORT

When Dhruva Mahārāja saw Lord Viṣṇu, he declined to take any benedictions from Him, for he was fully satisfied by seeing the Lord. Nonetheless, the Lord is so kind that because Dhruva Mahārāja, in the beginning, had desired a kingdom greater than his father's, he was promoted to Dhruvaloka, the best planet in the universe. Therefore in the *śāstra* it is said:

akāmaḥ sarva-kāmo vā
mokṣa-kāma udāra-dhīḥ

tīvreṇa bhakti-yogena
yajeta puruṣaṁ param

"A person who has broader intelligence, whether he is full of material desires, free from material desires, or desiring liberation, must by all means worship the supreme whole, the Personality of Godhead." (*Bhāg.* 2.3.10) One should engage in full devotional service. Then, even though he has no desires, whatever desires he previously had can all be fulfilled simply by his worship of the Lord. The actual devotee does not desire even liberation (*anyābhilāṣitā-śūnyam*). The Lord, however, fulfills the desire of the devotee by awarding him opulence that will never be destroyed. A *karmī's* opulence is destroyed, but the opulence of a devotee is never destroyed. A devotee becomes more and more opulent as he increases his devotional service to the Lord.

TEXT 75

आराध्यात्मप्रदं देवं स्वात्मानं जगदीश्वरम् ।
को वृणीत गुणस्पर्शं बुधः स्यान्नरकेऽपि यत् ॥७५॥

ārādhyātma-pradaṁ devaṁ
svātmānaṁ jagad-īśvaram
ko vṛṇīta guṇa-sparśaṁ
budhaḥ syān narake 'pi yat

ārādhya—after worshiping; *ātma-pradam*—who gives Himself; *devam*—the Lord; *sva-ātmānam*—the most dear; *jagat-īśvaram*—the Lord of the universe; *kaḥ*—what; *vṛṇīta*—would choose; *guṇa-sparśam*—material happiness; *budhaḥ*—intelligent person; *syāt*—is; *narake*—in hell; *api*—even; *yat*—which.

TRANSLATION

The ultimate goal of all ambitions is to become a servant of the Supreme Personality of Godhead. If an intelligent man serves the most dear Lord, who gives Himself to His devotees, how can he desire material happiness, which is available even in hell?

PURPORT

An intelligent man will never aspire to become a devotee to achieve material happiness. That is the test of a devotee. As Śrī Caitanya Mahāprabhu teaches:

na dhanaṁ na janaṁ na sundarīṁ
kavitāṁ vā jagad-īśa kāmaye
mama janmani janmanīśvare
bhavatād bhaktir ahaitukī tvayi

"O almighty Lord, I have no desire to accumulate wealth, nor do I desire beautiful women, nor do I want any number of followers. I only want Your causeless devotional service birth after birth." A pure devotee never begs the Lord for material happiness in the shape of riches, followers, a good wife or even *mukti.* The Lord promises, however, *yoga-kṣemaṁ vahāmy aham:* "I voluntarily bring everything necessary for My service."

TEXT 76

तदिदं मम दौर्जन्यं बालिशस्य महीयसि ।
क्षन्तुमर्हसि मातस्त्वं दिष्ट्या गर्भो मृतोत्थितः ॥७६॥

tad idaṁ mama daurjanyaṁ
bāliśasya mahīyasi
kṣantum arhasi mātas tvaṁ
diṣṭyā garbho mṛtotthitaḥ

tat—that; *idam*—this; *mama*—of me; *daurjanyam*—evil deed; *bāliśasya*—a fool; *mahīyasi*—O best of women; *kṣantum arhasi*—please excuse; *mātaḥ*—O mother; *tvam*—you; *diṣṭyā*—by fortune; *garbhaḥ*—the child within the womb; *mṛta*—killed; *utthitaḥ*—became alive.

TRANSLATION

O my mother, O best of all women, I am a fool. Kindly excuse me for whatever offenses I have committed. Your forty-nine sons have been born unhurt because of your devotional service. As an

enemy, I cut them to pieces, but because of your great devotional service they did not die.

TEXT 77

श्रीशुक उवाच
इन्द्रस्तयाभ्यनुज्ञातः शुद्धभावेन तुष्टया ।
मरुद्भिः सह तां नत्वा जगाम त्रिदिवं प्रभुः ॥७७॥

śrī-śuka uvāca
indras tayābhyanujñātaḥ
śuddha-bhāvena tuṣṭayā
marudbhiḥ saha tāṁ natvā
jagāma tri-divaṁ prabhuḥ

śrī-śukaḥ uvāca—Śrī Śukadeva Gosvāmī said; *indraḥ*—Indra; *tayā*—by her; *abhyanujñātaḥ*—being permitted; *śuddha-bhāvena*—by the good behavior; *tuṣṭayā*—satisfied; *marudbhiḥ saha*—with the Maruts; *tām*—to her; *natvā*—having offered obeisances; *jagāma*—he went; *tri-divam*—to the heavenly planets; *prabhuḥ*—the Lord.

TRANSLATION

Śrī Śukadeva Gosvāmī continued: Diti was extremely satisfied by Indra's good behavior. Then Indra offered his respects to his aunt with profuse obeisances, and with her permission he went away to the heavenly planets with his brothers the Maruts.

TEXT 78

एवं ते सर्वमाख्यातं यन्मां त्वं परिपृच्छसि ।
मङ्गलं मरुतां जन्म किं भूयः कथयामि ते ॥७८॥

evaṁ te sarvam ākhyātaṁ
yan māṁ tvaṁ paripṛcchasi
maṅgalaṁ marutāṁ janma
kiṁ bhūyaḥ kathayāmi te

evam—thus; *te*—to you; *sarvam*—all; *ākhyātam*—narrated; *yat*—which; *mām*—me; *tvam*—you; *paripṛcchasi*—asked; *maṅgalam*—auspicious; *marutām*—of the Maruts; *janma*—the birth; *kim*—what; *bhūyaḥ*—further; *kathayāmi*—shall I speak; *te*—to you.

TRANSLATION

My dear King Parīkṣit, I have replied as far as possible to the questions you have asked me, especially in regard to this pure, auspicious narration about the Maruts. Now you may inquire further, and I shall explain more.

Thus end the Bhaktivedanta purports to the Sixth Canto, Eighteenth Chapter, of the Śrīmad-Bhāgavatam, *entitled "Diti Vows to Kill King Indra."*

CHAPTER NINETEEN

Performing the Puṁsavana Ritualistic Ceremony

This chapter explains how Diti, Kaśyapa Muni's wife, executed Kaśyapa Muni's instructions on devotional service. During the first day of the bright fortnight of the moon in the month of Agrahāyaṇa (November–December), every woman, following in the footsteps of Diti and following the instructions of her own husband, should begin this *puṁsavana-vrata.* In the morning, after washing her teeth, bathing and thus becoming purified, she should hear about the birth mystery of the Maruts. Then, covering her body with a white dress and being properly ornamented, before breakfast she should worship Lord Viṣṇu and mother Lakṣmī, the goddess of fortune, Lord Viṣṇu's wife, by glorifying Lord Viṣṇu for His mercy, patience, prowess, ability, greatness and other glories and for how He can bestow all mystic benedictions. While offering the Lord all paraphernalia for worship, such as ornaments, a sacred thread, scents, nice flowers, incense and water for bathing and washing His feet, hands and mouth, one should invite the Lord with this *mantra: oṁ namo bhagavate mahā-puruṣāya mahānubhāvāya mahāvibhūti-pataye saha mahā-vibhūtibhir balim upaharāmi.* Then one should offer twelve oblations in the fire while chanting this *mantra: oṁ namo bhagavate mahā-puruṣāya mahāvibhūti-pataye svāhā.* One should offer obeisances while chanting this *mantra* ten times. Then one should chant the Lakṣmī-Nārāyaṇa *mantra.*

If either a pregnant woman or her husband regularly discharges this devotional service, both of them will receive the result. After continuing this process for one full year, the chaste wife should fast on the *pūrṇimā,* the full-moon day, of Kārttika. On the following day, the husband should worship the Lord as before and then observe a festival by cooking nice food and distributing *prasāda* to the *brāhmaṇas.* Then, with the permission of the *brāhmaṇas,* the husband and wife should take *prasāda.* This chapter ends by glorifying the results of the *puṁsavana* function.

TEXT 1

श्रीराजोवाच
व्रतं पुंसवनं ब्रह्मन् भवता यदुदीरितम् ।
तस्य वेदितुमिच्छामि येन विष्णुः प्रसीदति ॥ १ ॥

śrī-rājovāca
vrataṁ puṁsavanaṁ brahman
bhavatā yad udīritam
tasya veditum icchāmi
yena viṣṇuḥ prasīdati

śrī-rājā uvāca—Mahārāja Parīkṣit said; *vratam*—the vow; *puṁsavanam*—called *puṁsavana; brahman*—O *brāhmaṇa; bhavatā*—by you; *yat*—which; *udīritam*—was spoken of; *tasya*—of that; *veditum*—to know; *icchāmi*—I want; *yena*—by which; *viṣṇuḥ*—Lord Viṣṇu; *prasīdati*—is pleased.

TRANSLATION

Mahārāja Parīkṣit said: My dear lord, you have already spoken about the puṁsavana vow. Now I want to hear about it in detail, for I understand that by observing this vow one can please the Supreme Lord, Viṣṇu.

TEXTS 2–3

श्रीशुक उवाच
शुक्ले मार्गशिरे पक्षे योषिद्भर्तुरनुज्ञया ।
आरभेत व्रतमिदं सार्वकामिकमादितः ॥ २ ॥
निशम्य मरुतां जन्म ब्राह्मणाननुमन्त्र्य च ।
स्नात्वा शुक्लदती शुक्ले वसीतालङ्कृताम्बरे ।
पूजयेत्प्रातराशात्प्राग्भगवन्तं श्रिया सह ॥ ३ ॥

śrī-śuka uvāca
śukle mārgaśire pakṣe
yoṣid bhartur anujñayā
ārabheta vratam idaṁ
sārva-kāmikam āditaḥ

niśamya marutāṁ janma
brāhmaṇān anumantrya ca
snātvā śukla-datī śukle
vasītālaṅkṛtāmbare
pūjayet prātarāśāt prāg
bhagavantaṁ śriyā saha

śrī-śukaḥ uvāca—Śrī Śukadeva Gosvāmī said; *śukle*—bright; *mārgaśire*—during the month of November–December; *pakṣe*—during the fortnight; *yoṣit*—a woman; *bhartuḥ*—of the husband; *anujñayā*—with the permission; *ārabheta*—should begin; *vratam*—vow; *idam*—this; *sārva-kāmikam*—which fulfills all desires; *āditaḥ*—from the first day; *niśamya*—hearing; *marutām*—of the Maruts; *janma*—the birth; *brāhmaṇān*—the *brāhmaṇas; anumantrya*—taking instruction from; *ca*—and; *snātvā*—bathing; *śukla-datī*—having cleaned the teeth; *śukle*—white; *vasīta*—should put on; *alaṅkṛtā*—wearing ornaments; *ambare*—garments; *pūjayet*—should worship; *prātaḥ-āśāt prāk*—before breakfast; *bhagavantam*—the Supreme Personality of Godhead; *śriyā saha*—with the goddess of fortune.

TRANSLATION

Śukadeva Gosvāmī said: On the first day of the bright fortnight of the month of Agrahāyaṇa [November–December], following the instructions of her husband, a woman should begin this regulative devotional service with a vow of penance, for it can fulfill all one's desires. Before beginning the worship of Lord Viṣṇu, the woman should hear the story of how the Maruts were born. Under the instructions of qualified brāhmaṇas, in the morning she should wash her teeth, bathe, and dress herself with white

cloth and ornaments, and before taking breakfast she should worship Lord Viṣṇu and Lakṣmī.

TEXT 4

अलं ते निरपेक्षाय पूर्णकाम नमोऽस्तु ते ।
महाविभूतिपतये नमः सकलसिद्धये ॥ ४ ॥

alaṁ te nirapekṣāya
pūrṇa-kāma namo 'stu te
mahāvibhūti-pataye
namaḥ sakala-siddhaye

alam—enough; *te*—to You; *nirapekṣāya*—indifferent; *pūrṇa-kāma*—O Lord, whose desire is always fulfilled; *namaḥ*—obeisances; *astu*—may there be; *te*—unto You; *mahā-vibhūti*—of Lakṣmī; *pataye*—unto the husband; *namaḥ*—obeisances; *sakala-siddhaye*—unto the master of all mystic perfections.

TRANSLATION

[She should then pray to the Lord as follows] My dear Lord, You are full in all opulences, but I do not beg You for opulence. I simply offer my respectful obeisances unto You. You are the husband and master of Lakṣmīdevī, the goddess of fortune, who has all opulences. Therefore You are the master of all mystic yoga. I simply offer my obeisances unto You.

PURPORT

A devotee knows how to appreciate the Supreme Personality of Godhead.

oṁ pūrṇam adaḥ pūrṇam idaṁ
pūrṇāt pūrṇam udacyate
pūrṇasya pūrṇam ādāya
pūrṇam evāvaśiṣyate

"The Personality of Godhead is perfect and complete, and because He is completely perfect, all emanations from Him, such as this phenomenal world, are perfectly equipped as complete wholes. Whatever is produced of the complete whole is also complete in itself. Because He is the complete whole, even though so many complete units emanate from Him, He remains the complete balance." Therefore, to take shelter of the Supreme Lord is required. Whatever a devotee needs will be supplied by the complete Supreme Personality of Godhead (*teṣāṁ nityābhiyuktānāṁ yoga-kṣemaṁ vahāmy aham*). Therefore a pure devotee will not ask anything from the Lord. He simply offers the Lord his respectful obeisances, and the Lord is prepared to accept whatever the devotee can secure to worship Him, even *patraṁ puṣpaṁ phalaṁ toyam*—a leaf, flower, fruit or water. There is no need to artificially exert oneself. It is better to be plain and simple and with respectful obeisances offer to the Lord whatever one can secure. The Lord is completely able to bless the devotee with all opulences.

TEXT 5

यथा त्वं कृपया भूत्या तेजसा महिमौजसा ।
जुष्ट ईश गुणैः सर्वैस्ततोऽसि भगवान् प्रभुः ॥ ५ ॥

yathā tvaṁ kṛpayā bhūtyā
tejasā mahimaujasā
juṣṭa īśa guṇaiḥ sarvais
tato 'si bhagavān prabhuḥ

yathā—as; *tvam*—You; *kṛpayā*—with mercy; *bhūtyā*—with opulences; *tejasā*—with prowess; *mahima-ojasā*—with glory and strength; *juṣṭaḥ*—endowed; *īśa*—O my Lord; *guṇaiḥ*—with transcendental qualities; *sarvaiḥ*—all; *tataḥ*—therefore; *asi*—You are; *bhagavān*—the Supreme Personality of Godhead; *prabhuḥ*—the master.

TRANSLATION

O my Lord, because You are endowed with causeless mercy, all opulences, all prowess and all glories, strength and transcendental qualities, You are the Supreme Personality of Godhead, the master of everyone.

PURPORT

In this verse the words *tato 'si bhagavān prabhuḥ* mean "Therefore You are the Supreme Personality of Godhead, the master of everyone." The Supreme Personality of Godhead is endowed with all six opulences in full, and moreover He is extremely kind to His devotee. Although He is full in Himself, He nonetheless wants all the living entities to surrender unto Him so that they may engage in His service. Thus He becomes satisfied. Although He is full in Himself, He nonetheless becomes pleased when His devotee offers Him *patraṁ puṣpaṁ phalaṁ toyam*—a leaf, flower, fruit or water—in devotion. Sometimes the Lord, as the child of mother Yaśodā, requests His devotee for some food, as if He were very hungry. Sometimes He tells His devotee in a dream that His temple and His garden are now very old and that He cannot enjoy them very nicely. Thus He requests the devotee to repair them. Sometimes He is buried in the earth, and as if unable to come out Himself, He requests His devotee to rescue Him. Sometimes He requests His devotee to preach His glories all over the world, although He alone is quite competent to perform this task. Even though the Supreme Personality of Godhead is endowed with all possessions and is self-sufficient, He depends on His devotees. Therefore the relationship of the Lord with His devotees is extremely confidential. Only the devotee can perceive how the Lord, although full in Himself, depends on His devotee for some particular work. This is explained in *Bhagavad-gītā* (11.33), where the Lord tells Arjuna, *nimitta-mātraṁ bhava savyasācin:* "O Arjuna, merely be an instrument in the fight." Lord Kṛṣṇa had the competence to win the Battle of Kurukṣetra, but nonetheless He induced His devotee Arjuna to fight and become the cause of victory. Śrī Caitanya Mahāprabhu was quite competent enough to spread His name and mission all over the world, but still He depended upon His devotee to do this work. Considering all these points, the most important aspect of the Supreme Lord's self-sufficiency is that He depends on His devotees. This is called His causeless mercy. The devotee who has perceived this causeless mercy of the Supreme Personality of Godhead by realization can understand the master and the servant.

TEXT 6

विष्णुपत्नि महामाये महापुरुषलक्षणे ।
प्रीयेथा मे महाभागे लोकमातर्नमोऽस्तु ते ॥ ६ ॥

viṣṇu-patni mahā-māye
mahāpuruṣa-lakṣaṇe
prīyethā me mahā-bhāge
loka-mātar namo 'stu te

viṣṇu-patni—O wife of Lord Viṣṇu; *mahā-māye*—O energy of Lord Viṣṇu; *mahā-puruṣa-lakṣaṇe*—possessing the qualities and opulences of Lord Viṣṇu; *prīyethāḥ*—kindly be pleased; *me*—upon me; *mahā-bhāge*—O goddess of fortune; *loka-mātaḥ*—O mother of the world; *namaḥ*—obeisances; *astu*—may there be; *te*—unto you.

TRANSLATION

[After profusely offering obeisances unto Lord Viṣṇu, the devotee should offer respectful obeisances unto mother Lakṣmī, the goddess of fortune, and pray as follows.] O wife of Lord Viṣṇu, O internal energy of Lord Viṣṇu, you are as good as Lord Viṣṇu Himself, for you have all of His qualities and opulences. O goddess of fortune, please be kind to me. O mother of the entire world, I offer my respectful obeisances unto you.

PURPORT

The Lord has multifarious potencies (*parāsya śaktir vividhaiva śrūyate*). Since mother Lakṣmī, the goddess of fortune, is the Lord's very precious potency, she is addressed here as *mahā-māye.* The word *māyā* means *śakti.* Lord Viṣṇu, the Supreme, cannot exhibit His power everywhere without His principal energy. It is said, *śakti śaktimān abheda:* the power and the powerful are identical. Therefore mother Lakṣmī, the goddess of fortune, is the constant companion of Lord Viṣṇu; they remain together constantly. One cannot keep Lakṣmī in one's home without Lord Viṣṇu. To think that one can do so is very dangerous. To keep Lakṣmī, or the riches of the Lord, without the service of the Lord is always dangerous, for then Lakṣmī becomes the illusory energy. With Lord Viṣṇu, however, Lakṣmī is the spiritual energy.

TEXT 7

ॐ नमो भगवते महापुरुषाय महानुभावाय महाविभूतिपतये सह
महाविभूतिभिर्बलिमुपहरामीति । अनेनाहरहर्मन्त्रेण विष्णोरावाहनार्घ्य-

पाद्योपस्पर्शनस्नानवासउपवीतविभूषणगन्धपुष्पधूपदीपोपहाराद्युपचारान्
सुसमाहितोपाहरेत् ॥ ७ ॥

*oṁ namo bhagavate mahā-puruṣāya mahānubhāvāya mahāvibhūti-
pataye saha mahā-vibhūtibhir balim upaharāmīti. anenāhar-ahar
mantreṇa viṣṇor āvāhanārghya-pādyopasparśana-snāna-vāsa-upavīta-
vibhūṣaṇa-gandha-puṣpa-dhūpa-dīpopahārādy-upacārān susamā-
hitopāharet.*

oṁ—O my Lord; *namaḥ*—obeisances; *bhagavate*—unto the Supreme Personality of Godhead, full with six opulences; *mahā-puruṣāya*—the best of enjoyers; *mahā-anubhāvāya*—the most powerful; *mahā-vibhūti*—of the goddess of fortune; *pataye*—the husband; *saha*—with; *mahā-vibhūtibhiḥ*—associates; *balim*—presentations; *upaharāmi*—I am offering; *iti*—thus; *anena*—by this; *ahaḥ-ahaḥ*—every day; *mantreṇa—mantra; viṣṇoḥ*—of Lord Viṣṇu; *āvāhana*—invocations; *arghya-pādya-upasparśana*—water for washing the hands, feet and mouth; *snāna*—water for bathing; *vāsa*—garments; *upavīta*—a sacred thread; *vibhūṣaṇa*—ornaments; *gandha*—scents; *puṣpa*—flowers; *dhūpa*—incense; *dīpa*—lamps; *upahāra*—gifts; *ādi*—and so on; *upacārān*—presentations; *su-samāhitā*—with great attention; *upāharet*—she must offer.

TRANSLATION

"My Lord Viṣṇu, full in six opulences, You are the best of all enjoyers and the most powerful. O husband of mother Lakṣmī, I offer my respectful obeisances unto You, who are accompanied by many associates, such as Viśvaksena. I offer all the paraphernalia for worshiping You." One should chant this mantra every day with great attention while worshiping Lord Viṣṇu with all paraphernalia, such as water for washing His feet, hands and mouth and water for His bath. One must offer Him various presentations for His worship, such as garments, a sacred thread, ornaments, scents, flowers, incense and lamps.

PURPORT

This *mantra* is very important. Anyone engaged in Deity worship should chant this *mantra,* as quoted above, beginning with *oṁ namo bhagavate mahā-puruṣāya.*

TEXT 8

हविःशेषं च जुहुयादनले द्वादशाहुतीः ।
ॐ नमो भगवते महापुरुषाय महाविभूतिपतये स्वाहेति ॥ ८ ॥

haviḥ-śeṣaṁ ca juhuyād
anale dvādaśāhutīḥ
oṁ namo bhagavate mahā-puruṣāya mahāvibhūti-pataye svāheti

haviḥ-śeṣam—remnants of the offering; *ca*—and; *juhuyāt*—one should offer; *anale*—in the fire; *dvādaśa*—twelve; *āhutīḥ*—oblations; *oṁ*—O my Lord; *namaḥ*—obeisances; *bhagavate*—unto the Supreme Personality of Godhead; *mahā-puruṣāya*—the supreme enjoyer; *mahā-vibhūti*—of the goddess of fortune; *pataye*—the husband; *svāhā*—hail; *iti*—thus.

TRANSLATION

Śukadeva Gosvāmī continued: After worshiping the Lord with all the paraphernalia mentioned above, one should chant the following mantra while offering twelve oblations of ghee on the sacred fire: oṁ namo bhagavate mahā-puruṣāya mahāvibhūti-pataye svāhā.

TEXT 9

श्रियं विष्णुं च वरदावाशिषां प्रभवावुभौ ।
भक्त्या सम्पूजयेन्नित्यं यदीच्छेत्सर्वसम्पदः ॥ ९ ॥

śriyaṁ viṣṇuṁ ca varadāv
āśiṣāṁ prabhavāv ubhau
bhaktyā sampūjayen nityaṁ
yadīcchet sarva-sampadaḥ

śriyam—the goddess of fortune; *viṣṇum*—Lord Viṣṇu; *ca*—and; *vara-dau*—the bestowers of benedictions; *āśiṣām*—of blessings; *prabhavau*—the sources; *ubhau*—both; *bhaktyā*—with devotion; *sampūjayet*—should worship; *nityam*—daily; *yadi*—if; *icchet*—desires; *sarva*—all; *sampadaḥ*—opulences.

TRANSLATION

If one desires all opulences, his duty is to daily worship Lord Viṣṇu with His wife, Lakṣmī. With great devotion one should worship Him according to the above-mentioned process. Lord Viṣṇu and the goddess of fortune are an immensely powerful combination. They are the bestowers of all benedictions and the sources of all good fortune. Therefore the duty of everyone is to worship Lakṣmī-Nārāyaṇa.

PURPORT

Lakṣmī-Nārāyaṇa—Lord Viṣṇu and mother Lakṣmī—are always situated in everyone's heart (*īśvaraḥ sarva-bhūtānāṁ hṛd-deśe 'rjuna tiṣṭhati*). However, because nondevotees do not realize that Lord Viṣṇu stays with His eternal consort, Lakṣmī, within the hearts of all living entities, they are not endowed with the opulence of Lord Viṣṇu. Unscrupulous men sometimes address a poor man as *daridra-nārāyaṇa*, or "poor Nārāyaṇa." This is most unscientific. Lord Viṣṇu and Lakṣmī are always situated in everyone's heart, but this does not mean that everyone is Nārāyaṇa, especially not those in poverty. This is a most abominable term to use in connection with Nārāyaṇa. Nārāyaṇa never becomes poor, and therefore He can never be called *daridra-nārāyaṇa*. Nārāyaṇa is certainly situated in everyone's heart, but He is neither poor nor rich. Only unscrupulous persons who do not know the opulence of Nārāyaṇa try to afflict Him with poverty.

TEXT 10

प्रणमेद्दण्डवद्भूमौ भक्तिप्रह्वेण चेतसा ।
दशवारं जपेन्मन्त्रं ततः स्तोत्रमुदीरयेत् ॥१०॥

praṇamed daṇḍavad bhūmau
bhakti-prahveṇa cetasā
daśa-vāraṁ japen mantraṁ
tataḥ stotram udīrayet

praṇamet—should offer obeisances; *daṇḍa-vat*—like a stick; *bhūmau*—on the ground; *bhakti*—through devotion; *prahveṇa*—humble; *cetasā*—with a mind; *daśa-vāram*—ten times; *japet*—should utter; *mantram*—the *mantra; tataḥ*—then; *stotram*—prayer; *udīrayet*—should chant.

TRANSLATION

One should offer obeisances unto the Lord with a mind humbled through devotion. While offering daṇḍavats by falling on the ground like a rod, one should chant the above mantra ten times. Then one should chant the following prayer.

TEXT 11

युवां तु विश्वस्य विभू जगतः कारणं परम् ।
इयं हि प्रकृतिः सूक्ष्मा मायाशक्तिर्दुरत्यया ।।११।।

yuvāṁ tu viśvasya vibhū
jagataḥ kāraṇaṁ param
iyaṁ hi prakṛtiḥ sūkṣmā
māyā-śaktir duratyayā

yuvām—both of you; *tu*—indeed; *viśvasya*—of the universe; *vibhū*—the proprietors; *jagataḥ*—of the universe; *kāraṇam*—the cause; *param*—supreme; *iyam*—this; *hi*—certainly; *prakṛtiḥ*—energy; *sūkṣmā*—difficult to understand; *māyā-śaktiḥ*—the internal energy; *duratyayā*—difficult to overcome.

TRANSLATION

My Lord Viṣṇu and mother Lakṣmī, goddess of fortune, you are the proprietors of the entire creation. Indeed, you are the cause of

the creation. Mother Lakṣmī is extremely difficult to understand because she is so powerful that the jurisdiction of her power is difficult to overcome. Mother Lakṣmī is represented in the material world as the external energy, but actually she is always the internal energy of the Lord.

TEXT 12

तस्या अधीश्वरः साक्षात्त्वमेव पुरुषः परः ।
त्वं सर्वयज्ञ इज्येयं क्रियेयं फलभुग्भवान् ॥१२॥

tasyā adhīśvaraḥ sākṣāt
tvam eva puruṣaḥ paraḥ
tvaṁ sarva-yajña ijyeyaṁ
kriyeyaṁ phala-bhug bhavān

tasyāḥ—of her; *adhīśvaraḥ*—the master; *sākṣāt*—directly; *tvam*—You; *eva*—certainly; *puruṣaḥ*—the person; *paraḥ*—supreme; *tvam*—You; *sarva-yajñaḥ*—personified sacrifice; *ijyā*—worship; *iyam*—this (Lakṣmī); *kriyā*—activities; *iyam*—this; *phala-bhuk*—the enjoyer of the fruits; *bhavān*—You.

TRANSLATION

My Lord, You are the master of energy, and therefore You are the Supreme Person. You are sacrifice [yajña] personified. Lakṣmī, the embodiment of spiritual activities, is the original form of worship offered unto You, whereas You are the enjoyer of all sacrifices.

TEXT 13

गुणव्यक्तिरियं देवी व्यञ्जको गुणभुग्भवान् ।
त्वं हि सर्वशरीर्यात्मा श्रीः शरीरेन्द्रियाशयाः ।
नामरूपे भगवती प्रत्ययस्त्वमपाश्रयः ॥१३॥

guṇa-vyaktir iyaṁ devī
vyañjako guṇa-bhug bhavān
tvaṁ hi sarva-śarīry ātmā
śrīḥ śarīrendriyāśayāḥ

nāma-rūpe bhagavatī
pratyayas tvam apāśrayaḥ

guṇa-vyaktiḥ—the reservoir of qualities; *iyam*—this; *devī*—goddess; *vyañjakaḥ*—manifester; *guṇa-bhuk*—the enjoyer of the qualities; *bhavān*—You; *tvam*—You; *hi*—indeed; *sarva-śarīrī ātmā*—the Supersoul of all living entities; *śrīḥ*—the goddess of fortune; *śarīra*—the body; *indriya*—senses; *āśayāḥ*—and the mind; *nāma*—name; *rūpe*—and form; *bhagavatī*—Lakṣmī; *pratyayaḥ*—the cause of manifestation; *tvam*—You; *apāśrayaḥ*—the support.

TRANSLATION

Mother Lakṣmī, who is here, is the reservoir of all spiritual qualities, whereas You manifest and enjoy all these qualities. Indeed, You are actually the enjoyer of everything. You live as the Supersoul of all living entities, and the goddess of fortune is the form of their bodies, senses and minds. She also has a holy name and form, whereas You are the support of all such names and forms and the cause for their manifestation.

PURPORT

Madhvācārya, the *ācārya* of the Tattvavādīs, has described this verse in the following way: "Viṣṇu is described as *yajña* personified, and mother Lakṣmī is described as spiritual activities and the original form of worship. In fact, they represent spiritual activities and the Supersoul of all *yajña.* Lord Viṣṇu is the Supersoul even of Lakṣmīdevī, but no one can be the Supersoul of Lord Viṣṇu, for Lord Viṣṇu Himself is the spiritual Supersoul of everyone."

According to Madhvācārya, there are two *tattvas,* or factors. One is independent, and the other is dependent. The first *tattva* is the Supreme Lord, Viṣṇu, and the second is the *jīva-tattva.* Lakṣmīdevī, being dependent on Lord Viṣṇu, is sometimes counted among the *jīvas.* The Gauḍīya Vaiṣṇavas, however, describe Lakṣmīdevī in accordance with the following two verses from the *Prameya-ratnāvalī* of Baladeva Vidyābhūṣaṇa. The first verse is a quotation from the *Viṣṇu Purāṇa.*

nityaiva sā jagan-mātā
viṣṇoḥ śrīr anapāyinī

yathā sarva-gato viṣṇus
tathaiveyaṁ dvijottama

viṣṇoḥ syuḥ śaktayas tisras
tāsu yā kīrtitā parā
saiva śrīs tad-abhinneti
prāha śiṣyān prabhur mahān

" 'O best of the *brāhmaṇas*, Lakṣmījī is the constant companion of the Supreme Personality of Godhead, Viṣṇu, and therefore she is called *anapāyinī*. She is the mother of all creation. As Lord Viṣṇu is all-pervading, His spiritual potency, mother Lakṣmī, is also all-pervading.' Lord Viṣṇu has three principal potencies—internal, external and marginal. Śrī Caitanya Mahāprabhu has accepted *parā-śakti*, the spiritual energy of the Lord, as being identical with the Lord. Thus she is also included in the independent *viṣṇu-tattva*."

In the *Kānti-mālā* commentary on the *Prameya-ratnāvalī* there is this statement: *nanu kvacit nitya-mukta-jīvatvaṁ lakṣmyāḥ svīkṛtaṁ, tatrāha,—prāheti. nityaiveti padye sarva-vyāpti-kathanena kalā-kāṣṭhety ādi-padya-dvaye, śuddho 'pīty uktā ca mahāprabhunā sva-śiṣyān prati lakṣmyā bhagavad-advaitam upadiṣṭam. kvacid yat tasyās tu dvaitam uktaṁ, tat tu tad-āviṣṭa-nitya-mukta-jīvam ādāya saṅgatamas tu.* "Although some authoritative Vaiṣṇava disciplic successions count the goddess of fortune among the ever-liberated living entities (*jīvas*) in Vaikuṇṭha, Śrī Caitanya Mahāprabhu, in accordance with the statement in the *Viṣṇu Purāṇa*, has described Lakṣmī as being identical with the *viṣṇu-tattva*. The correct conclusion is that the descriptions of Lakṣmī as being different from Viṣṇu are stated when an eternally liberated living entity is imbued with the quality of Lakṣmī; they do not pertain to mother Lakṣmī, the eternal consort of Lord Viṣṇu."

TEXT 14

यथा युवां त्रिलोकस्य वरदौ परमेष्ठिनौ ।
तथा म उत्तमश्लोक सन्तु सत्या महाशिषः ॥१४॥

yathā yuvāṁ tri-lokasya
varadau parameṣṭhinau

tathā ma uttamaśloka
santu satyā mahāśiṣaḥ

yathā—since; *yuvām*—both of you; *tri-lokasya*—of the three worlds; *vara-dau*—givers of benedictions; *parame-ṣṭhinau*—the supreme rulers; *tathā*—therefore; *me*—my; *uttama-śloka*—O Lord, who are praised with excellent verses; *santu*—may become; *satyāḥ*—fulfilled; *mahā-āśiṣaḥ*—great ambitions.

TRANSLATION

You are both the supreme rulers and benedictors of the three worlds. Therefore, my Lord, Uttamaśloka, may my ambitions be fulfilled by Your grace.

TEXT 15

इत्यभिष्टूय वरदं श्रीनिवासं श्रिया सह ।
तन्निःसार्योपहरणं दत्त्वाचमनमर्चयेत् ॥१५॥

ity abhiṣṭūya varadaṁ
śrīnivāsaṁ śriyā saha
tan niḥsāryopaharaṇaṁ
dattvācamanam arcayet

iti—thus; *abhiṣṭūya*—offering prayers; *vara-dam*—who bestows benedictions; *śrī-nivāsam*—unto Lord Viṣṇu, the abode of the goddess of fortune; *śriyā saha*—with Lakṣmī; *tat*—then; *niḥsārya*—removing; *upaharaṇam*—the paraphernalia for worship; *dattvā*—after offering; *ācamanam*—water for washing the hands and mouth; *arcayet*—one should worship.

TRANSLATION

Śrī Śukadeva Gosvāmī continued: Thus one should worship Lord Viṣṇu, who is known as Śrīnivāsa, along with mother Lakṣmī, the goddess of fortune, by offering prayers according to the process mentioned above. After removing all the paraphernalia of worship, one should offer them water to wash their hands and mouths, and then one should worship them again.

TEXT 16

ततः स्तुवीत स्तोत्रेण भक्तिप्रह्वेण चेतसा ।
यज्ञोच्छिष्टमवघ्राय पुनरभ्यर्चयेद्धरिम् ॥१६॥

tataḥ stuvīta stotreṇa
bhakti-prahveṇa cetasā
yajñocchiṣṭam avaghrāya
punar abhyarcayed dharim

tataḥ—then; *stuvīta*—one should praise; *stotreṇa*—with prayers; *bhakti*—with devotion; *prahveṇa*—humble; *cetasā*—with a mind; *yajña-ucchiṣṭam*—the remnants of sacrifice; *avaghrāya*—smelling; *punaḥ*—again; *abhyarcayet*—one should worship; *harim*—Lord Viṣṇu.

TRANSLATION

Thereafter, with devotion and humility, one should offer prayers to the Lord and mother Lakṣmī. Then one should smell the remnants of the food offered and then again worship the Lord and Lakṣmījī.

TEXT 17

पतिं च परया भक्त्या महापुरुषचेतसा ।
प्रियैस्तैस्तैरुपनमेत् प्रेमशीलः स्वयं पतिः ।
बिभृयात् सर्वकर्माणि पत्न्या उच्चावचानि च ॥१७॥

patiṁ ca parayā bhaktyā
mahāpuruṣa-cetasā
priyais tais tair upanamet
prema-śīlaḥ svayaṁ patiḥ
bibhṛyāt sarva-karmāṇi
patnyā uccāvacāni ca

patim—the husband; *ca*—and; *parayā*—supreme; *bhaktyā*—with devotion; *mahā-puruṣa-cetasā*—accepting as the Supreme Person; *priyaiḥ*—dear; *taiḥ taiḥ*—by those (offerings); *upanamet*—should worship; *prema-śīlaḥ*—being affectionate; *svayam*—himself; *patiḥ*—the husband; *bibhṛyāt*—should execute; *sarva-karmāṇi*—all activities; *patnyāḥ*—of the wife; *ucca-avacāni*—high and low; *ca*—also.

TRANSLATION

Accepting her husband as the representative of the Supreme Person, a wife should worship him with unalloyed devotion by offering him prasāda. The husband, being very pleased with his wife, should engage himself in the affairs of his family.

PURPORT

The family relationship of husband and wife should be established spiritually according to the process mentioned above.

TEXT 18

कृतमेकतरेणापि दम्पत्योरुभयोरपि ।
पत्न्यां कुर्यादनर्हायां पतिरेतत् समाहितः ॥१८॥

kṛtam ekatareṇāpi
dam-patyor ubhayor api
patnyāṁ kuryād anarhāyāṁ
patir etat samāhitaḥ

kṛtam—executed; *ekatareṇa*—by one; *api*—even; *dam-patyoḥ*—of the wife and husband; *ubhayoḥ*—of both; *api*—still; *patnyām*—when the wife; *kuryāt*—he should execute; *anarhāyām*—is unable; *patiḥ*—the husband; *etat*—this; *samāhitaḥ*—with attention.

TRANSLATION

Between the husband and wife, one person is sufficient to execute this devotional service. Because of their good relationship, both of them will enjoy the result. Therefore if the wife is unable to execute this process, the husband should carefully do so, and the faithful wife will share the result.

PURPORT

The relationship between husband and wife is firmly established when the wife is faithful and the husband sincere. Then even if the wife, being weaker, is unable to execute devotional service with her husband, if she is chaste and sincere she shares half of her husband's activities.

TEXTS 19–20

विष्णोर्व्रतमिदं बिभ्रन्न विहन्यात् कथञ्चन ।
विप्रान् स्त्रियो वीरवतीः स्रग्गन्धबलिमण्डनैः ।
अर्चेदहरहर्भक्त्या देवं नियममास्थिता ॥१९॥
उद्वास्य देवं स्वे धाम्नि तन्निवेदितमग्रतः ।
अद्यादात्मविशुद्ध्यर्थं सर्वकामसमृद्धये ॥२०॥

viṣṇor vratam idaṁ bibhran
na vihanyāt kathañcana
viprān striyo vīravatīḥ
srag-gandha-bali-maṇḍanaiḥ
arced ahar-ahar bhaktyā
devaṁ niyamam āsthitā

udvāsya devaṁ sve dhāmni
tan-niveditam agrataḥ
adyād ātma-viśuddhy-arthaṁ
sarva-kāma-samṛddhaye

viṣṇoḥ—of Lord Viṣṇu; *vratam*—vow; *idam*—this; *bibhrat*—executing; *na*—not; *vihanyāt*—should break; *kathañcana*—for any reason; *viprān*—the *brāhmaṇas; striyaḥ*—women; *vīra-vatīḥ*—who have their husband and sons; *srak*—with garlands; *gandha*—sandalwood; *bali*—offerings of food; *maṇḍanaiḥ*—and with ornaments; *arcet*—one should worship; *ahaḥ-ahaḥ*—daily; *bhaktyā*—with devotion; *devam*—Lord Viṣṇu; *niyamam*—the regulative principles; *āsthitā*—following; *udvāsya*—placing; *devam*—the Lord; *sve*—in His own; *dhāmni*—resting place; *tat*—to Him; *niveditam*—what was offered; *agrataḥ*—after dividing first among the others; *adyāt*—one should eat; *ātma-viśuddhi-artham*—for self-purification; *sarva-kāma*—all desires; *samṛddhaye*—for fulfilling.

TRANSLATION

One should accept this viṣṇu-vrata, which is a vow in devotional service, and should not deviate from its execution to engage in anything else. By offering the remnants of prasāda, flower garlands, sandalwood pulp and ornaments, one should daily worship the brāhmaṇas and worship women who peacefully live with their husbands and children. Every day the wife must continue following the regulative principles to worship Lord Viṣṇu with great devotion. Thereafter, Lord Viṣṇu should be laid in His bed, and then one should take prasāda. In this way, husband and wife will be purified and will have all their desires fulfilled.

TEXT 21

एतेन पूजाविधिना मासान् द्वादश हायनम् ।
नीत्वाथोपरमेत्साध्वी कार्तिके चरमेऽहनि ॥२१॥

etena pūjā-vidhinā
māsān dvādaśa hāyanam
nītvāthoparamet sādhvī
kārtike carame 'hani

etena—with this; *pūjā-vidhinā*—regulated worship; *māsān dvādaśa*—twelve months; *hāyanam*—a year; *nītvā*—after passing; *atha*—then; *uparamet*—should fast; *sādhvī*—the chaste wife; *kārtike*—in Kārttika; *carame ahani*—on the final day.

TRANSLATION

The chaste wife must perform such devotional service continuously for one year. After one year passes, she should fast on the full-moon day in the month of Kārttika [October-November].

TEXT 22

श्वोभूतेऽप उपस्पृश्य कृष्णमभ्यर्च्य पूर्ववत् ।
पयःश्रृतेन जुहुयाच्चरुणा सह सर्पिषा ।
पाकयज्ञविधानेन द्वादशैवाहुतीः पतिः ॥२२॥

śvo-bhūte 'pa upaspṛśya
kṛṣṇam abhyarcya pūrvavat
payaḥ-śṛtena juhuyāc
caruṇā saha sarpiṣā
pāka-yajña-vidhānena
dvādaśaivāhutīḥ patiḥ

śvaḥ-bhūte—on the following morning; *apaḥ*—water; *upaspṛśya*—contacting; *kṛṣṇam*—Lord Kṛṣṇa; *abhyarcya*—worshiping; *pūrva-vat*—as previously; *payaḥ-śṛtena*—with boiled milk; *juhuyāt*—one should offer; *caruṇā*—with an offering of sweet rice; *saha*—with; *sarpiṣā*—ghee; *pāka-yajña-vidhānena*—according to the injunctions of the *Gṛhya-sūtras; dvādaśa*—twelve; *eva*—indeed; *āhutīḥ*—oblations; *patiḥ*—the husband.

TRANSLATION

On the morning of the next day, one should wash oneself, and after worshiping Lord Kṛṣṇa as before, one should cook as one cooks for festivals as stated in the Gṛhya-sūtras. Sweet rice should be cooked with ghee, and with this preparation the husband should offer oblations to the fire twelve times.

TEXT 23

आशिषः शिरसादाय द्विजैः प्रीतैः समीरिताः ।
प्रणम्य शिरसा भक्त्या भुञ्जीत तदनुज्ञया ॥२३॥

āśiṣaḥ śirasādāya
dvijaiḥ prītaiḥ samīritāḥ
praṇamya śirasā bhaktyā
bhuñjīta tad-anujñayā

āśiṣaḥ—blessings; *śirasā*—with the head; *ādāya*—accepting; *dvi-jaiḥ*—by the *brāhmaṇas; prītaiḥ*—who are pleased; *samīritāḥ*—spoken; *praṇamya*—after offering obeisances; *śirasā*—with the head; *bhaktyā*—with devotion; *bhuñjīta*—he should eat; *tat-anujñayā*—with their permission.

TRANSLATION

Thereafter, he should satisfy the brāhmaṇas. When the satisfied brāhmaṇas bestow their blessings, he should devotedly offer them respectful obeisances with his head, and with their permission he should take prasāda.

TEXT 24

आचार्यमग्रतः कृत्वा वाग्यतः सह बन्धुभिः ।
दद्यात्पत्न्यै चरोः शेषं सुप्रजास्त्वं सुसौभगम् ॥२४॥

ācāryam agrataḥ kṛtvā
vāg-yataḥ saha bandhubhiḥ
dadyāt patnyai caroḥ śeṣaṁ
suprajāstvaṁ susaubhagam

ācāryam—the *ācārya; agrataḥ*—first of all; *kṛtvā*—receiving properly; *vāk-yataḥ*—controlling speech; *saha*—with; *bandhubhiḥ*—friends and relatives; *dadyāt*—he should give; *patnyai*—to the wife; *caroḥ*—of the oblation of sweet rice; *śeṣam*—the remnant; *su-prajāstvam*—which insures good progeny; *su-saubhagam*—which insures good fortune.

TRANSLATION

Before taking his meal, the husband must first seat the ācārya comfortably, and, along with his relatives and friends, should control his speech and offer prasāda to the guru. Then the wife should eat the remnants of the oblation of sweet rice cooked with ghee. Eating the remnants insures a learned, devoted son and all good fortune.

TEXT 25

एतच्चरित्वा विधिवद्व्रतं विभो
रभीप्सितार्थं लभते पुमानिह ।
स्त्री चैतदास्थाय लभेत सौभगं
श्रियं प्रजां जीवपतिं यशो गृहम् ॥२५॥

etac caritvā vidhivad vrataṁ vibhor
abhīpsitārthaṁ labhate pumān iha
strī caitad āsthāya labheta saubhagaṁ
śriyaṁ prajāṁ jīva-patiṁ yaśo gṛham

etat—this; *caritvā*—performing; *vidhi-vat*—according to the injunctions of *śāstra; vratam*—vow; *vibhoḥ*—from the Lord; *abhīpsita*—desired; *artham*—object; *labhate*—gets; *pumān*—a man; *iha*—in this life; *strī*—a woman; *ca*—and; *etat*—this; *āsthāya*—performing; *labheta*—can get; *saubhagam*—good fortune; *śriyam*—opulence; *prajām*—progeny; *jīva-patim*—a husband with a long duration of life; *yaśaḥ*—good reputation; *gṛham*—home.

TRANSLATION

If this vow or ritualistic ceremony is observed according to the description of śāstra, even in this life a man will be able to achieve all the benedictions he desires from the Lord. A wife who performs this ritualistic ceremony will surely receive good fortune, opulence, sons, a long-living husband, a good reputation and a good home.

PURPORT

In Bengal even today if a woman lives for a long time with her husband, she is considered very fortunate. A woman generally desires a good husband, good children, a good home, prosperity, opulence and so on. As recommended in this verse, a woman will receive all these desirable benedictions, and a man will also be able to receive all benedictions, from the Supreme Personality of Godhead. Thus by performing this particular type of *vrata*, a man and a woman in Kṛṣṇa consciousness will be happy in this material world, and because of being Kṛṣṇa conscious they will be promoted to the spiritual world.

TEXTS 26–28

कन्या च विन्देत समग्रलक्षणं
पतिं त्ववीरा हतकिल्बिषां गतिम् ।
मृतप्रजा जीवसुता धनेश्वरी
सुदुर्भगा सुभगा रूपमग्र्यम् ॥२६॥
विन्देद् विरूपा विरुजा विमुच्यते
य आमयावीन्द्रियकल्यदेहम् ।
एतत्पठन्नभ्युदये च कर्म
ण्यनन्ततृप्तिः पितृदेवतानाम् ॥२७॥
तुष्टाः प्रयच्छन्ति समस्तकामान्
होमावसाने हुतभुक् श्रीहरिश्च ।
राजन् महन्मरुतां जन्म पुण्यं
दितेर्व्रतं चाभिहितं महत्ते ॥२८॥

kanyā ca vindeta samagra-lakṣaṇaṁ
patiṁ tv avīrā hata-kilbiṣāṁ gatim
mṛta-prajā jīva-sutā dhaneśvarī
sudurbhagā subhagā rūpam agryam

vinded virūpā virujā vimucyate
ya āmayāvīndriya-kalya-deham
etat paṭhann abhyudaye ca karmaṇy
ananta-tṛptiḥ pitṛ-devatānām

tuṣṭāḥ prayacchanti samasta-kāmān
homāvasāne huta-bhuk śrī-hariś ca
rājan mahan marutāṁ janma puṇyaṁ
diter vrataṁ cābhihitaṁ mahat te

kanyā—an unmarried girl; *ca*—and; *vindeta*—can get; *samagra-lakṣaṇam*—possessing all good qualities; *patim*—a husband; *tu*—and; *avīrā*—a woman without a husband or son; *hata-kilbiṣām*—free from fault; *gatim*—the destination; *mṛta-prajā*—a woman whose children are dead; *jīva-sutā*—a woman whose child has a long duration of life; *dhana-īśvarī*—possessing wealth; *su-durbhagā*—unfortunate; *su-bhagā*—fortunate; *rūpam*—beauty; *agryam*—excellent; *vindet*—can get; *virūpā*—an ugly woman; *virujā*—from the disease; *vimucyate*—is freed; *yaḥ*—he who; *āmayā-vī*—a diseased man; *indriya-kalya-deham*—an able body; *etat*—this; *paṭhan*—reciting; *abhyudaye ca karmaṇi*—and in a sacrificial ceremony in which oblations are offered to the forefathers and demigods; *ananta*—unlimited; *tṛptiḥ*—satisfaction; *pitṛ-devatānām*—of the forefathers and demigods; *tuṣṭāḥ*—being pleased; *prayacchanti*—they bestow; *samasta*—all; *kāmān*—desires; *homa-avasāne*—on the completion of the ceremony; *huta-bhuk*—the enjoyer of the sacrifice; *śrī-hariḥ*—Lord Viṣṇu; *ca*—also; *rājan*—O King; *mahat*—great; *marutām*—of the Maruts; *janma*—birth; *puṇyam*—pious; *diteḥ*—of Diti; *vratam*—the vow; *ca*—also; *abhihitam*—explained; *mahat*—great; *te*—to you.

TRANSLATION

If an unmarried girl observes this vrata, she will be able to get a very good husband. If a woman who is avīrā—who has no husband or son—executes this ritualistic ceremony, she can be promoted to the spiritual world. A woman whose children have died after birth can get a child with a long duration of life and also become very fortunate in possessing wealth. If a woman is unfortunate she will become fortunate, and if ugly she will become beautiful. By observing this vrata, a diseased man can gain relief from his disease and have an able body with which to work. If one recites this narration while offering oblations to the pitās and demigods, especially during the śrāddha ceremony, the demigods and inhabitants of Pitṛloka will be extremely pleased with him and bestow upon him the fulfillment of all desires. After one performs this ritualistic ceremony, Lord Viṣṇu and His wife, mother Lakṣmī, the goddess of fortune, are very pleased with him. O King Parīkṣit,

now I have completely described how Diti performed this ceremony and had good children—the Maruts—and a happy life. I have tried to explain this to you as elaborately as possible.

Thus end the Bhaktivedanta purports of the Sixth Canto, Nineteenth Chapter, of the Śrīmad-Bhāgavatam, *entitled "Performing the Puṁsavana Ritualistic Ceremony."*

END OF THE SIXTH CANTO

Appendixes

The Author

His Divine Grace A. C. Bhaktivedanta Swami Prabhupāda appeared in this world in 1896 in Calcutta, India. He first met his spiritual master, Śrīla Bhaktisiddhānta Sarasvatī Gosvāmī, in Calcutta in 1922. Bhaktisiddhānta Sarasvatī, a prominent devotional scholar and the founder of sixty-four Gauḍīya Maṭhas (Vedic institutes), liked this educated young man and convinced him to dedicate his life to teaching Vedic knowledge. Śrīla Prabhupāda became his student, and eleven years later (1933) at Allahabad he became his formally initiated disciple.

At their first meeting, in 1922, Śrīla Bhaktisiddhānta Sarasvatī Ṭhākura requested Śrīla Prabhupāda to broadcast Vedic knowledge through the English language. In the years that followed, Śrīla Prabhupāda wrote a commentary on the *Bhagavad-gītā*, assisted the Gauḍīya Maṭha in its work and, in 1944, without assistance, started an English fortnightly magazine, edited it, typed the manuscripts and checked the galley proofs. He even distributed the individual copies freely and struggled to maintain the publication. Once begun, the magazine never stopped; it is now being continued by his disciples in the West.

Recognizing Śrīla Prabhupāda's philosophical learning and devotion, the Gauḍīya Vaiṣṇava Society honored him in 1947 with the title "Bhaktivedanta." In 1950, at the age of fifty-four, Śrīla Prabhupāda retired from married life, and four years later he adopted the *vānaprastha* (retired) order to devote more time to his studies and writing. Śrīla Prabhupāda traveled to the holy city of Vṛndāvana, where he lived in very humble circumstances in the historic medieval temple of Rādhā-Dāmodara. There he engaged for several years in deep study and writing. He accepted the renounced order of life (*sannyāsa*) in 1959. At Rādhā-Dāmodara, Śrīla Prabhupāda began work on his life's masterpiece: a multivolume translation and commentary on the eighteen thousand verse *Śrīmad-Bhāgavatam* (*Bhāgavata Purāṇa*). He also wrote *Easy Journey to Other Planets*.

After publishing three volumes of *Bhāgavatam*, Śrīla Prabhupāda came to the United States, in 1965, to fulfill the mission of his spiritual master. Since that time, His Divine Grace has written over forty volumes of authoritative translations, commentaries and summary studies of the philosophical and religious classics of India.

In 1965, when he first arrived by freighter in New York City, Śrīla Prabhupāda was practically penniless. It was after almost a year of great difficulty that he established the International Society for Krishna Consciousness in July of 1966. Under his careful guidance, the Society has grown within a decade to a worldwide confederation of almost one hundred *āśramas*, schools, temples, institutes and farm communities.

In 1968, Śrīla Prabhupāda created New Vṛndāvana, an experimental Vedic community in the hills of West Virginia. Inspired by the success of New Vṛndāvana, now a thriving farm community of more than one thousand acres, his students have since founded several similar communities in the United States and abroad.

In 1972, His Divine Grace introduced the Vedic system of primary and secondary education in the West by founding the Gurukula school in Dallas, Texas. The school began with 3 children in 1972, and by the beginning of 1975 the enrollment had grown to 150.

Śrīla Prabhupāda has also inspired the construction of a large international center at Śrīdhāma Māyāpur in West Bengal, India, which is also the site for a planned Institute of Vedic Studies. A similar project is the magnificent Kṛṣṇa-Balarāma Temple and International Guest House in Vṛndāvana, India. These are centers where Westerners can live to gain firsthand experience of Vedic culture.

Śrīla Prabhupāda's most significant contribution, however, is his books. Highly respected by the academic community for their authoritativeness, depth and clarity, they are used as standard textbooks in numerous college courses. His writings have been translated into eleven languages. The Bhaktivedanta Book Trust, established in 1972 exclusively to publish the works of His Divine Grace, has thus become the world's largest publisher of books in the field of Indian religion and philosophy. Its latest project is the publishing of Śrīla Prabhupāda's most recent work: a seventeen-volume translation and commentary—completed by Śrīla Prabhupāda in only eighteen months—on the Bengali religious classic *Śrī Caitanya-caritāmṛta.*

In the past ten years, in spite of his advanced age, Śrīla Prabhupāda has circled the globe twelve times on lecture tours that have taken him to six continents. In spite of such a vigorous schedule, Śrīla Prabhupāda continues to write prolifically. His writings constitute a veritable library of Vedic philosophy, religion, literature and culture.

References

The purports of *Śrīmad-Bhāgavatam* are all confirmed by standard Vedic authorities. The following authentic scriptures are specifically cited in this volume.

Bhagavad-gītā, 2, 7, 18, 54, 58, 65, 84, 87, 90, 91, 93, 99, 100, 105, 108, 119, 120, 125, 126, 127, 128, 134, 135, 139, 148, 150, 151, 152, 153, 155, 158, 173, 180, 182, 183–185, 194, 200, 215, 232, 235, 239, 243, 263, 273, 274, 275, 278.

Bhakti-rasāmṛta-sindhu, 56, 102, 129, 147, 191

Brahma-saṁhitā, 44, 100, 122, 123, 124, 147, 182, 195, 199

Bṛhan-nāradīya Purāṇa, 140

Caitanya-caritāmṛta, 86, 160, 196, 207

Cāṇakya-śloka, 14, 27, 34, 239

Īśopaniṣad, 12, 132, 272–273

Nārada-pañcarātra, 129–130

Padma Purāṇa, 116, 149, 207

Prameya-ratnāvalī, 281–282

Prema-vivarta, 158

Śikṣāṣṭaka, 174–175, 178, 192–193, 204, 266

Śrīmad-Bhāgavatam, 7, 8, 13, 67, 109, 115, 119, 126, 130, 132, 136, 137, 138, 149, 182, 197–198, 206, 229–230, 237, 246, 262, 264–265

Glossary

A

Ācārya—a spiritual master who teaches by example.
Adhibhautika—misery inflicted by other living beings.
Adhidaivika—miseries of nature inflicted by demigods.
Adhyātmika—misery caused by the body or mind.
Ānandamaya—(lit., full of bliss), spiritual realization; Kṛṣṇa consciousness.
Aṇimā—the mystic power to become as small as an atom.
Annamaya—(lit., consisting of food), consciousness absorbed only in eating.
Ārati—a ceremony for greeting the Lord with offerings of food, lamps, fans, flowers and incense.
Arcanā—the devotional practice of Deity worship.
Āśrama—a spiritual order of life.
Asura—atheistic demons.
Avatāra—a descent of the Supreme Lord.

B

Bhagavad-gītā—the basic directions for spiritual life spoken by the Lord Himself.
Bhagavān—the Supreme Lord, who possesses six opulences: wealth, strength, fame, beauty, knowledge and renunciation.
Bhakta—a devotee.
Bhakti-yoga—linking with the Supreme Lord in ecstatic devotional service.
Brahmacarya—celibate student life; the first order of Vedic spiritual life.
Brahman—the Absolute Truth; especially, the impersonal aspect of the Absolute.
Brāhmaṇa—a person in the mode of goodness; first Vedic social order.

C

Cāraṇaloka—the heavenly planet of the Cāraṇa demigods.

D

Dharma—eternal occupational duty; religious principles.

E

Ekādaśī—a special fast day for increased remembrance of Kṛṣṇa, which comes on the eleventh day of both the waxing and waning moon.

G

Goloka (Kṛṣṇaloka)—the highest spiritual planet, containing Kṛṣṇa's personal abodes, Dvārakā, Mathurā and Vṛndāvana.
Gopīs—Kṛṣṇa's cowherd girl friends who are His most confidential servitors.
Gṛhastha—regulated householder life; the second order of Vedic spiritual life.
Guru—a spiritual master or superior person.

H

Hare Kṛṣṇa *mantra*—*See: Mahā-mantra*

J

Jīva-tattva—the living entities, who are small parts of the Lord.
Jñānī—one who cultivates knowledge by empirical speculation.

K

Kali-yuga (Age of Kali)—the present age, which is characterized by quarrel. It is last in the cycle of four, and began five thousand years ago.
Karatālas—hand cymbals used in *kīrtana.*
Karma—fruitive action, for which there is always reaction, good or bad.
Karmī—one who is satisfied with working hard for flickering sense gratification.
Kīrtana—chanting the glories of the Supreme Lord.
Kṛṣṇaloka—*See:* Goloka
Kṣatriyas—a warrior or administrator; the second Vedic social order.

L

Laghimā—the mystic power to become as light as a feather.

M

Mahābhārata—the history of greater India compiled by Śrīla Vyāsadeva. It includes *Bhagavad-gītā.*

Mahā-mantra—the great chanting for deliverance: Hare Kṛṣṇa, Hare Kṛṣṇa, Kṛṣṇa Kṛṣṇa, Hare Hare/ Hare Rāma, Hare Rāma, Rāma Rāma, Hare Hare.

Mahat-tattva—the total material energy before the manifestation of diverse elements.

Manomaya—(lit., consisting of mind), consciousness absorbed in mental activity.

Mantra—a sound vibration that can deliver the mind from illusion.

Mathurā—Lord Kṛṣṇa's abode, surrounding Vṛndāvana, where He took birth and later returned to after performing His Vṛndāvana pastimes.

Māyā—(mā—not; *yā*—this), illusion; forgetfulness of one's relationship with Kṛṣṇa.

Māyāvādīs—impersonalist philosophers who say that the Lord cannot have a transcendental body.

Mṛdaṅga—a clay drum used for congregational chanting.

P

Paramātmā—Lord Viṣṇu expanded into everyone's heart.

Paramparā—the chain of spiritual masters in disciplic succession.

Prāṇamaya—(lit., consisting of life), consciousness absorbed in maintaining one's bodily existence.

Prasāda—food spiritualized by being offered to the Lord.

Purāṇas—Vedic supplements in the form of histories.

R

Ṛṣi—sage or mystic.

S

Sac-cid-ānanda-vigraha—the Lord's transcendental form, which is eternal, full of knowledge and bliss.

Samādhi—fixed mind for understanding the self; trance; absorption in the Supreme.

Saṅkīrtana—public chanting of the names of God, the approved *yoga* process for this age.
Sannyāsa—renounced life; the fourth order of Vedic spiritual life.
Śāstras—revealed scriptures.
Siddhaloka—heavenly planet where residents have all eight mystic powers.
Śravaṇaṁ kīrtanaṁ viṣṇoḥ—the devotional processes of hearing and chanting about Lord Viṣṇu.
Śūdra—a laborer; the fourth of the Vedic social orders.
Svāmī—one who controls his mind and senses; title of one in the renounced order of life.

T

Tapasya—austerity; accepting some voluntary inconvenience for a higher purpose.
Tilaka—auspicious clay marks that sanctify a devotee's body as a temple of the Lord.

V

Vaikuṇṭha—the spiritual world, where there is no anxiety.
Vaiṣṇava—a devotee of Lord Viṣṇu, or Kṛṣṇa.
Vaiśyas—farmers and merchants; the third Vedic social order.
Vānaprastha—one who has retired from family life; the third order of Vedic spiritual life.
Varṇāśrama—the Vedic social system of four social and four spiritual orders.
Vedas—the original revealed scriptures, first spoken by the Lord Himself.
Vidyādharas—a race of celestial beings.
Vijñānamaya—(lit., full of knowledge), consciousness of the self as different from matter.
Viṣṇu, Lord—Kṛṣṇa's first expansion for the creation and maintenance of the material universes.
Vṛndāvana—Kṛṣṇa's personal abode, where He fully manifests His quality of sweetness.
Vyāsadeva—Kṛṣṇa's incarnation, at the end of Dvāpara-yuga, for compiling the *Vedas*.

Y

Yajña—sacrifice, work done for the satisfaction of Lord Viṣṇu.

Yogī—a transcendentalist who, in one way or another, is striving for union with the Supreme.

Yugas—ages in the life of a universe, occuring in a repeated cycle of four.

GENEALOGICAL TABLE

The Descendants of Kaśyapa Muni

This chart shows the descendants of Kaśyapa Muni, whose father, Marīci, was born from the mind of Lord Brahmā, the first created being in the universe. Kaśyapa's wives helped to populate the universe with different species of life. Two of his wives, Diti and Aditi, are especially important: Diti was the mother of many great demons, and Aditi, many great demigods. An incarnation of the Supreme Personality of Godhead, Urukrama, also appeared from Aditi's womb.

Kaśyapa +

- Timi → aquatics
- Vinatā → Garuḍa, Anūru (Aruṇa)
- Kadrū → serpents
- Pataṅgī → birds
- Yāminī → locusts
- Kāṣṭhā → single-hooved animals
- Ariṣṭā → Gandharvas
- Surasā → Rākṣasas
- Ilā → creepers & trees
- Muni → angels
- Surabhi → cow, buffalo, *etc.*
- Tāmrā → large birds of prey
- Krodhavaśā → mosquitoes, serpents (dandaśūka & others)
- Saramā → ferocious animals
- Diti → { Hiraṇyākṣa + Upadānavī, Hiraṇyakaśipu + Kayādhu, Maruts }
  - Hiraṇyakaśipu + Kayādhu → { Saṁhlāda + Kṛti, Anuhlāda + Sūryā, Hlāda + Dhamani, Prahlāda + NS, Siṁhikā }
    - Saṁhlāda + Kṛti → Pañcajana
    - Anuhlāda + Sūryā → Bāṣkala, Mahiṣa
    - Hlāda + Dhamani → Vātāpi, Ilvala
    - Prahlāda + NS → Virocana + NS → Bali + Aśanā → { Bāṇa & 99 others }
- Danu → { Ariṣṭa, Anutāpana, Dvimūrdhā, Śambara, Vipracitti, Dhūmrakeśa, Aruṇa, Vibhāvasu, Ayomukha, Svarbhānu + NS, Vṛṣaparvā + NS, Śaṅkuśirā, Kapila, Durjaya, Pulomā, Vaiśvānara + NS, Hayagrīva (demon), Ekacakra, Virūpākṣa }
  - Vipracitti + Siṁhikā → Rāhu & the one hundred Ketus
  - Svarbhānu + NS → Suprabā + Namuci
  - Vṛṣaparvā + NS → Śarmiṣṭhā + Yayāti
  - Vaiśvānara + NS → { Upadānavī, Hayaśirā + Kratu, Pulomā, Kālakā }
    - { Pulomā, Kālakā } Kaśyapa → { the Paulomas & the Kālakeyas, *headed by* Nivātakavaca }

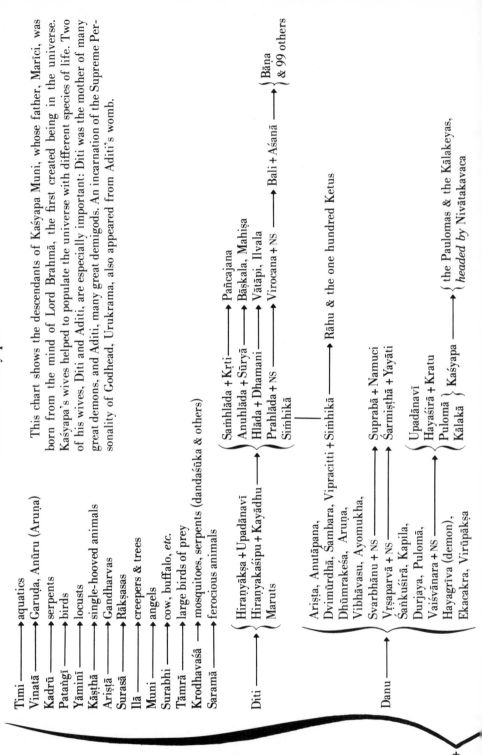

Aditi →

- Bhaga + Siddhi → Mahimā, Vibhu, Prabhu & Āśī
- Savitā + Pṛśni → Agnihotra, Paśu, Soma, Cāturmāsya, the 5 Mahāyajñas, & Sāvitrī, Vyāhṛti, Trayī
- Vidhātā + Kriyā → the 5 Purīṣyas (fire gods)
- Varuṇa — (from an anthill) → Vālmīki
- Varuṇa + Carṣaṇī → Bhṛgu (in second birth)
- Varuṇa & Mitra — (no mother) → Agastya, Vasiṣṭha (common sons of Varuṇa & Mitra)
- Mitra + Revatī → Utsarga, Ariṣṭa, Pippala
- Urukrama + Kīrti → Bṛhatśloka + NS → Saubhaga & many others
- Dhātā +
  - Kuhū → Sāyam
  - Sinīvālī → Darśa
  - Rākā → Prātaḥ
  - Anumati → Pūrṇamāsa
- Tvaṣṭā + Racanā → Sanniveśa, Viśvarūpa
- Aryamā + Mātṛkā → scholars & human beings
- Vivasvān +
  - Chāyā → Śanaiścara, Sāvarṇi Manu, Tapatī + Saṁvaraṇa
  - Saṁjñā → Yama, Śrāddhadeva & R. Yamunā (Yamī) → Aśvinī-kumāras
- Indra + Paulomī → Jayanta, Ṛṣabha, Mīḍhuṣa
- Pūṣā

+ indicates marriage ties
→ indicates offspring
NS not specified

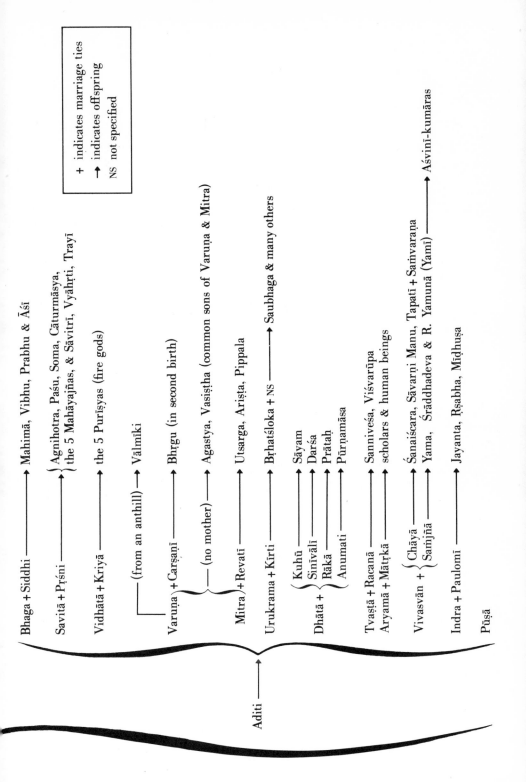

Sanskrit Pronunciation Guide

Vowels

अ a आ ā इ i ई ī उ u ऊ ū ऋ ṛ ॠ ṝ

ऌ ḷ ए e ऐ ai ओ o औ au

ं ṁ *(anusvāra)* ः ḥ *(visarga)*

Consonants

Gutturals:	क ka	ख kha	ग ga	घ gha	ङ ṅa
Palatals:	च ca	छ cha	ज ja	झ jha	ञ ña
Cerebrals:	ट ṭa	ठ ṭha	ड ḍa	ढ ḍha	ण ṇa
Dentals:	त ta	थ tha	द da	ध dha	न na
Labials:	प pa	फ pha	ब ba	भ bha	म ma
Semivowels:	य ya	र ra	ल la	व va	
Sibilants:	श śa	ष ṣa	स sa		
Aspirate:	ह ha	ऽ ' *(avagraha)* – the apostrophe			

The vowels above should be pronounced as follows:

a – like the *a* in org*a*n or the *u* in b*u*t.
ā – like the *a* in f*a*r but held twice as long as short *a*.
i – like the *i* in p*i*n.
ī – like the *i* in p*i*que but held twice as long as short *i*.
u – like the *u* in p*u*sh.
ū – like the *u* in r*u*le but held twice as long as short *u*.

ṛ – like the *ri* in *rim*.
ṝ – like *ree* in *reed*.
ḷ – like *l* followed by *ṛ* (*lṛ*).
e – like the *e* in th*ey*.
ai – like the *ai* in *ai*sle.
o – like the *o* in g*o*.
au – like the *ow* in h*ow*.
ṁ (*anusvāra*) – a resonant nasal like the *n* in the French word *bon*.
ḥ (*visarga*) – a final *h*-sound: *aḥ* is pronounced like *aha; iḥ* like *ihi*.

The consonants are pronounced as follows:

k – as in *k*ite
kh – as in Ec*kh*art
g – as in *g*ive
gh – as in di*g-h*ard
ṅ – as in si*ng*
c – as in *ch*air
ch – as in staun*ch-h*eart
j – as in *j*oy
jh – as in he*dgeh*og
ñ – as in ca*ny*on
ṭ – as in *t*ub
ṭh – as in ligh*t-h*eart
ḍ – as in *d*ove
ḍha- as in re*d-h*ot
ṇ – as r*na* (prepare to say the *r* and say *na*).

Cerebrals are pronounced with tongue to roof of mouth, but the following dentals are pronounced with tongue against teeth:

t – as in *t*ub but with tongue against teeth.
th – as in ligh*t-h*eart but with tongue against teeth.
d – as in *d*ove but with tongue against teeth.
dh – as in re*d-h*ot but with tongue against teeth.
n – as in *n*ut but with tongue between teeth.
p – as in *p*ine
ph – as in u*ph*ill (not *f*)
b – as in *b*ird
bh – as in ru*b-h*ard
m – as in *m*other
y – as in *y*es
r – as in *r*un
l – as in *l*ight
v – as in *v*ine
ś (palatal) – as in the *s* in the German word *sprechen*
ṣ (cerebral) – as the *sh* in *sh*ine
s – as in *s*un
h – as in *h*ome

There is no strong accentuation of syllables in Sanskrit, only a flowing of short and long (twice as long as the short) syllables.

Index of Sanskrit Verses

This index constitutes a complete listing of the first and third lines of each of the Sanskrit poetry verses and the first line of each Sanskrit prose verse of this volume of *Śrīmad-Bhāgavatam*, arranged in English alphabetical order. In the first column the Sanskrit transliteration is given, and in the second and third columns respectively the chapter-verse reference and page number for each verse are to be found.

A

abhayaṁ cāpy anīhāyāṁ	16.59	160
abhīkṣṇaṁ labdha-mānānāṁ	14.41	34
ācāryam agrataḥ kṛtvā	19.24	289
ādāv ante 'pi ca sattvānāṁ	16.36	121
adhunā putriṇāṁ tāpo	15.21	70
adyād ātma-viśuddhy-arthaṁ	19.20	286
agastyaś ca vasiṣṭhaś ca	18.5	213
āgatya tulya-vyasanāḥ suduḥkhitās	14.49	39
agnihotraṁ paśuṁ somaṁ	18.1	211
agnīn purīṣyān ādhatta	18.4	212
ahaṁ te putra-kāmasya	15.17	67
ahaṁ vai sarva-bhūtāni	16.51	148
aho adharmaḥ sumahān	18.38	235
aho arthendriyārāmo	18.39	236
aho vidhātas tvam atīva bāliśo	14.54	42
ajita jitaḥ sama-matibhiḥ	16.34	117
aklinna-hṛdayaṁ pāpaṁ	18.24	225
alaṁ te nirapekṣāya	19.4	272
āliṅgyāṅkīkṛtāṁ devīṁ	17.5	468
amba te 'haṁ vyavasitam	18.71	261
amṛtyuṁ mṛta-putrāhaṁ	18.37	234
anāma-rūpaś cin-mātraḥ	16.21	103
ananya-bhāvān pārṣadān	18.64	257
ānapatyena duḥkhena	14.39	33
anarcitāsaṁyata-vāk	18.50	248
anuhrādasya sūryāyāṁ	18.16	219
andhe tamasi magnasya	15.16	65
añjas tarema bhavatāpraja-dustaraṁ	14.56	45
aṅkīkṛtya striyaṁ cāste	17.7	170
antar bahiś ca vitataṁ	16.23	104
anugrahāya bhavataḥ	15.19	67
anveti vyatiricyeta	16.56	156
apāntaratamā vyāso	15.12	63
apatyam icchanty acaraṁ	18.69	260
api dārāḥ prajāmātyā	14.19	19
api te 'nāmayaṁ svasti	14.17	17
ārabheta vratam idaṁ	19.2	271
ārādhanaṁ bhagavata	18.74	264
ārādhyātma-pradaṁ devaṁ	18.75	265
arced ahar-ahar bhaktyā	19.19	286
āśāsānasya tasyedaṁ	18.26	226
āsīd rājā sārvabhaumaḥ	14.10	12
āśiṣaḥ śirasādāya	19.23	288
āśiṣaṁ ca varārohāṁ	18.2	211
asmad-vidhānāṁ duṣṭānāṁ	17.11	175
aspṛṣṭa-vāry-adhautāṅghriḥ	18.60	255
āste mukhyaḥ sabhāyāṁ vai	17.6	170
āśvāsya bhagavān itthaṁ	16.65	164
atad-arham anusmṛtya	15.18	67
ataḥ pāpīyasīṁ yonim	17.15	179
atha bhagavan vayam adhunā	16.45	141
atha deva-ṛṣī rājan	16.1	80
athāha nṛpatim rājan	14.29	26
atha kāla upāvṛtte	14.32	29
atha kaśyapa-dāyādān	18.10	216
atha prasādaye na tvāṁ	17.24	189
atha tasmai prapannāya	16.17	97
athendram āha tātāham	18.69	260
ātmamāyā-guṇair viśvam	16.9	89
ātmanaḥ prīyate nātmā	14.21	21
ātmānam eka-deśa-sthaṁ	16.53	153
ātmānaṁ prakṛtiṣv addhā	14.18	19

J

K

L

M

General Index

Numerals in boldface type indicate references to translations of the verses of *Śrīmad-Bhāgavatam.*

A

Abhinnatvaṁ nāma-nāminoḥ
quoted, 151
Abortion
atonement for, 96
at contraceptive's failure, 55
Absolute Truth
devotee's vs. *jñānī's* approach to, 197–198
features of, three defined, **97,** 107, 149
See also: Supreme Lord
Ācārya. See: Spiritual master
Activities
caused by the Lord, 151
illusion of soul concerning, 58
material, as mental concoction, **72–74**
pious and forbidden, 149
understanding, from the Lord, 150
See also: Karma
Acyuta, Kṛṣṇa's forms as, 100
Aditi, descendants of, **210–216**
Advaita, Kṛṣṇa's forms as, 100
Advaitam acyutam anādim ananta-rūpam
quoted, 102
verse quoted, 120, 197
Āgamāpāyino 'nityās
verse quoted, 100
Agastya Muni, **213, 214**
Vātāpi served to, **219**
Agents of the Lord, father, king, etc., as, **58**
Age of Kali. *See:* Kali-yuga
Agnihotra, **211**
Ahaituky apratihatā, 118
verse quoted, 130
Aham ādir hi devānām
quoted, 123
Ahaṁ vai sarva-bhūtāni
quoted, 150–151
Ahaṅkāra itīyaṁ me
verse quoted, 150
Ahaṅkāraṁ balaṁ darpaṁ
verse quoted, 135
Ahaṅkāra-vimūḍhātmā
verse quoted, 58, 183
Air. *See:* Elements, material
Airplane as example of false creation, 120–121
Ajāmila, attachment of, compared to a woman's attachment to husband, 232
Ajo 'pi sann avyayātmā
verse quoted, 215
Akāmaḥ sarva-kāmo vā
verse quoted, 126, 264–265
Akarmaṇaś ca boddhavyaṁ
verse quoted, 150
Alphabet, true purpose of, 115
Amāninā mānadena
verse quoted, 175, 178
Ānanda, in Kṛṣṇa, 101–**102**
Ānandamayo 'bhyāsāt
quoted, 101
Ananta, Kṛṣṇa as, **124**–125
Anantadeva
See also: Anantadeva, quotations from
Citraketu instructed by, **146–164**
described, **113**
disappears, **164, 166–167**
universes held by, **145**
Anantadeva, quotations from
on cause of material and spiritual energies. Himself as, **152**
on Deity form of Himself, **148**
on fruitive activities, **160–161, 162**
on Indians in spiritual life, **159**
on knowledge in living entities, **157**
on living entity's forgetfulness, **158**

B

D

Dadāmi buddhi-yogaṁ tam
quoted, 149
Daityas defined, **217**
Daiva-netra, 182
Daivī hy eṣā guṇamayī
verse quoted, 180
Dakṣa, Citraketu unlike, 171
Dām-patye 'bhirucir hetuḥ
quoted, 237
Daṇḍavats to Lakṣmī-Nārāyaṇa, **279**
Daṇḍo mitraṁ ca tasyaitāḥ
verse quoted, 18
"*Daridra-nārāyaṇa,*" 278
Darśa, **212**
Dattātreya, **64**
Death in material relationships, **52–**53
Dehino 'smin yathā dehe
quoted, 18, 54, 87
Deity of the Supreme Lord, **148**
Deity worship of the Supreme Lord, 116, 141, 143, **276–**277
Demigods
criticizing, an offense, 173
defined, 222
long lives of, 235
ninety million, 8
as parts of the Lord, **232**
reciting *puṁsavana-vrata* pleases, **292**
as secondary actors, **145**
worship of, condemned, **125–126**
See also: Indra; Maruts; *other names of individual demigods*
Demons, reformation of, 222
Desires
of devotees, *yogīs* and *jñānīs,* 118–119
of devotees to go to the Lord, 182
devotional service fulfills, 112, **263–264**
material, absent in devotional service, 56
material, body given by, 60–61
material, unhappiness from, **160–162**
material, worship of the Lord with, 126–128
Destiny in getting children, **55**
Detachment. *See:* Renunciation
Devala, **64**
Śukadeva heard of Vṛtrāsura from, **11**
Devotees of the Supreme Lord
accept everything as mercy, 182
appreciate the Lord, 272
behavior of, **201, 204**
Caitanya Mahāprabhu's happiness as, 196
dear to the Lord, **201**
demigods respected by, 126
depend on the Lord, 272–273
desire nothing material, **264–266**
desires of, the Lord fulfills, **263–264**
duty and activities of, 69
enemies of, punished by the Lord, 91–92
envy avoided by, 246
food not eaten by, **247**
goal of, 111, 182
hearing from, necessity of, 207
humility of, 174–175, 178, **204**
incapability in, 107
jñānīs inferior to, 6, 118
karma transcended by, 182
knowledge in, 151, **188–189**, 197, 198
the Lord conquered by, **117–**119
the Lord depends on, 274
the Lord favors, 91–92
the Lord seen by, 142, **146–149**
the Lord's lotus feet served by, **107**
as *mahā-pauruṣīya,* 68–69
material conditions do not affect, **68–**69, 74
Māyāvādīs inferior to, 6, 118
meeting, as fortune, 86
obligated feeling of, to the Lord, 130
opulence of, 111–112
pride disqualifies, 174
pure. *See:* Pure devotees of the Supreme Lord
purpose of, **62–**65
rarity of, **3–4,** 8–9
renunciation in, 182, 186, **192,** 195
security of, in difficulty, 205–206
service of, accepted, 109
Śiva glorifies, **192–194, 197, 201**

E

I

J

K

L

M

Q

R

T

W

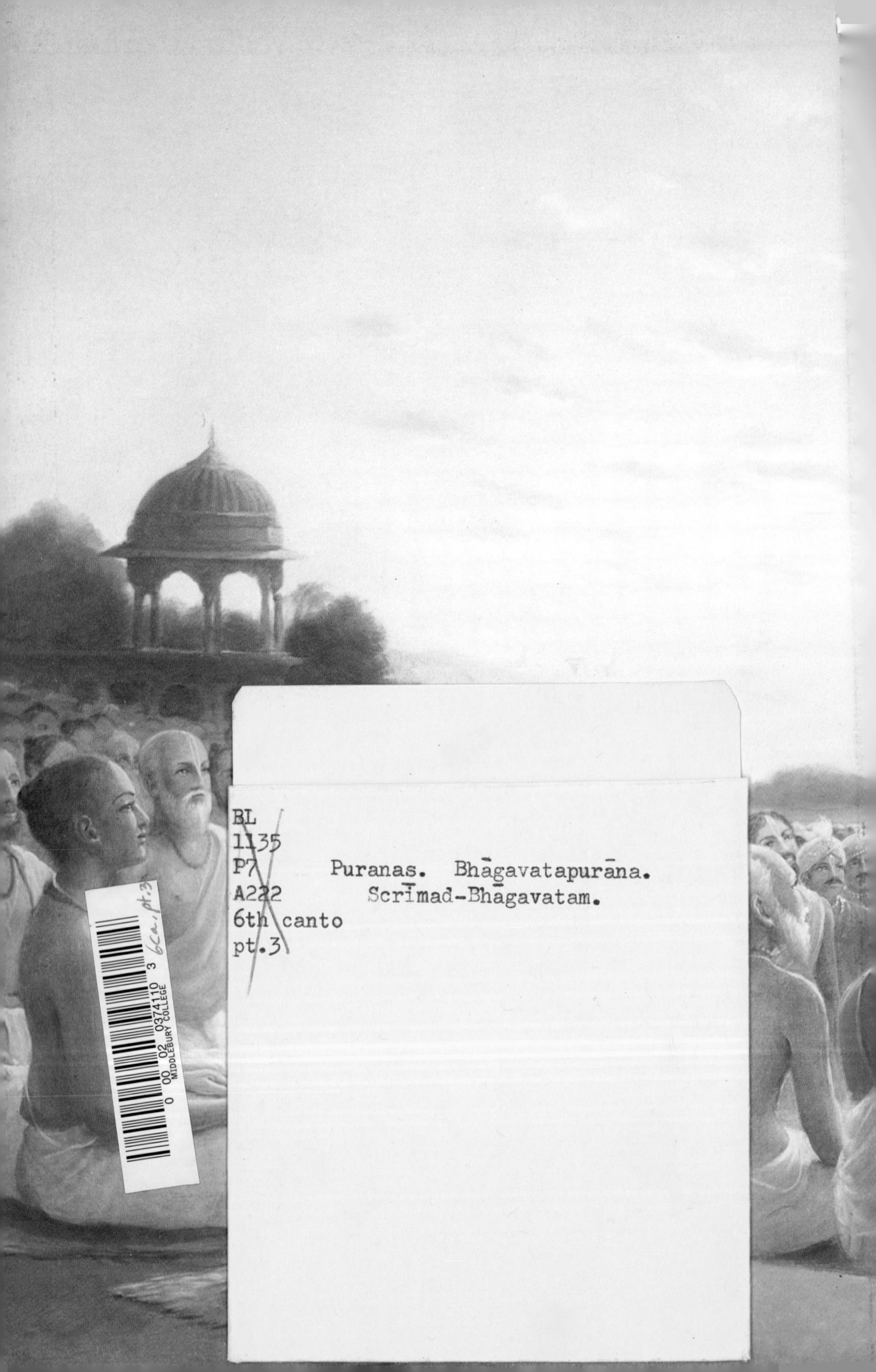